By Testimony

*"And they overcame him because of the blood of the Lamb and because of the **word of their testimony**…"*
Revelation 12:11

Incredible and Powerful Testimonies of Restored Marriages

Dan and Erin Thiele

Eighth Edition, Revised

Cover Design by Dallas Thiele • Restore Ministries Productions

By the Word of Their Testimony
Incredible and Powerful Testimonies

By Dan and Erin Thiele

Published by:
Restore Ministries Productions
POB 830
Ozark, MO 65721 U.S.A.

The materials from Restore Ministries are used to stop divorce and to restore families. For more information, visit us at: www.RestsoreMinistries.net.

All rights reserved. No part of this book may be reproduced or transmitted in any form or by any means, electronic or mechanical, including photocopying, recording or by any information storage and retrieval system without written permission from the author, except for the inclusion of brief quotations in a review.

Unless otherwise indicated, most Scripture verses are taken from the New American Standard Bible (NAS). Scripture quotations marked KJV are taken from the King James Version of the Bible.

Copyright © 2005 by Dan and Erin Thiele

First Printing: 2001
Second Printing: 2002
Third Printing: 2002
Fourth Printing: 2003
Fifth Printing: 2004 Revised
Sixth Printing: 2004 Completely Revised
Seventh Printing: 2004 Revised
Eighth Printing: 2005 Completely Revised

Library of Congress Control number: 2004195507

ISBN 1-931800-06-5

Printed in the U.S.A. by
Morris Publishing
3212 East Highway 30
Kearney, NE 68847
1-800-650-7888

TABLE OF CONTENTS

YOUR DIVINE APPOINTMENT 4

1. NOTHING IS IMPOSSIBLE *WITH* GOD! 10
2. HOW GOD RESTORED OUR MARRIAGE 12
3. WONDERFUL TESTIMONIES 15

   NEED HELP? 242

   ABOUT THE AUTHORS 243

   AT LAST THERE'S HOPE! 244

Introduction

Your Divine Appointment

*"I was **crying** to the LORD with my voice,
And He **answered me** from His holy mountain"
Psalm 3:4.*

Have you been searching for marriage help? It's not by chance, nor is it by coincidence, that you are reading this booklet. God has heard your cry for help in your marriage dilemma. He predestined this DIVINE APPOINTMENT to give you the hope that you so desperately need right now!

If you have been told that your marriage is hopeless or that without your spouse's help your marriage cannot be restored, then this is the book you need. Read this over and over so you will begin to believe that God is MORE than able to restore ANY marriage, including YOURS!

For ALL the testimonies of those who once had "seemingly" hopeless marriages that are now restored, go to our website – MarriageHelpOnLine.com to read those that we have received since the printing of this book that we post on our website.

We know and understand what you are going through since WE, and MANY others who have come to our ministry for help, have a restored marriage and family! No matter what others have told you, your marriage is NOT hopeless!! We KNOW, after twelve years of ministry, that God is able to restore ANY marriage, even YOURS!

If you have been crying out to God for more help, someone who understands, someone you can talk to, then join our Internet Restoration Fellowship OnLine and receive an ePartner (email partner) who will help you see your marriage through to restoration. Since beginning this fellowship, we have seen more marriages restored on a regular basis than we ever thought possible!

"My partner was scheduled to go to his final divorce hearing and asked me to fast and pray with him. Only two days after my wife told me she wanted to come home, my ePartner's wife went to the attorney and canceled their divorce!! Both our wives chose to stop the divorce and restore the marriage in the very same week!! I was two weeks away from a divorce and my ePartner was only 3 days from the court date!"

So, if you are really serious in your desire to restore your marriage, then our fellowship is the answer. For more information or to join, go to our website. We would love for you to be a part of our Restoration Fellowship!

Who are we and what are we hoping to do?

Restore Ministries helps those who have found themselves in a hopeless situation: men and women whose spouse is in adultery, has left them, has filed for divorce, or any other seemingly impossible marital situation. They have often sought help, but everyone (many times even their pastors) has told them it was hopeless. We believe that no marriage is hopeless – regardless of the circumstances. We offer hope, help and encouragement through our website, our Restoration Fellowship, and a variety of resources.

Erin Thiele founded Restore Ministries in 1990 a year after her husband, Dan, left her for another woman. Even her own pastor (and all the other pastors she spoke to from many denominations) told her that her marriage was hopeless. Yet after seeking the Lord and searching His Word, she knew that it was the Lord's desire to restore her marriage. She promised the Lord that if He would restore her marriage to Dan she would spend the rest of her life proclaiming the truth that "nothing is impossible with God." Just two years after Dan left, and even after Dan divorced her, the Lord kept His word and restored Erin's hopeless marriage "suddenly" in January of 1991. This ministry is the fulfillment of her promise to the Lord.

Erin's ministry to women grew beyond her local area after her first book *How God Can and Will Restore Your Marriage* was published by a Christian publisher and sent all over the world in 1996. Three years later the Lord called her husband, Dan, to join her in ministry when they printed and sent out the men's version of the same book. These books soon became the publisher's most requested books (over their 600 other publications). Restore Ministries began to self-publish their resources when the publisher told the Thieles that they were unable to keep up with the demand for their books.

In 1999 their ministry went up on the Internet and Restore Ministries became an international ministry overnight. Their ministry grew at a phenomenal rate at this point; each month for the first six months on the Internet they doubled or tripled the number of men and women they were ministering to.

In 2001, when they were unable to keep up with the growth, the Thieles established Restoration Fellowship to minister more effectively to the needs of those seriously seeking restoration. Within a year the fellowship grew to over 400 committed members and increases by an average of five members a day with members from all over the world.

Restore Ministries has never sought advertising or paid for placement in search engines but has instead grown by word of mouth. Though often ostracized by the established church, because of those who have cried out to God for help when their own church, pastor, family and friends offered them no hope or support, it has given hope and has been the oasis in the desert for the desperate, the hurting, the rejected.

Often accused of being extreme, radical, out-of-balance or legalistic, the message in all of their resources is founded firmly on the Word of God, encouraging those seeking restoration to live the message that Jesus proclaimed, beginning with the familiar Beatitudes.

Their ministry teaches the good news of God's Word to bring healing to the brokenhearted, comfort to those in pain, and freedom to prisoners of despondency and sin through the truth of His Word, giving them the hope that is "against all hope" through the Power of Jesus Christ, the Mighty Counselor and Good Shepherd.

To date Dan and Erin have published 10 books and 21 videos in an effort to minister to the hurting all over the world with the intent of creating a deeper and more intimate walk with the Lord that results in the hurting healed, the bound freed, the naked clothed, the lost saved and broken marriages restored. They minister to men and women from 15 countries including Switzerland, Hong Kong, New Zealand, Sweden, Philippines, Brazil and Germany, with large followings in Australia, Canada, and Africa. Dan and Erin's books have been translated into Spanish, Portuguese, Tagalog (Filipino), and is currently being translated into Afrikaans, French, Italian, Malayalam (So, India).

Jesus said that you "will know them by their fruits." This book *By the Word of Their Testimony* is filled with testimonies of hopeless marriages that were restored, marriages that give glory to God and to the Power of His Word. This book grows at such a phenomenal rate that they are unable to keep up with reprinting due to the number of testimonies that pour into their office. If you have any doubt about the validly of their ministry, you won't after reading this awesome book. It will show you not only hopeless marriages that were restored, but more importantly, it will show you men and women who have been completely transformed into God-lovers and are now committed on-fire Christians, many of whom were saved through this ministry.

Below is a small sampling of the letters of gratitude that Restore Ministries has received. Please note when you read the letters that they give all the praise and glory to the Lord. This ministry was founded and continues to grow on the premise that "if He be lifted up, He will draw all men to Himself" and "the Lord will share His glory with no man."

"Let Another Praise You" Proverbs 27:2

"Thank You so much LORD . . . for giving all of us Erin and Dan to assist You in bringing families together after enduring such hard times. The praise goes to the LORD; many thanks and blessings to Restore Ministries and their family for the work they do to help deliver His word in ways that many can understand. My wife of 17 years divorced me but she now has been home for three weeks after a year and a half of being divorced and 21 months apart!" C.B.

"Erin, I want to thank you for what you do to help marriages. I am so thankful that God has restored my marriage and as I continue to seek Him, I now think I know what you mean.... BE STILL AND KNOW THAT I AM GOD!! My marriage was restored!! I had cried out to God for help because when I went to my pastor and asked what I could do he just looked sad and said it was up to my husband, but by the Grace of God I found Restore Ministries!!!" BJ.

"Erin, I want to thank you so much for being so honest with all of us. Thank you for allowing the Lord to change you, and for allowing Him to help you spread the truth. My husband is home almost one year to the day after the Lord allowed him to leave! I

was contentious, controlling, angry, suspicious, hurt, bitter, had committed adultery, and was ready to kill myself when he left. Would you believe that now he keeps telling me how lucky he is to have married me and wants to 'show me off' to his friends and family?!!" M.P.

"Praise God! Thank You Jesus, and thank you Restore Ministries for the guidance to get myself in tune with God's will!! God can and will restore if we let Him! IF WE LET JESUS DO IT, HE WILL DO IT!! PRAISE GOD!! PRAISE GOD!! Our home is finally 'home' again, and Restore Ministries helped me see that it's not what I think or what the world thinks, BUT WHAT GOD WANTS ME TO THINK AND DO! Don't listen to people's opinions; go to God! Do what the Lord says and it will work!" D.D.

"Praise God with every breath that He gives us. I thank God for this wonderful ministry that I found when I was at my lowest. Erin and Dan, you have been like John the Baptist to me, pointing me in the direction of God, my first love. My husband is home, PTL!! He is more affectionate and considerate and tells our family that we must put God first! I can't help but cry tears of joy when I think about how far God has brought me and to know that God loves me even with all my shortcomings. Who wouldn't serve a God like this?" K.T.

"I am convinced also, as Erin is, that 'marriage crises' are not about the marriage, but are actually 'spiritual crises' in disguise. For those of you out there who are wondering if you need to apply all the Biblical principles that Erin suggests: JUST DO IT! My husband has been home now for a little over one month, and has shared with me one story after another that confirms this wisdom of following God's way!!" K.B.

"Erin, I thought my husband and I were happily married until this summer when he grew cold and distant. I did not understand or react well to this and it quickly escalated into him telling me he doesn't love me and never did and even once that he hated me. I was drowning in despair and wanted to save my marriage but could find no help. Erin is so right about counseling—it only made things worse!! (And my minor is in psychology!) A Christian friend led me to your site and I immediately embraced God and the teachings. I was saved through the prayer I found on your website." M.B.

We put this book together because we believe that as you spend some time reading these incredible and awesome testimonies of seemingly hopeless marriages that were miraculously restored, you will be encouraged and know without a doubt...

NOTHING IS IMPOSSIBLE WITH GOD!!

Chapter 1

Nothing is Impossible *with* God!

*"Looking at them, Jesus said,
'With people it is impossible,
but not with God;
for all things are possible with God.'"
Mark 10:27*

"And they overcame him because of the blood of the Lamb and because of the **word of THEIR testimony**, and they did not love their life even to death." Rev. 12:11.

The following testimonies are filled with miracles of men and women who took God at His Word and believed that "nothing was impossible with God!" Those who have had the miracle of a restored marriage have several things in common. All "delighted themselves in the Lord" and He gave them "the desires of their heart." All of them "hoped against hope" when their situation seemed hopeless.

All of them "fought the good fight" and "finished their course." All of them were determined "not to be overcome with evil" but instead to "overcome evil with good." All were willing to "bless their enemies" and to pray for them that "despitefully used and persecuted them." All "turned the other cheek" and "walked the extra mile." All realized that it was "God who removed lover and friend far from" them and it was God who "made them a loathing" to their spouse. All of them understood and believed that it is NOT the will of man (or woman) but the "will of God" who would "turn the heart" whichever way He chose.

All refused to fight in "the flesh" but chose to battle "in the spirit." None were concerned to protect themselves, but trusted themselves "to Him who judges righteously." All of their trust was "in the Lord" because their trust was "the Lord." All released their attorneys (if that was part of their testing) since they "would rather be wronged or defrauded." All of them "got out of the way of wickedness" and "let the unbeliever leave" since they "were called to peace." All refused to do "evil for evil or insult for insult." All loved their spouse who may have been unfaithful because they knew that "love never fails."

This is the same journey that the Lord took me on back in 1989. That year I made a promise to God that if He would restore my marriage to my husband, I would devote my life to telling others about Him and His desire and ability to restore ANY marriage no matter what the circumstances. The Lord was faithful and restored my marriage, suddenly, two years later after a divorce. (Yes! AFTER a divorce!) Now I faithfully, with the Lord's continued help, love, support, and guidance, spread the GOOD news that nothing—NOT A THING—is impossible with God!

It is important to know that our ministry was FOUNDED to help all those who were told by pastors and Christian friends that their situations were HOPELESS. Those who come to us for hope are facing a spouse who is deep in adultery, who has moved out (often in with the other person), who has already filed for divorce or whose divorce has gone through. 99% of those who come, come alone for help since their spouse is not interested in saving their marriage, but is desperately trying to get out. Over 95% claim that they are Christians and most are married to Christians. Over half are in some type of Christian service and many of the men who are involved with other woman are pastors who have left not only their wife and children, but their church as well.

If you, or if someone you know, is facing devastation in their marriage, there is hope. Read these awesome testimonies that prove that God is MORE than able to restore ANY marriage!

———————— **Chapter 2** ————————

How God Restored Our Marriage
by Dan Thiele

"O Lord God of hosts,
restore us;
Cause Your face to shine upon us,
and we will be saved"
Psalm 80:19

In January of 1989, I left Erin for another woman. However, the Lord gave Erin the heart and endurance to stand for our marriage. It was during this fiery trial that Erin became a new woman. She studied the Bible concerning marriage and began to apply the principles in her life. Like the three youths who were thrown into the fiery furnace, Erin too became "loosed" of things in her life that had her "bound." She also found herself walking with another, her precious Lord. (See Daniel 3:25.)

Everyone, even the most respected pastors in our city, told Erin that it was hopeless to fight against my desire to leave her and be with another woman. But Erin found in God's Word that "nothing is impossible with God"! (Luke 1:37) It was during this time that she founded Restore Ministries to help those who also wanted their marriages restored. She began by sharing with each of them the Scriptures the Lord had shown her. Soon there were too many women to help individually, so she began to type out the Bible references. Some of the women who came had never held a Bible in their hands, so Erin began to type out entire verses and then make copies to minister to these hurting and abandoned women.

However, the more she helped other women, the worse her situation became. Her fiery furnace was turned up when I divorced Erin in October of 1990. However, the Lord gave Erin the peace she needed to not fight or contest the divorce, but to trust in her Lord. Undaunted, Erin continued to minister to other women by sharing the Word of God. She told the Lord that if He would restore her marriage to the man she loved, me, she would devote her life to helping women in marriage crises. That's when Erin put together a workbook for women, *A Wise Woman*.

Our marriage was miraculously restored due, in part, to Erin's obedience to not obtain an attorney. God delivered me when it was discovered that even though the judge had granted the divorce on October 30, the papers that had been filed by my attorney had to be overturned due to an error in the paperwork! This, to me, was the first sign from God that He would "somehow" deliver me from the cords that had me bound to the adulteress. Had Erin had an attorney, the divorce would not have been overturned. (To hear more of how Erin's prayers were answered, get our testimony tape.)

Erin, who had "hoped against all hope" (Rom. 4:18), received her miracle on January 29, 1991 at 11:10 p.m. when I returned home to Erin and our four children. This was after adultery, and after a divorce, over two years after I left her.

The Birth of Restore Ministries International

Over the next five years, the Lord blessed us with three more babies as Erin continued to minister to other women. In 1996 the first version of *How God Can and Will Restore Your Marriage*, which was taken out of *A Wise Woman* workbook, was published. Thousands of requests for the book started coming in to Restore Ministries and the publishers from all over the U.S. and from abroad.

Many books were sent to prisons all over the U.S. Men were being blessed with restored marriages after reading the restoration book for women! That's when Erin was led to write a version for men. Later she wrote (with very little of my help) a manual for men, *A Wise Man* accompany the men's restoration book.

Today, through Restore Ministries International, we now minister to men and women primarily over the Internet and through books, audiotapes, and videotapes.

I have seen in my life, and in so many we have helped, that God is more than able to heal and save any marriage!

I encourage you to read, reread and read over again these testimonies to build your faith and to BELIEVE the Lord's promises about restoring your marriage!

Mark those "seemingly" impossible situations that are similar to yours; and please, **don't** focus on how your situation is different. Of course it is! God is looking, actually "roaming to and fro throughout the WHOLE earth, looking for those whose hearts are completely His. To STRONGLY support you" to give you a testimony that is different, unique and "seemingly" impossible if it weren't for GOD!

This FAITHBUILDING book has first person and third person testimonies. Before we had a place to send in Praise Reports, we received our "testimonies" through many different sources. All of us love to hear it right from the person's own lips, so now we have first person testimonies. Whether in first or third person, al these testimonies give "glory to God"!

Chapter 3

Wonderful Testimonies

*"Your **testimonies** also are my delight;
They are my **counselors**"
Psalm 119:24*

Look to GOD!

I suffered (or so I thought) the worst marriage for almost five years. I could not see anything except that God had put my husband and me together just to torture each other. Everything about my husband made me sick. I had no love anymore for him, couldn't stand to be around him, and especially couldn't stand to be intimate.

I finally got so fed up that I started seeking a way out of the marriage, for I knew that God hated divorce. I searched for Scriptures and even sought for approval from other Christians.

One night as I was searching the Word, I asked the Lord for a sign and for my husband to come home and not start with me for no reason at all (as usual). I told the Lord that if he came home and started an argument, that would be the sign, as if it were okay for me to go ahead and file for a divorce the following day.

So guess what happened? Yep!! He came home and started with me, and that was all I needed to make me feel good about what I was planning to do. So I filed, had him put out by the police, and had him served papers. I hurt deeply inside because I knew then that I really did love him but hated his ways.

He immediately told me that he could not live in the same state with me. He left for Florida but called every day wanting to come back home. He even agreed to go to counseling.

On the following Monday, I called to put the divorce on hold and agreed to go to counseling, but would not let my husband come back home because I didn't see the changes that I thought were good enough. Counseling was a mess!! The counselor pretty much kicked us out. He told us that if we could not commit to each other and tell each other that we were both willing to try and give our best, then there was no reason to come back to his office.

WOW!! That was pretty harsh, and I didn't even care. By this time my heart was even harder than it had ever been before. What is worse, I am saved, sanctified, and Holy Ghost filled!! I am the Praise and Worship Leader at my church but could not get my marriage together!! How is that for HOLY?!!

My husband got called up on active duty with the National Guard and, even though his unit didn't have to go out of the country, they had to serve as security for about a year at another army unit. This distance caused him to slide even further back from the Lord, because he didn't have strong support from other men.

After about a year, God started dealing with me about my marriage. I needed to get this thing together!! At the beginning of 2004, I started praying for our marriage and for God to change me.

As I finally began to really want my marriage, my husband had changed his mind and now wanted a divorce! I wanted him to come home, but he did not want to anymore. I just couldn't understand.

One night I was searching the web for restored marriage testimonies. I clicked on the RMI link and read the intro. Talk about God speaking!! I felt like I had hit the jackpot! I truly could see this as a sign that God was going to restore our marriage. I immediately ordered the Resource Packet and joined the fellowship!! I could hardly wait to receive my packet! I was like a child with a brand new toy! I immediately started reading and eating the words!

It was as I began to seek the Lord and stand in the gap that I found out about the so-called OW (other woman)—one for whom my husband bought a cell phone and that I was never supposed to know about. I really relied on RMI and my ePartner. The first ePartner I got did not respond to my email, so I immediately got discouraged. But then I sent another request and was blessed to have found a true friend!! I thank God for her because she prayed for (and with me), which helped through all my fears and kept me encouraged.

She put a lot of things in perspective and helped me conquer that test!! This was so painful, especially now, because God had started breaking me and showing me how to forgive, filling me with his unconditional love. Love that loves even in the worst situation. Even in sin! My heart was pierced with indescribable pain! I cried for days and couldn't eat but was constantly in prayer. I soon began to realize that God was purifying me! It was painful but very well worth it!!

Every time I thought about the cell phone, which he purchased with a contract, or it would ring, I got mad. I constantly let the devil defeat me with that cell phone! All I could see was that he was divorcing me and was going to go be with her. By this time my husband was constantly telling me that he was back to be with me and to stop worrying about something that I couldn't change. (His telling me that did not help me; he could have been lying for all I knew.)

One morning while praying (before I found RMI), the Spirit told me to go to 1 Peter 3:1: "In the same way, you wives, be submissive to your own husbands so that even if any of them are disobedient to the word, they may be won without a word by the behavior of their wives." As I read, I knew what it was saying but at the same time I didn't. I asked God over and over, "What does this mean?" Then, as I started reading my resources, there it was!!!

Learning to say "not a word" was so hard! Yes, I failed that test many times!! (Thank You, Lord, for being so forgiving.) I also learned what it really means to be in subjection and submissive to my husband. My hardest test was being submissive and obedient while there was a divorce pending, and knowing about the OW.

When my husband told me that he did not see us being able to start over unless we got a divorce first, God showed me that He was in control and we would start over without a divorce. God showed me that my husband's heart was truly in His hands and He would turn it sooner than I would think!

After finding RMI and my constantly seeking the Lord, my husband and I grew closer and closer. We spent every day together. God showed me His power in many, many situations.

God had given me so many confirmations that He had already restored my marriage and, even with a divorce hearing scheduled for May 25, I had no doubt that God was going to restore our marriage. I was full of faith. My ePartner was full of faith. One of my closest friends at work was full of faith. All we were waiting for was the manifestation—the true sign: the divorce cancellation!!

On Sunday, May 2, my husband told me that he loved me!! PTL!!

And then on Thursday, May 6, he spoke the words that I had been waiting to hear: "I am not going to go through with the divorce." PTL!! Hallelujah!

On Mother's Day, he gave me back my original wedding rings, which I had declared I would never wear again and said that, if he wanted me back, he would have to buy me a new set. When I saw those rings, they were new enough for me. He even put them on my finger himself. He has moved back home and that in itself is WONDERFUL, because he had told me that he did not want to come back to this same apartment. But look at GOD....

I encourage everyone to hold onto every promise of the Lord, for He is faithful and will do exceedingly abundantly above all that you could ask or even just think about! Trust me—I know! Don't give up—the end result is so much worth the wait and even the pain!!

All the resources are wonderful but I truly found the *How God Can and Will Restore Your Marriage* and *A Wise Woman* to be the most helpful! They immediately made me see myself and caused me to repent for many, many things, and many, many times.

I truly thank God because even when my ePartner saw the signs of restoration, she did not get jealous—she just prayed even harder for the complete restoration and manifestation of restoration. I love you, Laura, a dear friend for life!! God has promised you restoration and He will do just what He said!! Get ready, get ready, get ready! Your blessing is coming!!

Clarissa, RESTORED in Georgia

Restoration! God has Changed my Life!

In October of 2003, the worst possible thing I could imagine happened. My husband of 12 years told me that he wanted to leave. I was devastated, and didn't know what to do. Desperately, I began searching and praying for something to show me what I needed to do to gain back the man I loved. I found Restore Ministries over the Internet a few weeks later. I know it was the Lord who led me to the website. I immediately ordered the *Restore Your Marriage* and *A Wise Woman*. What a blessing! I read and read until I couldn't read any more. God started showing me all that I had done to cause my husband to leave our home. I was contentious, spiritually prideful, and arrogant. God convicted me of my sins, and I pleaded with Him to help me change. Praise God, He had mercy on me and changed my life!

As I continued to pray and fast, I noticed my husband's heart softening towards me a few months later. He began spending more time at our home and staying for longer periods of time. Around Christmastime, the Lord worked a miracle. He led my husband to spend the night so that our children would not have to be without him on Christmas Day! Praise the Lord! After that, and into the New Year, he started to spend less time with the OW and more with the children and me. We started to communicate as husband and wife again, and a month later, he decided to give our marriage another chance. He said that he did not want to see 12 years of marriage wasted away, and realized his life was turning upside down without us!

On February 19, 2004 my husband moved back home! We are learning to seek the Lord first in everything we do. As I look back, I realize that the Lord was not my first love. My husband was. I learned that I had to release my husband and my marriage to God in order to see any kind of turnaround. When I did, it worked! God is so very gracious, awesome and loving. I thank Him for allowing me another chance to be the wife I was called to be. I pray that each day brings about further blessings from the Lord and that I never lose sight of Him again. My desire is to serve Him day and night for the rest of my life.

I also want to thank Restore Ministries and my prayer partner for not giving up on me. You encouraged me, supported me, and rebuked me. You helped me to not be fearful and to continue to believe that my husband would one day return. God bless you, Erin, for your ministry! May the Lord continue to keep you in His tender care.

Yvette, RESTORED in Pennsylvania

Jesus Raised Her Marriage from the Dead!

Praise the Lord, in order for the Lord to get my attention, He removed my husband from me two and a half years ago. My old life and marriage had to be destroyed for God to begin something new in my life and marriage.

I was a "Christian girl" all my life—a Pentecostal going to church on Sundays and tearing down my household as a foolish woman on other days. When my husband left in July of 2002 after our tenth anniversary, he told me he would never come back and he headed straight to his lawyer friends, who all decided that it was in his best interest to divorce me and start new life without me and our daughter, who was nine years old at that time.

At this point I knew he was serious and he was leaving. I was so desperate that I turned to my senior pastor for help. He and his wife just hugged me and that was it. I turned to all my church friends, but all they said was to forget about him.

From the beginning, when my husband left, God put in my heart that He would restore my marriage but I didn't know how. The Lord gave me John 11: Jesus raises Lazarus from the dead.

I knew He allowed my situation of separation and divorce for His glory. I went crazy and went to different bookstores, including Christian bookstores, but I couldn't find anything about restoring marriage. Then I starting going on Internet looking at different Christian sites about marriage. One night I was crying so hard as I was typing. It was the divine power of the mighty Abba Papa Almighty, my very being, my all and all—oh, I love Him and cannot praise Him enough! Hold my hand and type "restore marriage" and push the button "search." Praise the Lord—there it was!—the RMI website looking me right in the face! I screamed so loud and call my daughter to come and see what mama has found. We both were so excited—I knew God was behind all this.

The next day I called RMI and said, "I want to become a member," and I signed up right away. I ordered the *How God Can and Will Restore Your Marriage* book and other materials because I was so desperate, hoping against hope, and I was willing do whatever God wanted me to do! I didn't have the money but I charged it on a credit card—I would rather be buying something to do with the kingdom of God and in debt than spending on my worldly desires and debt.

As I sought the Lord, He drew near to me, and at the same time He removed people I was depending on and took them away from me. He changed me and taught me to depend on Him by running to Him when in need instead of to the arm of flesh.

He taught me to really pray—I mean pray like I never did before—and to fast. One of the biggest things He broke me of was never to talk about my situation to anyone but Him and Him alone.

As I obeyed Him on that, He was so faithful to me that most of my close friends at work didn't even know that my husband had been gone.

God has protected me and our little girl. He made me into a lover of His Word, and now I seek Him in everything I do in my life. Jesus has become not just my Savior but also my precious Lord and best friend, the Lover of my very soul and being. Glory to His powerful name: Jesus!

As I sought the Lord and became so close to Him, my situation didn't get better but worse. My husband went ahead and divorced me, even though the hate wall was down. I didn't hire any lawyer; I didn't have to because I have the best lawyer on my side—His name is Jesus.

God told me two months in advance as I was walking my dog in the park that the divorce would go through in order for my husband to heal. God said He would allow it, but "don't be afraid—I am with you." At that time I had the peace that passes all human understanding in my soul. But that didn't stop me from fasting and praying against that divorce going through. After the divorce, things turned around for good.

God taught me during this trial so much, including that God *is* faithful to His Word, and He is merciful and full of love. The resources from RMI—God used them to teach me, including the *How God Can and Will Restore Your Marriage* book, the *Wise Woman* workbook, and the "Be Encouraged" tapes and videos. I very much recommend them to everyone—they were a big part of my desire to restore my marriage. I knew that what God could do for you, sweet sister Erin, He could do for me too.

The two and a half years was difficult not just for me but for our little girl also. Finding out about the OW was hard—I felt helpless because I wasn't anything because I wasn't his wife legally, and I cried into the arm of God. My daughter was very sick because I could not afford groceries—I bought the cheapest frozen pizza, and she got sick from eating it. I had dropped her off to her daddy's place before I went work. He called me later and asked me what I fed her the night before. I answered "pizza." He asked where I got it, and I told him, and he got mad. I didn't say anything back to him—I just took all the insults and told him I would do better next time.

I went right into my Father's mighty arm and cried, emptying everything to Him. I said, "Father, he was with the OW eating dinner in the expensive place in town, buying good food, whole food, and taking expensive trips, and here I am doing the best I can to put food on the table for my precious baby girl and yet it is not good enough. Lord, I am the wife of his youth. I helped him through his college and even helped him through finishing his doctor's degree. But now to him I am nothing." I told God I don't care about any person or any thing anymore—all I want is just Him and me. And He held me and told me that "soon the wicked will be cut off and destroyed and you will go in and conquer the land." As He whispered this sweet promise into my ear four months ago, I fell asleep into His arms.

The turning point in our restoration was when I let God be God and just loved Him and asked Him to give me the grace to love my new husband with His unconditional love. God brought him to a point where nothing was working for him. He was so miserable with the OW, at his work, because my God built a wall around him and he could not find his lovers and could not overtake them. Then he said, "I will go back to my wife for it was better for me."

Those were his words, which he told me around June, when he invited me and our daughter to our summer cabin. He told me he had ended the relationship with the OW, and told her he has had a girlfriend all along, that she is his best friend and soul mate and he loves her and wants to be with her. I turned to him. "Who is that girl?" I asked. He turned to me with pure love in his eyes and said, "This girl is you." He told me, "You're the best. I don't know what else I was looking for." I was praising the Lord in my spirit as he was saying these things!

On Wednesday July 7 at 2:00 or 3:00 in the morning, the Lord woke me up to pray. I asked the Lord, "Pray for what and for who?" One of the lesson the Lord taught me during this trial was that He would wake me up in the middle of the night to pray for a certain person or situation. The Lord knew the typical questions I would ask: "Lord, now what, who, and why? Do I have pray, or can it wait until I am fully awake?" God always wins out.

Anyway, on that night He said, "Pray for your husband's deliverance." I said, "From what?" He said, "From the enemy." So I began praying half asleep, then the Lord said, "Stop praying and just keeping praising Me and thanking Me, for I have delivered him from the land of the enemy and I will bring him home to live in peace and safety."

Around 7:00 a.m., I got ready and got the house clean and I was so excited. And when I asked my daughter to get ready, she looked me and said, "Mom, you okay?" I said, "Yes I am." I told her that God woke me up and said He is bringing daddy today—daddy has been delivered from the land of the enemy!

Around 9:00 a.m., my new husband called. When our daughter answered the phone, he said, "I need to talk to Mom." I said hi, and he said, "I really need you. Would you come and take me home?" He was calling from his apartment. When I put down the phone, I began praising God with my daughter and our dog, jumping and shouting.

After that, I drove to his apartment and brought him home. He called his landlord to terminate his lease, even though he has to pay for an extra month. He called his family and told them about us. I know God brought him home—I had nothing to do with it. God did all the changes in me, and He will continue to change me more into His image every day. Glory and honor to His holy name!! I bless Him! Thank You, Jesus, for your sacrifice—one more marriage has been restored!

Daisy, RESTORED in Wisconsin

Dear Reader,

It gives me such joy to introduce this testimony to you this month. God never ceases to thrill me with who He is. He is a God who is sovereign, for it was almost exactly two years ago that I saw Lisa at the Fourth of July celebration at our church, where she told me that the Lord had restored her marriage!

One morning after church, I was waiting for a woman I was to meet so I could give her a copy of the RYM book. While I was waiting, one of our altar workers, who knew my testimony and about our ministry, brought a woman over to me and said she needed to talk to me. But Lisa didn't talk—she just began to weep with her head down. So I took her hands and began to share with her that God was about to help her, that God could restore her marriage, and many other things that the Holy Spirit spoke through me that I don't remember.

The more I spoke, the more her tears fell, on my hands and on my feet. I prayed with her and then at the close said that I had been waiting for a woman to give the RYM book to, but I believed that God knew all the time that Lisa was coming and the book was for her. She wept even more, we hugged, and I did not see her again.

Then some time later, our pastor shared that a woman had her marriage restored, whose husband had been gone for years. Though I speak to many in our church about restoration (we attend a mega church), I knew it had to be "her." Months went by and as she came to mind, I kept asking the Lord to reveal if Lisa was the woman who had restoration. I knew I would never be able to find her because I really didn't know what she looked like, since she cried the entire time with her head down.

Then two years ago, Lisa came up to me and said that her marriage was restored!

Since that time I have been blessed to see Lisa and her husband sitting in the front of the church. Once I ran into them coming out after a service and I made a point of introducing myself to her husband. Lisa looked worried at first, thinking I might reveal how we knew each other, but I was just so thrilled to be shaking the hand of a miracle.

You will be blessed as she shares her heart and her testimony with you today. Erin

Restored through Humility!

Five years ago, my husband and I got married. A few months after that, I found out that he had someone else, and he told me that he felt it best to get a divorce. I was devastated and, needless to say, depressed. This went on for almost two and a half years. During those years, I continued to go to church and read Scripture, mostly the Psalms and Proverbs.

During that time, God took me to the wilderness to where only He and I spent time together. Only through total brokenness did God really begin to speak to me. I had so many bad habits that involved control and anger. He had to get rid of those before He could really work in my marriage. I kept reading about the restored marriages and wondered why mine was not happening. Now I realize that through brokenness, prayer, and fasting God breaks through to us. He was there all of the time, yet with my tainted view of life, I never really saw what He was doing.

I found Restore Ministries through a woman at our church who led me to Erin. Erin prayed with me and gave me a Restore Your Marriage book that was originally intended for someone else—the Lord knew I needed it desperately! I also recommend the *A Wise Woman*. The Scriptures were especially helpful.

God began to change me and soften my heart. He taught me humbleness (something I have never been very good at) and He taught me to look to Him and not at my circumstances. He taught me to run to His Word and not my friends. Better yet, He taught me to pray instead of speaking my mind immediately! During this past two and a half years that my husband has been back home, our relationship improves every day. I see God working on my husband's heart in areas that I have been praying about for a long time. He continues to work on my heart because the enemy loves to creep in and steal my joy if he can.

God's Word kept telling me to "*wait*." I hated that word at one time. I even told the Lord that I didn't like *waiting*. His loving patience kept me waiting. Waiting on Him, waiting until my heart was ready for what He had in store for me, waiting for the Lord to work on my husband's heart. "Be still and know that I am God"—that was something that God really had to teach me. I am a person of action and wanting to fix things, right now! God's Word (especially the Psalms) helped me to realize that waiting on God is the only way to have victory in any circumstance.

I can remember when the OW would call the house or my husband would leave to go call her. I would begin praising the Lord and telling Him how much I loved Him. When I didn't know what to say, I would repeat over and over, "By Your grace, Lord, cover me in Your grace...."

Oftentimes, my husband would come in more loving or would want to spend time with me. Also, it often turned out that he wasn't doing what I feared the most. I truly believe that by praising the Lord during those times, the enemy was sent back to where he belongs. Prayer and praise break the bonds of the enemy!!

I would say that the turning point of my marriage restoration was when I took my eyes *off* of my marriage and put them on the Lord. Things didn't happen overnight for me. It has been a slow process, but I think that I know why: God knows my temperament, my strong will, and my control issues. I believe that God brings my marriage along at a pace that He knows is best for me and my husband. I continually pray for His wisdom, His guidance, His eyes to see with, and a heart like Jesus'. He continues to show me how He is restoring our marriage one day at a time.

I praise the Lord because He loves me enough to teach me His ways as I seek His guidance. My husband wants to be with me, He wants to go to church with me, and He gets more and more involved with time. He speaks of us growing old together and makes plans for our lives in the future. He is becoming more sensitive to my needs and wants. He also communicates to me in a way that helps ease any insecurity that may linger from what happened in the past.

God has truly been transforming both of us, which is my prayer. I see God working in our lives in ways that only the Lord knows how! He is such a faithful God Who really loves us and knows us!

Lisa, RESTORED in Missouri

Restored! And He Alone is the Pearl of Great Price!!

Praise the Lord! He has glorified Himself through the work He has done in our marriage—and in me! I thank Him for the testimony He has given me and pray that He would receive all the glory for what is written here.

First, I must say that I do not deserve anything that He has done! The reason my marriage was such a mess to begin with was because of my own sin and selfishness. This marriage is my second one. My first marriage ended in divorce after I was in adultery. After my divorce, I am ashamed to say, I continued to live a lifestyle that was desperately wicked. Even though I had two young daughters, I made parties, men, and drinking my life, and I encouraged other women in the same lifestyle! Worse, I used abortion as birth control. (Even an unbeliever would be horrified to hear how many abortions I had, which goes to show that even those who call themselves "pro-choice" know deep down that abortion is an abomination to God.)

I became heavily involved in New Age and Eastern spirituality and truly believed I could control my own future. Sadly, at the time, I thought I was happy, in control, at peace, and the life of the party. (It never occurred to me to wonder whether "peacefulness" could really coexist with "life of the party.") Now I realize how spiritually dead I really was!

When I met the man who would become my second husband, we didn't date long before we became intimate. Not only did I become pregnant, but I deceptively chose to become pregnant because I wanted another child! (Why this time and not the others? I really must have thought I was playing god!) I did not expect him to marry me and selfishly made every decision for my own purposes. I also lied to him and did not tell him of my deception. He graciously asked me to marry him, though, because of his love for his son, his desire to make an honorable decision, and his love for me (which, however imperfect, was certainly more mature than my love for him!).

We were married by three people: a Greek Orthodox monk in full regalia, a New Age priestess (for lack of a better term), and a female pastor of a very liberal church (that proclaimed not salvation through Jesus Christ alone but "tolerance and social justice"). During our wedding ceremony, we promised to love and adore each other, but only after we first loved ourselves!! No traditional vows for us!

The fruit was evident immediately: At our wedding reception, we ended up in a huge argument, and I selfishly walked out of my own reception, dragging my friends with me. Praise God—He used one of them to tell me point-blank that my self-centered New Age beliefs and the sinful life I was living without God were the reasons things had gotten so bad! A few days later, I prayed to God to save me from my own sin. I wasn't sure He was real, but I asked Him to show me and save me if He was.

As a child, I had "accepted Christ" many times, but in retrospect I see that what was so obviously missing was an understanding of my sin! Back then, I was a "good girl"—I didn't see any sin anywhere. Ironically, I had often listened to testimonies in church from people whom God had delivered from terrible sins—drugs, alcohol, prostitution, etc.—and I remember thinking that I wanted a testimony like that and how sad it was that "I would never have one." God in all His wisdom (and certainly not without a sense of humor) must have taken that as a prayer, because I now have that kind of testimony—one that glorifies Him and Him alone!

After I prayed and asked God to save me, He definitely showed me He was real. I had asked specific questions of Him in my prayer that day, and within a week He had answered all of them! I knew beyond a shadow of a doubt that He was real, and that the shed blood of Jesus Christ had saved me from all of my sins!

He began to show Himself to me on our honeymoon. My husband and I went to a beach house in South Carolina, where we fought constantly. (Can you imagine what my husband thought? That I had "planned" all along to "change all the rules" as soon as we were married!) But our time away became my honeymoon with Jesus, and He began to transform me as I read His Word every day.

He also showed me that it was His timing when He called me to Himself, and the fact that it was after our wedding (had it been a week before, we probably wouldn't have married!) meant that I was to remain married, that God had a plan and a purpose for this marriage. When things got bad later and people told me we were unequally yoked, I could honestly tell them that we were very equally yoked when we married, and it was clearly His will that we remain together.

When we got back from our honeymoon, the Lord convicted me that I needed to tell my husband the truth about our son, that I had become pregnant on purpose. It was one of the hardest things I have ever had to do, but I knew that I had to be obedient and leave the results in God's hand. Unfortunately, after I confessed, things got worse, not better. I never doubted that I had done the right thing by telling him, yet admitting my willful deception seemed to be the beginning of a root of bitterness and distrust in my husband's heart that only grew worse (and I certainly couldn't blame him!). I see now that I was probably the most contentious woman who ever lived—we were invariably arguing about something, no doubt because I was constantly criticizing him!

On top of that, I was like the adulterous woman—my feet were never home. One weekend, after being away on business, I returned home and felt something was amiss. I noticed a woman's hair on our couch (bright red—not my color!) and immediately accused my husband of having someone over. He admitted that a woman had been in our house but said that it was innocent. (The children had been with him, and in retrospect I am sure he was speaking the truth. I obviously didn't know or take to heart the fact that "love believes all things.") Immediately I kicked him out of the house to make a point that I would not be treated "that way," then I proceeded to shame him by telling everyone I knew what he had "done."

There had also been physical altercations, which I first provoked and then used to get sympathy from anyone who would listen. There was also a lot of drinking, but instead of "love covering all transgressions" (Prov. 10:12, 1Pet. 4:8), I slandered my husband by talking loudly about that too! Of course my friends and even people in the church told me to practice "tough love," to take a stand against being "treated that way," and said that my husband would "never change" if I continued to "enable" him. I don't repeat this to slander my husband now but instead to show you that God wants to glorify Himself even in situations like these that seem impossible—but I didn't give God a chance! He certainly didn't need to defend someone who was already busy defending herself, or to be righteousness for one who was so self-righteous! By listening to the world (wanting to have my "ears tickled"), I continued to justify my own sinful behavior.

What a Pharisee I was! I told others of my husband's sins but could not see my own contentiousness, jealousy, self-righteousness, and insubordination (1 Sam 15:23). God showed me later that my "tough love" stance was actually manipulation!

He also later showed me that I was responsible for the times my husband had become physical ("a fool's mouth calls for blows," Prov. 18:6). In fact, I had provoked it every time! Once I learned to control my tongue, God took care of the rest. God had shown me earlier through Scripture that if my husband were truly a threat, He could remove him immediately. But obviously He didn't because it wasn't my husband who was so bad but me!!

I also learned later that the times when he has a few drinks are times that God has chosen for me to be away from my husband (He removes "lover and friend far from me," Ps. 88:18) in order to have me all to Himself—I am to be in the Word during those times, praying and rejoicing for my time alone with Him!

After about two months of my husband's being out of the house, I felt led by the Lord to fast, something I had never done before. By the middle of the second day, I knew beyond a doubt that I was to ask my husband to return home—and that I never should have asked him to leave in the first place.

Things got better for a time, but again I fell into the trap of distrusting, snooping, and following up on everything my husband said or did—and it became almost an obsession. We tried counseling on several occasions, which came to nothing and in fact often made things worse. I did have a single moment of truth with one counselor, who told me, "You may not be able to trust your husband, but you can trust God." That convicted me for a short period of time, but then (with the counselor's blessing!) I was back trying my own hand at controlling the situation.

My distrust came to a head a few years later, when I ended up asking God to show me whether my husband was or had been in adultery (I obviously forgot to pray about the future!). I promised to let go and trust Him if the answer He gave me was "no"—and it was! Immediately God enabled me to stop all of my snooping, and I began for the first time to really live by faith. The verse "For your Maker is your Husband" (Isa. 54:5) became real to me—it was (and still is!) one of my favorite verses in the Bible.

For the next six months, things got better. My faith continued to grow, and my relationship with the Lord was becoming more intimate. I was trusting Him in a new way. And then one night, I was prompted to pray in a way I never had before, for any hidden things to come to light. I was thinking in my mind of pornography or something similar, having no idea what God actually had in store. My last prayer before falling asleep that night (prayed with a real sense of not necessarily trepidation but expectancy that something was about to happen) was that God would "bring all things done in darkness to light."

The next morning at 4:00 a.m., while it was still dark outside, I was awakened by first our home phone, then my cell phone, and then my office phone ringing. I didn't know it until I checked messages later that morning, but God had answered my prayer before the sun even rose! It was the husband of the OW, calling to tell me that my husband had been in adultery with his wife. I remember an incredible calm coming over me, I think because I knew that this was God's answer to my prayer the night before, and He had prepared my heart for such a time as this.

My husband had seen the name on the caller ID and thought I was going to ask him to leave, as I had done before. Instead, I asked him to sit down with me and I told him I forgave him!! He cried, told me how sorry he was, and said he could not believe that I could forgive him for what he had done. It had to be God's very own mercy flowing through me, because it was real and something I could never have manufactured myself, even if I had wanted to! I didn't have to "will" myself to say anything—the words just came out, gracious and loving and merciful. The other reason I know that it was from the Lord is because it was permanent! Although I've had to extend forgiveness for other things, I have not had to continue to "re-forgive" my husband for that morning or anything leading up to it.

I became pregnant the same day my husband began his relationship with the OW. My husband says now that it was probably no accident that I miscarried the same week he ended it (which was before I found out what was going on); he truly felt that the loss of our child was a punishment for his sin. However, not only did God graciously allow me to "miss" all of the signs of the OW during that time, but He blessed me amazingly through a pregnancy that lasted only ten weeks! I was given the gift of delivering, seeing, holding, and burying our tiny baby, perfectly formed and the size of my thumb! God used the same event that seared my husband's conscience to bless me (Titus 1:15).

In just a few short weeks, that little person was already fulfilling the purpose God had planned for him since before the beginning of time, and God granted me favor by allowing me to carry that sweet child who is at this very moment in the presence of Jesus! God showed me His incredible mercy and forgiveness during that time, not only for my sin of having children out of wedlock but also for the sin of aborting His perfect creations before they were born. Although I knew I was already forgiven, He blessed me by letting me see this perfect baby and showed me that I not only have a whole "family" of children in His presence at this very moment, but in fact they are already waiting to greet me whenever He takes me home! I am amazed and humbled at God's mercy—that He would forgive me so completely that I can now rejoice at this fact with tears of hope and joy instead of tears of mourning!

I don't know for sure—His ways are so much higher than my ways—but to have experienced God's mercy so completely during that time may also have prepared my heart so that I could offer that same tender love and mercy to my husband.

The amazing thing is that when God allowed me to forgive my husband, He also turned my husband's heart so that he forgave me for all of my sins against him both before and during our marriage! That alone made the entire trial worthwhile! I truly believe there is great power in forgiveness—and, as I learned through RMI, there is not much that is more alluring!

We had a wonderful month after what I would now call our "restoration." We went away for a long weekend with our boys and it truly felt like the honeymoon we never had! As if confirming God's will for our marriage, a woman who didn't even know us approached me at the hot springs and told me what a beautiful family we had—she said that she could "tell" that there was truly something special in our marriage! God was beginning to show me that He had plans to fulfill the "desires of my heart" for my husband and our family.

I would like to be able to tell you that our trial stopped there and we lived happily ever after, but unfortunately things again took a turn for the worse. Everyone, even many of my Christian friends, began to tell me that I couldn't possibly forgive "so easily," that we would surely have to "talk about" and "work through our issues" or our marriage would never "really get better." Can you believe that after all that God had shown me about the dangers (and futility) of psychology and counseling (Isa. 30:1–3, Jer. 8:22, Isa. 5:13), I still took the bait?!! Within six weeks, after being told by our pastors that we should see a "professional counselor" instead of meeting with them (our first choice), we were back in counseling, dredging up the past and venting our feelings (Prov. 29:11, Phil. 3:13–14) instead of rejoicing in what God had done.

I even saw the old counselor one time (who I later discovered was going through a divorce herself) and took her advice to chat with another woman whose husband was unfaithful. After talking to these two women, I insisted that my husband take a lie detector test to "prove" that the OW was really out of the picture! Since my husband was eager to do anything to please me, he agreed. Immediately afterward, God impressed upon me the verse "some trust in horses and chariots, but we trust in the Lord our God" (Ps. 20:7). I realized that not only had I let my husband down by my ridiculous demands, but, even worse, I had let God down by placing my trust not in Him alone but in physical "evidence" I could see (which He certainly controlled anyway—Prov. 16:33—but that possibility escaped me at the time). I know, I know—you'd think I would have figured out by now that "friendship with the world is hostility toward God"! But I am foolish and stubborn and it takes me longer than most.... Praise God that He is patient and never gives up!

After a few months of counseling, by God's grace, my husband had the wisdom to see that we were going nowhere, always looking into ourselves instead of at God. On top of that, we were sick at the money we had to spend to get "advice" from those who were "peddling the Word of God," when the Mighty Counselor gives His counsel and wisdom freely to all who ask!! How much wiser would we have been had we gone to Him alone in the first place, and had I looked to older women to guide me in how to be a godly wife!

About that time, by God's divine providence, I "happened to" stumble across the Restore Ministries website, unexpectedly and out of the blue! I ordered the resources, including the Wise Woman workbook, which completely convicted me of all I was still doing wrong. I set to work to begin doing all of the things that I had never known about before! I was completely convicted of my contentiousness and asked God to help me stop arguing. I began to treat my husband as the spiritual leader of our home, deferring to him in everything he asked, and even insisting that my teenage girls do so also. ("What is wrong with you, Mom? Why don't you stand up for yourself?!" They thought I had gone off the deep end.)

I had never thought much about the verse that God turns the king's heart like channels of water (Prov. 21:1), but once I got a hold of that, everything changed! I also praised and thanked God that Erin showed me that God is the head of Christ, and "Christ is the head of EVERY man" (1 Cor. 11:3)! Knowing those two verses, I began to take everything to God in prayer, and what a difference it made! When I took my concerns to God first, He began to turn my husband's heart on specific issues without my ever saying a word!! He even began to turn my husband's heart toward me, with a tenderness and sweetness that I didn't know he still had!

(At one point, I suggested that home schooling my eighth grade daughter might be the answer to some issues she was having at school. Her dad said no, my husband said no, and she insisted she would run away from home if I tried. I didn't say another word to anyone but took it to God in prayer. Within three days, all three of them had changed their minds and all came to me, asking me to home school her for a season!)

I give all praise and glory to God for how He is changing me and drawing me closer to Himself. I praise Him for His Word ("Thy Word is Truth," John 17:17) and thank Him that He equipped Erin to painstakingly take the time to pull together all of the Scriptures about being a godly wife and mother—it is truly a blessing to have them all right at hand when a trial comes! I praise Him for Erin's unwavering commitment to speaking the Truth in love, and for not ever compromising or watering down God's Word. I am a living testimony to the fact that God wants us to trust completely in Him—without any doubting, doublemindedness, or friendship with the world. It is only when I trust in God alone that I can truly say, "The joy of the Lord is my strength"!

Yes, Jesus demands radical obedience, but where else would I go if not to Him (John 6:68)—He has the words of eternal life! I praise Him for His infinite grace and mercy when I fall short; He enables me to keep getting back up, and His mercies are new every morning! I can trust that He will complete every good work He has begun, and His grace is sufficient for me.

I must admit, it's a bit scary to write all of this down and put it "out there" for others to read, but I pray that what I write will give hope to others that He can forgive ANY sin, and that they would know how wide and long and high and deep is the love and forgiveness of Christ. "This is a faithful saying and worthy of all acceptance, that Christ Jesus came into the world to save sinners, of whom I am chief" (1 Tim. 1:15).

Most of all, I praise Him for the shed blood of Jesus, which covers my sins and enables me to have a relationship with my Maker and Creator! Nothing compares to the unspeakable joy of knowing Him, of sitting at the feet of Jesus and learning from Him. To me, He alone is the pearl of great price, worth any cost!

Michele RESTORED in Colorado RMI Fellowship Member and RMI Publishing Director

Restored AFTER He Divorced and Remarried the OW!

In 1998, I walked out of an 11-year marriage. I left a physically challenged wife and two young children and moved over 1,000 miles away to begin a new life.

Within 10 hours of arriving in town, I had been hired for two jobs. I honestly believed the Lord had blessed my leaving! I was sending financial support to my wife and was involved in a local church.

Two months after I left, one of my co-workers encouraged me to look through the personal ads in a local paper. Mostly to humor my co-worker, I looked through the ads and called one of the women. Although I knew from the beginning that this was not a relationship that God had for me, I continued to see the woman.

I divorced my wife and became more involved with this new woman and her four sons. I stayed active in church and did my best to encourage the boys to attend church also. The woman was very controlling and demanded that we move frequently.

In 2002, we married. My entire relationship with my second wife was tough. So often God showed me my sin, but I was blind to it. Even the woman's parents tried to show me things she was doing, but I ignored all the signs.

At one point my second wife got hold of my employer's credit card number and charged some of her bills. This resulted in my getting arrested and incarcerated.

During this time the Lord truly ministered to me. He showed me the error of my ways. It took quite a while; in fact, I believe it took my being incarcerated for the Lord to show me my sin. The Lord showed me that my second wife had simply used me. During my incarceration, I made it clear to my second wife that our relationship was over. I knew what she had done and was well aware of her cheating.

While I was incarcerated, I stayed in God's Word. The Psalms and the Proverbs especially strengthened me. The Lord showed me about commitment, faithfulness, and true love.

The Lord led me to contact my ex-wife regarding reconciliation. After much prayer, I did call my ex-wife and we prayed together. We spent a lot of time in prayer, and as we progressed in our reconciliation the Lord made my incarceration easier.

The turning point of our restoration was when my first wife told me she had been in prayer that we would reconcile; at that point, I knew it was God's will!

When I was released, I filed for divorce and returned to Tennessee to be closer to my first wife and our children. Our reconciliation went very well. The divorce from my second wife came very quickly, and on April 18, 2004, I remarried the wife of my youth! We have grown closer than we had ever been, and now our relationship is as God intended marriage to be!

For others seeking to restore their marriage, I would point them to prayer and standing on God's Word alone! What He has done for me, He also can do for others. I give Him all the glory and honor for restoring my marriage to the wife of my youth!

Ian, RESTORED in Tennessee

GOD HAS CHANGED ME!

My husband and I went through a period where things had gotten very rocky in our marriage. One issue for my husband, at that time, was my weight. I was smaller throughout most of our marriage, but after my pregnancy and being in a car accident, I had gained a lot of weight and started to have back problems.

Then, after the birth of my baby, my total focus was my little girl and I just didn't have the same zeal to serve in ministry. All of these things were causing problems in my marriage. My husband felt as though I didn't want to do anything with anyone, or go anywhere. My mom even tried to encourage me to get going. The reality was that I had gotten lazy and comfortable, but I didn't really believe that that this was case. My husband began to stay at work longer, and would not want to come home until late.

To make things even worse, my mother passed away. I felt and behaved as though my husband was not there for me when my Mom died, but he really was. For example, he made all the arrangements for our family because we were all so in shock. I resented that he was always doing things for the church, but not for home. I wanted him with me 24/7, but of course, that was impossible. My behavior almost ruined my marriage.

One day we talked and my husband told me how he felt about everything. I went totally off. I was furious. I couldn't believe he was thinking of himself after all that I've been through, but the problem was actually me. Finally he said he felt like leaving and he did leave the house.

I allowed the devil to come against me with all kinds of thoughts, and the rage really began. I got out a pen and paper and divided all of our bills and was ready to sell the house—I was going to let him go. Please keep in mind, that my husband is a good and righteous man, who loves God, and is very respectful. But I just wasn't getting the attention that I wanted. So when I told my husband of the plan I came up with, he said that "I just said that's how I felt, but I didn't say I wanted to do all of that!" Right then the Holy Spirit began to deal with me.

The Holy Spirit told me to go back to what initially attracted my husband, and to what we use to do before our work in the ministry ever began. I had to repent, because I realized that I was not submissive most of the time. We would never agree and I would never submit—I wasn't even trying. God told me to change not for my husband, but for Him. If I loved Him, then I would do it. So I did, and God begin to turn my marriage around quickly.

The turning point of my restoration was when I began to get closer to God and allow God to show me how to take care of my body. I begin to exercise and to eat healthy, and I noticed my husband's response to me beginning to change. God also change me in area of respecting my husband more, and learning to keep my mouth shut.

God showed me to follow my husband, and let him be the spiritual leader of our home. Before I use to get frustrated with my husband when it came to the ministry, but now, I pray and give it to God and rejoice. My friend gave me the *Restore Your Marriage* book. I know your resources work because I see the fruit of them in the lives of my friend and her husband.

My husband and I have confessed our vows again to each other again and have promised that divorce is a dirty, profane word and not allowed to be used in our mouth when it comes to our marriage.

Although we have little things come up here and there, I praise God because now it is none of the past problems ever happened in our marriage. I am telling others about your website and my husband and I are both sharing what God has done is our lives, so that others will have hope.

Ruth, RESTORED in Florida

Fought the Good Fight!

My husband had moved out and was living with the OW, a co-worker. He was not happy and felt unwanted in our 20+ years of marriage. Prior to deciding to fight for our marriage, I had sent him emails quoting Scripture and pointing out his sins and faults. That was the wrong way to handle things! He has since shared with me that it just made him mad and confirmed for him that he had done the right thing by leaving.

After approximately six weeks of separation and moving toward divorce, I realized that divorce did not have to be the answer. I decided to "fight the good fight." I was doing it alone with my prayers. A pastor friend across the country referred me to the Restore Ministries website. I immediately ordered the *Restore Your Marriage* book and read it within a couple of days.

I did not immediately release my attorney or sign the agreement at the end of that chapter. I had a hard time with the thought of dismissing my attorney, but I prayed about it, and within a couple of days I knew that I needed to follow through. A burden was lifted from me once I released my attorney. Ladies, you have to take that step! My outlook changed immediately.

I knew that God would restore our marriage; it was only a matter of days before I began to see changes in myself and would stop to think about what I had done to change. I realized it was not me— it was God working in awesome ways! The changes came after I began to realize the things I had done wrong, prayed for God to change me, and prayed for our marriage. I had to turn it all over to God and trust Him completely.

My husband began to notice little changes when he stopped by briefly for the kids or the mail. A mutual friend was also telling him how much I had changed. I asked him to forgive me for my contentiousness in the past. Getting past those ways was a relief to me; it is so much better to live a non-contentious life! Life is much more enjoyable, and I am happier too. Of course, this also comes from having the Spirit living within me!

My husband couldn't imagine that the changes were real and that I wasn't putting on a front, trying to get him back for the wrong reasons. We did not talk much but would occasionally email to discuss the kids. Just as Erin mentioned in her book, he tested me at times when he talked to me. I felt this happen on several occasions where he would say something to see if I would react. I did not react as I would have in the past, which showed him that I was a new person.

There were several different events coming up over the holidays, and I prayed in desperation for our marriage to be restored so we could attend together as husband and wife. It didn't happen. The kids and I were with my family in a resort area for Christmas, and I had invited my husband, letting him know he could join us at any time during the week. I prayed that he would show up on Christmas— it was the only thing I wanted! I went to bed crying and praying, but also realizing that it would happen in God's timing, not mine. Once I acknowledged to God that He alone could know when we were both ready, that's when restoration happened.

It was December 28 and my husband showed up at the resort. I did not expect it, and my husband didn't know until 30 minutes prior to leaving our hometown for the resort that he would return home. He wasn't sure why he was there, but I assured him it was God who had brought him.

Ladies, be sure to turn it all over to God. When you are waiting and having a rough day, pray and pray some more! If it weren't for my faith, for our awesome God, and for prayer, I would not have gotten through! Do not fight in the flesh—it will only frustrate you and slow your restoration. I found that so many things happened just as Erin said they would in the *RYM* book. I followed her advice, read the Scriptures, and prayed, and that is what got me through. It will get you through also.

"If God brings you to it, He will bring you through it." All of this happened for a reason. God had a plan, and now my husband and I are so much happier. We are living for God, we have a great marriage, and it just gets better every day!

Thank you, Dan and Erin, for your ministry. It is so awesome how you have helped so many marriages, ours included! God is wonderful, and what a gift He has given the two of you!

Lydia, RESTORED in Colorado

God's Timing is Perfect!

My marriage was in trouble before I even realized we had problems. My husband seemed distant from me, but I figured this was work-related since he was experiencing difficulty on his job. Little did I know that the devil had entered to steal, kill and destroy my marriage.

In May 2003, my husband had an affair and wanted a divorce. We went to two counselors who told us there was no hope for our marriage. After this, my husband went to live with his parents and actually filed for divorce. I prayed and prayed and asked many friends pray for us as well. Although I didn't know about RMI at that time, I began to apply some of the principles that I later discovered are outlined in the *God Can and Will Restore Your Marriage* book. We made one more attempt at counseling, and the counselor asked my husband some tough questions. At the end of the session, he still wanted a divorce. But to my surprise, the very next day my husband called me and asked me for a date. We went out and he said he changed his mind about the divorce that was filed! He shortly moved back home. How I praised God!

We were in counseling and things seemed to be going well. I thought my marriage was restored. However, six months later, my husband told me he'd had another affair and he needed to move out again with his parents. I was devastated and angry. I wondered why my marriage wasn't restored? Why did he have to leave again? Two days after my husband left, I found RMI through a prayer request chain that I had submitted on the Internet. As I read though the materials, I began to find out why my husband left me again. For one, I wasn't as close to God as I thought I was. I was a devout Catholic and went to church every Sunday, but did not have a personal relationship with Jesus. And two, I realized that I needed some changing!

As I read through and studied the RMI materials, I learned many things. I realized I was the contemptuous wife and also a Pharisee. I discovered that I made a mistake in becoming suspicious of my husband a month before he left, and "testing" him about things. I learned not to ask my husband questions and snoop around for information. Before, I didn't allow my husband to be the head of the house as evidenced by him always calling me "the boss". So, I learned to keep quiet with my husband and not tell him how to do things. The RMI materials helped to see that I needed be the heart of the home and submissive to my husband in everything. I bought a

Bible and began to read it. As I began to walk with the Lord, whenever I had an attack from Satan, I would open up my Bible at random and it never failed that there would be a passage that would jump out at me addressing the very problem that I was facing. It was amazing!

God showed me that I was going through the seasons like Erin stated on one of the tapes. I had never fasted before and so I did a three day fast. The day after my fast, my husband called me and came over and told me for the first time that he missed me and we were intimate. This was the end of winter and the beginning of spring because after that, we started talking a few times a week that slowly progressed to talking everyday. Then, we started to see each other a few times a week, which also increased as time went by. I noticed that I was able to keep quiet and not be the contemptuous wife! It happened very naturally. I knew this was God at work! A turning point of my restoration came for me on Easter Sunday 2004. My husband was taking a nap in our bed for the first time since he left. I took out my Bible and a passage came to me from John 16:19-23. It said that my grief will be turned to joy in a little while and when it turns to joy, no one will take my joy away from me and that what I ask of the Father in Jesus' name, He will give it to me. I then knew that in a "little while" my grief would be turned to joy and all I needed to do was wait and also rest in the Lord.

A little while after this, on a Monday, my husband told me that he was thinking about coming back home. I rejoiced! A week later I was getting anxious and again on a Monday, my husband told me again he was thinking about coming home. I waited. The devil attacked me with thoughts and told me that my marriage was like a piece of fine china with a crack that would never be fixed. I cried out to God and asked Him for help. God answered and told me he would not just fix my marriage but He would make it new (Rev 21:5)! The following week Monday, my husband told me he would be coming home next week. I was so excited!

However, the devil attacked the very next day with circumstances that made me question whether my husband was really going to come home. Again, I turned to scripture and read a verse in Esther saying "...gathering together with joy and happiness before God, they shall celebrate these days on the fourteenth and fifteenth of the month..." I thought to myself that my husband could not come home on the weekend (which was the 15th) because he said that he would be coming home next week. I should not have underestimated God's power because He gave me my miracle. On Friday, the 14th, my husband told me that he was going to be coming home the next day, on the 15th! I was so happy and just amazed at what God can do. Then another surprise, my husband came home on the 14th at 9:00 p.m.! My husband didn't even wait for the next day! God was with me for the entire journey and He delivered a surprise to me right at the very end! WOW! My husband told me that he missed me, that he loves me and that he never stopped loving that he and me likes the way that I make him feel!

I really liked and used many of the materials from Restore Ministries, including the *Restore Your Marriage* book, *A Wise Woman* workbook, all the "Be Encouraged" tapes, the Allure video, the Husband Returning Home video and the Queen Esther video. I didn't buy all these at once. I believe that God prompted me to buy the items when He knew I would need them. For example, I felt like my husband was getting closer to returning home, so I bought the Husband Returning Home video. The very day that the tape arrived, my husband told me that he was thinking about coming back home! God's timing is perfect!

When I look back at all of the passages in the Bible that God gave me during this process and put them together, it's like a story unfolding. I thank God that during this journey the He taught me to stay focused on Him and trust that He is more than able to take care of the situation. I know that this time my husband is home for good! Things are different from when he came home before and I have God's word on it this time!

Mary Beth, RESTORED in Indiana

It Happened for a Reason – God had a Plan!!

My husband had moved out and was living with the OW, a co-worker. He was not happy and felt unwanted in our 20+ years of marriage. Prior to deciding to fight for our marriage, I had sent him emails quoting Scripture and pointing out his sins and faults. That was the wrong way to handle things! He has since shared with me that it just made him mad and confirmed for him that he had done the right thing by leaving.

After approximately six weeks of separation and moving toward divorce, I realized that divorce did not have to be the answer. I decided to "fight the good fight." I was doing it alone with my prayers. A pastor friend across the country referred me to the Restore Ministries website. I immediately ordered the "Restore Your Marriage" book and read it within a couple of days.

I did not immediately release my attorney or sign the agreement at the end of that chapter. I had a hard time with the thought of dismissing my attorney, but I prayed about it, and within a couple of days I knew that I needed to follow through. A burden was lifted from me once I released my attorney. Ladies, you have to take that step! My outlook changed immediately.

I knew that God would restore our marriage; it was only a matter of days before I began to see changes in myself and would stop to think about what I had done to change. I realized it was not me—it was God working in awesome ways! The changes came after I began to realize the things I had done wrong, prayed for God to change me, and prayed for our marriage. I had to turn it all over to God and trust Him completely.

My husband began to notice little changes when he stopped by briefly for the kids or the mail. A mutual friend was also telling him how much I had changed. I asked him to forgive me for my contentiousness in the past. Getting past those ways was a relief to me; it is so much better to live a non-contentious life! Life is much more enjoyable, and I am happier too. Of course, this also comes from having the Spirit living within me!

My husband couldn't imagine that the changes were real and that I wasn't putting on a front, trying to get him back for the wrong reasons. We did not talk much but would occasionally email to discuss the kids. Just as Erin mentioned in her book, he tested me at times when he talked to me. I felt this happen on several occasions where he would say something to see if I would react. I did not react as I would have in the past, which showed him that I was a new person.

There were several different events coming up over the holidays, and I prayed in desperation for our marriage to be restored so we could attend together as husband and wife. It didn't happen. The kids and I were with my family in a resort area for Christmas, and I had invited my husband, letting him know he could join us at any time during the week. I prayed that he would show up on Christmas—it was the only thing I wanted! I went to bed crying and praying, but also realizing that it would happen in God's timing, not mine. Once I acknowledged to God that He alone could know when we were both ready, that's when restoration happened.

It was December 28 and my husband showed up at the resort. I did not expect it, and my husband didn't know until 30 minutes prior to leaving our hometown for the resort that he would return home. He wasn't sure why he was there, but I assured him it was God who had brought him.

Ladies, be sure to turn it all over to God. When you are waiting and having a rough day, pray and pray some more! If it weren't for my faith, for our awesome God, and for prayer, I would not have gotten through! Do not fight in the flesh—it will only frustrate you and slow your restoration. I found that so many things happened just as Erin said they would in the *RYM* book. I followed her advice, read the Scriptures, and prayed, and that is what got me through. It will get you through also.

"If God brings you to it, He will bring you through it." All of this happened for a reason. God had a plan, and now my husband and I are so much happier. We are living for God, we have a great marriage, and it just gets better every day!

Thank you, Dan and Erin, for your ministry. It is so awesome how you have helped so many marriages, ours included! God is wonderful, and what a gift He has given the two of you!

Lydia, RESTORED in New Mexico

Miracle Restoration Deep in the Heart(s) of Texas!

I discovered Restore Ministries when I was looking for answers, stumbling upon the website. It served to confirm to me what the Holy Spirit was beckoning me to do . . . do not divorce, let him go, and believe for your marriage. Erin's book filled in the blanks! Thank you!

God changed me before changing my situation. I first learned how to become humble and keep my mouth shut. I learned to lean on the Lord and the Lord only! I had to learn to submit to my husband, although it was against what my flesh was telling me to do. It took every ounce of faith to lean on the Lord and submit to my husband, especially when it seemed detrimental to my circumstance. Keeping my mouth shut, I ran to the Lord. I also learned about the power of fasting.

Ministry resources I have include *How God Can and Will Restore Your Marriage* and *A Wise Woman* and the "Be Encouraged!" videotapes. I highly recommend each of these resources. I have already passed the book along to my sister-in-law who is going through great marital difficulties. I have recommended the website numerous times.

One evening, as I sat on my balcony, I reviewed the events in my life over the past year—it seemed as though everything was spiraling downward. My marriage seemed nonexistent as my husband and I, although still living together, were worlds apart. I felt I had fallen out of love with him months ago and vice versa. It had been a long time since we were intimate.

I chuckled thinking that we were like roommates who shared a bed. Who knew where he was and what he was doing? Did I even care? I recounted in the last twelve months how much debt we were in, how little money we had, and that what money we did have I spent club-hopping, drinking, and hanging out with my girlfriends. My parent's were often doing our job of raising our son as he stayed with them three to five days a week.

Inside were a huge void and a heavy burden that plagued me every day and night. I remembered how I used to love the Lord with all my heart and here I was feeling as though He were a long lost friend. Then I started to wonder what would happen if Christ came back tomorrow. I knew without a doubt I would be left behind.

I instantly began to think about maybe praying again, but would He listen? Then without hesitation, I got down on my knees and rededicated my life to the Lord, asking Him to change me. As I prayed, I made the decision to stay in our marriage and work it out, but I asked the Lord to please give me "feelings" for my husband again or else I didn't see how it would work. I also prayed that He would change my husband and bring him back to the Lord.

In the following weeks, my hunger for the Lord grew insatiably. I began reading the Bible thoroughly for the first time. I was attending church regularly and tithing as the Bible instructs. In less than a month, my feelings for my husband had returned and I loved and was "in love" with my husband! It was miraculous since I hadn't felt that way for him since we first dated. I was just waiting and praying for the Lord to do the same to my husband. I believed for my husband's salvation.

One day as I was reading the Word and praying for the salvation of my husband and our marriage, the Lord showed me a chapter in Hosea. Briefly, the Lord tells Hosea to marry a promiscuous woman named Gomer. Gomer then leaves her husband to continue her promiscuous lifestyle with a string of men with the promise of greener grass on the other side. She goes through the trenches, eventually being sold as a slave. Hosea, while extremely heartbroken, is then commanded by the Lord to go and take her back as his wife despite her unbridled flaws.

After reading the account, I remembered thinking that it was interesting and amazing that the Lord would ask Hosea to marry and take back this woman who had a bad reputation and was unfaithful. It also ran through my mind that I supposed the Lord would have me do the same with my husband if I was in the same situation. However, I was not—at least that's what I thought at the time. I was sadly mistaken that since I had turned my life back to Jesus that the ball would reverse and begin rolling up the hill again. Boy, was I wrong.

A few months later, not only did our marriage take a turn for the worse, but I finally found out that he had been in adultery for a while. I thought once I confronted him that he would beg for forgiveness and make things right. Still wrong! He left and I was the one doing the begging and pleading for him to please not leave me.

I was stunned, shocked, empty, lonely, crushed, and my heart and self-worth were shattered. I thought, "Now what?" I thought the Bible taught that I had the right to divorce him and some well-meaning friends reminded me of just that. However, deep in my heart I wanted my marriage back, but I also thought it impossible.

My husband was convinced we married too young and we only married because I became pregnant while dating. To this day, although premarital sex is wrong and not biblical, I KNEW that I married him because he was my only love and "my soul mate." I also knew that he would never marry any woman simply because of a child. All in all, I knew it was a lie straight from the gates of hell.

The next day after I found out about the OW, I called an on-fire Christian friend. She shared with me that the Lord had told her that I was NOT to divorce my husband, but to let him go and wait on the Lord. Although I wanted to believe her, I was ridden with doubt, fear, and strong opposition in the spiritual and in the physical realms. I had so many questions: why, when, and how will this work out? Even through torturing emotional pain and anxiety, I committed to continue to trust and seek the Lord with all my heart. I "set my face like flint" and sought the Lord's will. After all, he didn't re-establish my love for my husband for no reason, right?

In the coming weeks and months, the Lord continued to confirm His will for me to believe for my marriage. It wasn't going to be a cakewalk and it would take much changing on my part. I had to learn about unconditional love (like Hosea). I had to banish any self-righteousness and pride on my part. I had to repent for my own mistakes, including premarital sins.

Accomplishing this feat truly required the ultimate essence of Jesus—love, sacrifice, obedience, and total humility! Wow, it was like the show "Extreme Makeover" (in the spiritual sense) where it takes a lot of pain to come out a brand new person. God was performing an extreme makeover inside of me.

In the meantime, my husband was off in fantasyland, free from the constraints of a wife and child waiting for him at home, vying for his attention. He called from time to time to check on us. He often asked for financial favors. I was working and supporting our child and myself while he was unemployed and living "the life." He would visit when the OW was at work. Although he would go out of his way not to lead me on, I would every once in awhile catch "a glimpse of what I saw in his eyes" when we were first dating.

The devil attacked spontaneously and suddenly when I least expected it after I had found my calm in God during this great storm. Once I found a burn hole in his underwear while doing laundry. I realized that it was from a candle. The devil allowed my emotions to do the rest.

Another time as I was looking for some tax papers, a love poem fell in my lap. It was from the OW to my husband. Again, I felt my very breath get knocked out of me and instantly I felt nauseous. I could go on and on and on, but my testimony is about victory and not about shame!

Finally, as was prophesied by a woman in a church revival, my breakthrough came! My husband moved home for the first time. I say first time because in the next six months was the most powerful spiritual tug of war yet. He was confused and literally moved in and back out with the OW, in and out, in and out, but more out than in, at least a half dozen times. I have to admit; it was the most painful part of the struggle, even more painful than the beginning when I first found out.

I faced rejection like a broken record; it played over and over again. Each time it felt like a painful blow in the stomach and a stab to my heart. However, I continued to believe in all the Lord had taught me through fasting, fervent prayer, and reading/reciting the Word. I probably shed the most tears and ate fewer meals at this time in my life than ever before. I often liken this last part of my trial as the "final exam." While my husband was being pulled back and forth by good and evil, it was as if the Lord allowed this critical time to test and stretch my stamina, my faith, and my perseverance. I felt much like Job as he underwent his last set of traumas or like the three boys in the furnace as the fire was turned up seven notches.

Praise God, while it was excruciatingly painful, I came out refined, pure, and consecrated! The whole storm was over a year and a half. Keep in mind though your test, in actuality, is a lifetime.

In the beginning, I had Christian counselors advise me to divorce him. I had a handful of supportive friends and prayer partners. In the end, I had one or two faithful, unwavering prayer partners, but in His wondrous mercy, I had Jesus before, during, and after the whole ordeal. Only God was able to restore an impossible situation!! He called something that was dead back to life!!

It has been almost two years since my husband came home permanently. It definitely took at least a full year to heal and overcome the damage done, but it is worth a new marriage in Christ and a broken divorce curse. Neither of us could be happier in our marriage.

My husband tells me daily that he loves me and he says he misses me when he's at work. I praise God for all that he taught me during my trial and now what seemed a curse was truly a masterpiece of a blessing from the Lord. He makes all things new!!

Kery, RESTORED in Texas

Impossibly Restored (by God Alone) and More!

After three years of praying and praying with Restore Ministries, my husband not only came home to our children and me, but received Jesus and was baptized and now is growing by leaps and bounds in Christ!! We are both renewed and restored, thanks to God!

The Lord had a lot of work to do on me so that I could learn how to love and how to pray for my husband; I had to get rid of all the hate, resentment and pain, first, as did my husband. We are both in love with the Lord and with each other now and want to work in a marriage ministry.

Throughout my trial, the principles from God's Word and RMI resources taught me perseverance, to never give up, endurance, and to KNOW that the Lord hears our prayers.

The resources I would recommend are: Restore Ministries and The Holy Bible!

Even when we do not realize it, God has heard our prayers and continues to work on our hearts. He is a faithful God Who keeps His promises to us when we are faithful. He is so worthy of our praise and worship!

There is no way our marriage could have been restored without God. We had been married 21 year when my husband left. He was angry, disillusioned, depressed and full of animosity. At the time, he said he was "done," but thankfully, the Lord had other plans. Thank You, Jesus!

Diane, RESTORED in California

God Moved So Quickly that I Didn't Get to Hear the Tapes!

There aren't words enough to praise God for who He is and what He alone can do! He is the God of the impossible! His love for us is deeper and wider and higher than we could ever imagine. He loves blessing us and asks so little in return. Obedience with faith and repentance bring healing.

This is my second marriage. I had been married once before (when I was not a believer) and left that marriage in hatred and anger. This time was completely different, because of God's grace!

When my husband was gone, the Lord continually encouraged me and showed me through Scriptures and through others that our marriage would be restored. He reminded me that it would be He who would soften my husband's heart as I sought and obeyed.

From the beginning, I was seeking and God was showing me what to do. Months before my husband left, I began praying for his brokenness. Six months later he lost his job and, eventually, decided to leave. It was at this time that God impressed upon me to wait on Him, to let my husband go—that like the prodigal he would return. God encouraged me to trust Him and let go of all control. He woke me and told me to fast and pray. He showed me that I was to be loving and gentle whenever we spoke. The Lord gave me His agape love for my husband, despite the circumstances. I didn't get angry with him but fell more in love while he was gone!

I never asked about the OW, but God woke me to pray every time there was temptation for him. My husband said he was physically faithful to me, and I know that's true because of what the Lord showed me. Early in my crisis, the Lord also showed me not to get a lawyer and to let the finances go, which was hard coming from a wealthy family who was pushing me to go after him. The Lord did lead me to write my husband one love letter, asking for his forgiveness.

During our separation, the single women's Sunday school class kept asking me to join them. I shared with them that I wasn't single but married, and—God willing—always would be! I found out about RMI when I was at church talking to a divorced woman; she gave me your pamphlet and shared her situation with me. I came home, immediately researched your website, and ordered the materials the very next day.

I ordered the first resource packet and right away I read the book on restoring your marriage, which is excellent. Although the Lord had impressed upon me that our marriage would be restored, my husband had filed for divorce, so I ordered the book on divorce as well. I responded without a lawyer, and—praise the Lord!—it is no longer in the court system! I have yet to listen to the tapes because God moved so quickly!

I again fasted and prayed for a week, as your book says to do. This just happened to be the week before I met with my husband for the first time in three months! I was the first to speak when we saw each other. I asked him for forgiveness, which really opened the door, and he cried.

Within twelve hours of our first conversation (a three-hour talk), he called and asked to return home! Twenty-four hours later, he asked all four of our children for forgiveness! He is now a changed man, always putting my needs first. I know now that the Lord used these trials to refine us so that we could both be the godly spouses He intends us to be.

It was your book that the Lord used to convict me of all my sins—playing my husband's Holy Spirit, being the leader in the home, being critical and judgmental, etc. I already had a close walk with the Lord, but these were areas that I had neglected, and I needed to put God first in all things. God spoke daily to my heart and gave me the strength and faith to obey. I have watched a miracle unfold, and I give Him all the glory!

God continues to change me daily. I am working through "A Wise Woman" and am in agreement with everything it teaches. As a Bible Study leader, I would love to offer it to other women as a study. I am excited to see God continue to move, and I hope and pray someday my husband (who hates that sort of thing) will ask to do the men's *A Wise Man*.

The two resources that I would most recommend are *How God Can and Will Restore Your Marriage* book and *A Wise Woman*. I'm sure your other resources are just as valuable, but those are what I read. I know God is going to use your ministry in incredible ways—in fact, He already has! My neighbors, who were missionaries for 20 years, have a restored marriage after the wife read your book in just one day!

I have already shared your website with at least ten women and want to tell the world about it. I am recommending your resources to friends in both difficult and good marriages—I think every woman should do the workbook no matter the state of her marriage! I am buying a copy for our son and daughter-in-law, as well as for our daughter who is falling in love. I wish every woman could have your workbook before she gets married!

He is the Healer and Restorer and Redeemer and Lover of our souls. I praise Him day and night, always and forever!!! Thank you, and God bless you and your ministry always.

Shelia, RESTORED in Colorado

Disastrous Circumstances, Yet God Delivers!

While I was looking for Christian websites for marriage restoration, not divorce recovery, because I believe God wanted ours and all marriages healed.

I had practiced the occult for most of my life, but after my husband left, God revealed Himself to me, delivering me from that bondage.

When I accepted Christ as my Savior, He changed me into the woman my husband wanted and needed all along. He led me to your site to show me He had not given up on my husband or marriage, and that He wanted me to stand in the gap.

God revealed His truth to me through His Word—you MUST know God's promises to claim His promises! NOTHING is impossible for our Lord to handle! Your resources helped by teaching me that your actions show God that you believe in Him. By wearing my wedding ring, letting my attorney go, and telling others my husband WOULD return, I affirmed that I trusted what God told me!

I only used your website as my only resource. The information led me to search God's Word and grow strong in it.

After being gone for eleven months, my wayward husband returned home! God was faithful to His Word and promises to lift me up when things looked hopeless, giving me the hope and strength I needed to stand in the gap for our marriage restoration. He gave me great peace and joy, and my husband said he saw in me "a new light."

My husband thought he had wanted the OW, but he didn't want her anymore. Furthermore, he saw himself being with our children and me, being truly happy. He knew God was calling him—you must put Him first.

I prayed for God to restore our marriage while my family was here, and God did more than I asked for by gathering my whole family one Sunday evening. My Mom and sister came from Alaska to visit my brother, who has brain cancer, and my husband's mom came from out of town to be with us!

Then my husband gathered everyone together and broke down before us, pleading forgiveness and said he was coming home! Just an hour before, my mom and brother had told me he was NOT coming home and that it was time to let him go! I told them that God told me otherwise and that I was to wait for His perfect timing. Within an hour, they witnessed the mighty hand of God working right before their eyes! Praise God—He is so awesome!

My husband asked to pray as we joined in a big circle. He came to "godly sorrow" right then—what an amazing thing for a family to witness!

My husband had told me all those months that he was happy with the OW, didn't love me, was NEVER coming home, and we would be divorced as soon as he could afford it. When he said those things, it hurt, but the Holy Spirit told me they were all lies, and to focus on Christ and His truth instead.

Don't ever give up! You may not see what God is doing with your spouses while they are away, but know that He is working! My husband revealed to his mom just last month (the first we started to see him changing) that his year with the OW was the most miserable he had ever had. He said he had made a huge mistake and wanted to come home, but didn't know how! He had been sleeping on the sofa at their home for a long time!

See, nothing is too hard for the Lord! Keep your eyes on Him, not on the circumstances around you. Be persistent in prayer, and believe it so you can receive it! Let God mold and make you into the person He wants you to be; then He will do the same for your beloved spouse!

Thank You, heavenly Father, for loving us so much and hearing our cries! Your truth really does change men's hearts and sets them free! All glory goes to God! May He bless you and bring your one-flesh mate back home to you soon!

Darla, RESTORED in Ohio

Amazing Successes to Restoration and Thereafter!

I was desperate for years before finding Restore Ministries—since 1995. I found you through another ministry that listed RMI as an alternative.

I realized how I had degraded my husband and myself with my mouth by telling everyone to pray and about our business. I told everyone all the bad things he was doing, and did not realize I was blind, poor, mean and domineering. I began to see my actions and sin. I was truly that Abigail wife; I was clean on the outside, but a liar and a manipulator on the inside.

God began to show me myself and continues to this day. I began to be kind and stand back and be grateful. Except for a very chosen few times in the beginning, I kept quiet. I watched the videos repeatedly. I remember Dan speaking of his Erin's kindness. It hurt to realize that my mouth was a pair of scissors.

I dishonored God and my husband and our family. I was a true hypocrite. I began to shut up. I wrote letters to all the people I had talked to and told them my own shortcomings and sins. I began to build my husband up in our daughter's eyes, and to love unconditionally.

I learned that all I ever had was Jesus Christ. I learned and read and reread *How God Can and Will Restore Your Marriage*. I also learned what a treasure my husband and family truly are and you can win the whole world, but if your family is not with you, it is hollow. Mostly, I realized not to deride nor ask questions of him.

I learned, through prayer, that God turned the situation around. I did not have to beg, nor did I have to threaten, nor did I have to scream. I had to let go, be kind and pray. I had serious changes to make and God is still making serious life changes in me. Truthfully, I have a long way to go.

As I started to change, God turned the situation around. When my husband came home, I had to visit the places and do the things he had done with her (the OW). I wanted to die on the inside. It was very painful. If I did not have RMI's videos, I would have cracked under the pressure.

I have the tapes, but I have passed some along, and have done the same with your books. A "Wise Woman" workbook just found a new home two weeks ago. All of them were much needed! The videos and *How God Can and Will Restore Your Marriage* were vital. My advice—"Get as much as you can!"

My husband has been home a little over a year now. It has been very difficult because the tests are harder. Ladies and men, do not give up. When I tell you it is harder, it is. However, it is only by the grace of God and everything that I have learned to remain at peace most of the time.

I praise God because my husband sleeps with his arms around me and holds my hands and constantly says he loves me. I praise God because there was a time when he never said those things.

I praise God because my husband has expressed a desire to work here at home in a converted garage shop, to start our own business. This is a gift from God because he did not even want or care about his tools anymore.

I can only give this exciting detail—I have been married for 25 years now. I used to beg my husband to read the Word of God with me. He now wakes me up sometimes, but he insists on reading the Bible and praying with me every morning since this past October!!! He reads and explains the Word to me.

I praise God because in past I would have corrected him. Now he corrects me! It is a joy. I still have a hard time with the reality of everything because it was so hard for 24 years. I can only thank Jesus Christ publicly. I can only thank God.

I had to stay home and not go to church for a while because I was waiting on God to lead my husband. That was most difficult. Before his return, I was in church and the Christian school almost daily. I was very agitated, but the Lord once again showed His goodness in the land of the living as seven months later He led my husband to church!! We have been there now one year!!! I give all of the glory to God.

Kelly, RESTORED in New York

Worth It All to Follow God to Restoration!

I found your website through another website when I was looking for someone who had results of a restored marriages.

I first learned that God heals all hurts and bitterness. Then, I learned to forgive my husband. When I became gentle and kind to him, he began to see the difference. I stayed away and never contacted him.

He always called me as I watched his heart turn back to our children and me.

I learned, too, that I had to stand on God's Word, especially when my husband didn't give us any chance for restoration. He had totally given up on us. The Lord blessed me with two women to help me believe when I became weary. I would go to your website and read the testimonies of marriages restored. Finally, I declared that one day I would be writing my testimony and here I am!

I purchased *How God Can and Will Restore Your Marriage* and *A Wise Woman*. I ordered copies for a friend and my brother, too. I wholeheartedly recommend both resources to encourage you in your walk.

I truly thank the Lord because He has been faithful to do what His Word says He would do. Not only that, but others around me have the opportunity to witness what the Lord did for us. It was long time, but the Lord kept giving me His Word.

In addition, He would send people to me—sometimes people I knew and other times not, to encourage them to believe. A couple a weeks ago as I was getting out of a friend's car, her five-year-old son said to me, "Sister, I thank the Lord that your husband is coming back."

Late December, my husband had a big fight with the OW. He packed his things, left her house, and moved in with a friend, but his friend's wife did not want him there. He had no other place to go. So, he called me a day later, quit his job, and came home after living out of state with the OW.

He was broken, but the "Wise Woman workbook" had prepared me for his return. Things were shaky in the beginning. I had learn to listen to the Holy Spirit telling me not to say anything about the things he does that I don't like, and to allow Him to complete the work He began in my husband. Praise the Lord!

G.S., RESTORED in Pennsylvania

Supernaturally Restored!

After being separated from my husband of seventeen years and near divorce, late one night I went online looking for encouragement to believe for our marriage. I went to a website and found a link to RMI.

I ordered Erin's book, the "Be Encouraged!" videos, and several other resources. They were my lifeline! Faithful each day, I watched the videos, listened to the book on tapes and read the book as well. I came to love and know Erin through the material. Her warmth and genuine love came shining through as if she were right there with me.

Although God had given me Scriptures for restoration before finding RMI, it was Erin and Dan's material that taught me the practical application of those principles. Without that instruction, I don't think I would have known what restoration behavior really looked like. I will forever be grateful for their teaching, as it equipped this saint to believe for her marriage and give the glory to the Lord.

The first thing I did was to repent of the sin the Lord had shown me I had committed in our marriage. I then committed myself to restoration, with a fervent resolve to stand my ground in Christ and not give the devil a foothold. I think choosing to be kind was very important. Not challenging my husband at every turn was vital.

As I placed my trust in Christ and expressed faith in my husband's judgment to handle things properly, not pushing him to help me financially or in any other way, God began to change his heart. Without a word from me, he became kinder and began to again support us financially.

Previously, it was weeks before the children heard from him at all. He then began to call at least every other day, then every day. God alone changed his heart. He had to change mine as well. You see, I had wanted a divorce. It represented freedom from pain to me and a fresh start or second chance to find a new life in the Lord.

But, once I knew the Lord was calling me to believe for restoration, I had to be obedient. My flesh wasn't willing at times, but my spirit was. God took that surrender and multiplied the fruit over and over. He taught me that I had made our difficult marriage an idol, instead of focusing on the Lord as my first love. That understanding made all the difference, even today.

I ordered Erin's recommended package from the start. The "Be Encouraged!" videos were my daily lifeline. When the enemy would attack through discouragement or disappointment, I would watch Erin and Dan's videos and understanding would come to me. The videos kept me from returning to my old patterns of anger, disrespect and fear.

I also purchased the books Facing Divorce and Workers at Home, the home schooling tapes, the CD testimony, the Women's Workbook and several tracts to hand out. Those resources were there to teach, support, encourage and remind me to continue to believe for our marriage.

Above all, I feel that the "Be Encouraged!" videos were the most effective, as well as the Question and Answer videos. I used the book (and still do) as a reference every day.

I am amazed at the faithfulness of God and give Him ALL the praise and glory for restoring our marriage and home. From the moment I felt His quiet voice speak to my heart about restoration, He made the way clear by providing RMI and its support. After eight months of separation, my husband returned home. Although restoration is difficult work, perhaps much harder than I had anticipated, I see the Lord's promised fruits coming from it in our children, spilling over into our community.

He has now called me to begin a restoration group in my area and I have been helping women consistently as He sends them my way. All glory to the Lord, for He alone can bring life to the lifeless! Our hopeless, dead marriage has been resurrected by the Holy Spirit and I will praise His name forever. And through His grace and mercy, our marriage will continue to grow.

He is no respecter of persons, so He will do the very same for any one of His children willing to surrender to Him and follow His Word. The enemy hates this move of God's Spirit and will fight you each step. Be aware as you walk this path and know that in the name of Jesus, you have victory over any schemes the enemy has for your family.

Continue in Christ and be encouraged! You are a rare and precious child of God, as you stand for sacred marriage in this evil day. God is faithful and He will bring His love back to you and your spouse.

Katie, RESTORED in Florida*

This restored marriage testimony is especially dear to me. Katie's* name is a name most anyone would recognize around the world. She came to us for help but because of her high profile name, she needed to be sure that her identity would be kept confidential.

Through our correspondence we became close friends and I was thrilled to see her marriage restored so quickly after she became a member of our fellowship! She has also offered to help us with our vision for RMI Home Fellowships.

Please keep Katie in your prayers as she helps us with our vision for this AWESOME way of getting the Good News out to the marital hurting in our communities! Erin

Alabama Restoration!

I was blessed that a friend shared the web address of RMI with me only about six weeks after my husband moved out. After finding RMI, I learned of my shortcomings and what I did wrong to contribute to my husband feeling that he needed to leave. God molded and changed me in His refining fire. But as the Word says, "He will never leave you nor forsake you."

The resources from RMI that I used were the *Restore Your Marriage* book, the *Wise Woman* workbook, *By the Word of Their Testimony*, the "Be Encouraged!" video series, *Workers at Home*, and the "Alluring and Unconditional Love" video.

These resources, in conjunction with the Bible, taught me that my husband was my God-ordained authority and taught me how to take my problems privately to God instead of to my husband. They taught me to win my husband "without a word," and that "many words" cause strife, anger, and confusion.

The *RYM* book taught me the fundamentals of restoration, including what I had done to cause this. It also showed me how God, without my spouse, could help bring about restoration.

The "Be Encouraged!" videos did exactly what they said—they encouraged me! I believed Dan when he said that my husband still loved me but that it was buried deep inside and would one day blossom. Those tapes kept me going. "Alluring and Unconditional Love" taught me how to love my husband and give to him unconditionally with love.

I would recommend the *Restore Your Marriage* book and the "Be Encouraged!" video series.

God is truly awesome! His Word does not return to Him void. Whatever the Bible says about marriage, speak it! It will not return void, but will accomplish exactly what it sets out to accomplish!

The eight months without my husband have been hard. We have four children and no family where I live. However, I knew that God was calling me to believe for our marriage, and I knew that I must do whatever God wanted me to do.

I followed the principles of Restore Ministries. I fasted and still fast. I have lost over 50 pounds and feel and look so much better.

My husband left and had almost nothing to do with me. As Erin instructed, we still had intimate moments, but it was obvious there was no emotion involved in it for him. But, I was being a submissive wife as God instructs, so I knew God would honor my being in HIS will. My husband made sure I understood the whole time he was gone that he was not coming back. He moved out and got his own house, and I did not even know where he lived! I praised God for what I did NOT see, because I know that God's ways are not our ways, and I know that His Word says He will not allow us to be put to shame.

I just knew that God had a plan, and I was content to let Him work His plan. Yes, it hurt. Yes, I cried out to God. Yes, I got weary sometimes. But, I never doubted for one moment that God would restore, because I knew that God did not want me to be double-minded.

Just two weeks ago, my husband told me that even though he knew it would hurt, he had to be honest and tell me that he did not want me or any other woman in his life—that he would be content to live the rest of his life alone. He also told me that he hurt every day and wished he were dead.

I prayed even more fervently after that, because it was obvious that Satan was trying his tricks again (to steal, kill, and destroy). I don't know about anyone else, but I was not letting Satan have my husband, our marriage, or anything else that my precious Savior already paid the price for with His precious blood shed on Calvary.

Then my husband, who had not even held a conversation with me in eight months, called and said through his tears, "I love you with all my heart and soul, and I want with all my heart for our marriage to be restored." We are now moving the whole family into his new house!! Praise God! He can do it! And He WILL do it!

Every night I prayed Job 33:14-18 over my husband and inserted my husband's name, and every morning I prayed the hedge of thorns. I prayed and praised so much that I finally understood what "pray without ceasing" really means!

Remember, saints, when you find out something that your mate is supposedly doing, and it hurts, and you want to call them and fuss about it, don't! It is the enemy trying to block your restoration! Usually, some type of breakthrough is right around the corner!

God Restores All over the World!

I found Restore Ministries while surfing the Internet, looking for positive words and expressions connected to marriage healing.

Our heavenly Father taught me first to KEEP MY MOUTH CLOSED, to not pursue my husband, but to pray fervently for him and not talk negatively to others about him. God taught me to submit to him in everything.

I started to find joy in my situation, to enjoy being a housewife, exploring what the children and I could do together. Before, I used to work, work and work and if I didn't work, I was exhausted. I had another woman looking after the children.

I learned the following:

We walk by faith, not by sight!

Delight yourself in the Lord, and He will give you the desires of your heart.

Submit yourself to your husband as unto the Lord; be subject to him in everything.

Reward evil with good.

God is not a respecter of persons.

Your fruits will show others whom you believe in.

The Lord's ways are so much higher than our ways; His thoughts higher than our thoughts.

The Word of the Lord NEVER returns void.

How God Can and Will Restore Your Marriage and *A Wise Woman* were the resources that helped me to become obedient (and it was very difficult for me to accept some of the sayings—I rebelled in the beginning!). They have been a continuous support, encouragement and means of breaking my resistance and disobedience, as they are very clear and demanding. I would recommend both of these resources.

I cannot express enough all that the Lord has done for us! In fact, I feel that the main thing that has happened to me is learning to trust in the Lord and stop doing things on my own. The further we progress into restoration, the more clearly the Lord stops me from DOING. He has given us ALL we ever imagined and so much more.

He has turned curse to blessing, night to day, rain to sun, and storm to peaceful quiet! Praise His holy name! His mercy endureth forever!

When I "met" Restore Ministries on the Internet, our marriage was in a crisis, tormented, full of quarrels, misunderstandings, separation and old grief. We have been married for nine years and have two children. Right from the beginning, there were problems. I filed for divorce three times. I loved my husband but always nagged at him, and worshipped my own depressions, my ability to work hard and also my intellect. I thought he was idle and unable, and told him so and tried all I could to change him.

In fact, changing him was the god that I worshipped every day. The results were: separation every year, my husband leaving us regularly, and financial breakdown. Nothing progressed.

As I studied Restore Ministries' resources and started to read the Bible regularly, submit, shut my mouth, and pray and fast, our situation turned around within three months. My husband then announced he would be coming back home. After two more months, he returned, and we immediately moved away from the country we had lived in as my husband desired.

My husband took over all responsibilities, began to build his own company, started an education and feels very satisfied here. The restoration process is progressing every day like the parable of the growing seed—it grows while we sleep. I have backslidden and made many mistakes along the way, but the Lord always forgives and allows me back into His presence.

The latest step along the way is that my husband has started to read his Bible and pray with us. PTL!

Elisa,* RESTORED in the United Kingdom

Restored Faster Than She Ever Imagined!

I found your ministry through another individual via the Internet. And as I fasted, prayed, and stayed in God's Word, He changed my situation more and more. He gave me everything I asked for sooner than I thought I would receive it! I learned that God is AWESOME, and that if I spend time with Him, He will answer my prayers! Praise God!

I will continue to spend time with the Lord fasting and praying because I know my husband and I have a long road ahead of us. However, I also know that we can do all things through Christ who strengthens us!

Principles that I learned are to pray a hedge of protection, a hedge of thorns, a wall of fire, and God's armor on my husband daily. Then, I learned to fast and to pray with authority. I also learned how important it is to be sincere in seeking the Lord.

I have several of RMI's resources. I have at least five of your books as well as your tapes (VHS and cassettes). They were all encouraging. I especially like the cassettes because I can listen to them as I drive.

I recommend *How God Can and Will Restore Your Marriage*. It is truly awesome and very encouraging! I bought the cassette version, also, because I needed to hear the information again and again and again.

Thank You, Jesus, for Restore Ministries! Thank You, Lord, for Erin and Dan! Thank You for my ePartner!

Lord Jesus, I cannot praise You enough for restoring our marriage. You are truly worthy to be praised! I give You the highest praise—hallelujah! I worship You, Lord! I praise Your name! I give You all the honor and the glory! LORD, I LOVE YOU!

Another Restoration by God!

When my husband left this past January, I searched for Christian prayer sites. A fellow Christian saw my request and sent me an email. He suggested your ministry. He also told me about your book, *How God Can and Will Restore Your Marriage*. Praise God!

Once I received your book, I began to look at my situation in a completely different way. Yes, I still cried, but I cried TO THE LORD instead of crying for my husband. Your book taught me a lot about myself and how I had to change! Praise God for opening my eyes to His Word!

Without the Lord leading me, I could never have gotten through each day feeling stronger in spirit. I finally let God take full control of my life and our marriage. Whenever I felt the urge to call my husband, I prayed. Yes, I left him a card for Valentine's Day, but the struggle got easier the more I read the Word and talked to God.

Your book gave me reason to believe our marriage would be restored when the Lord was ready to do His work. He taught me that even though my husband was giving up, I had to trust Him with my entire being. He taught me that I, too, was at fault because I was not perfect.

I had to forgive my husband. Hard? Yes, but not with prayer as God made it easier for me to have a forgiving heart. I learned that I needed to control my anger. I had to stand firm against the enemy, believing in the Lord to crush him and win my husband back.

Erin's book *How God Can and Will Restore Your Marriage* was the best money I ever spent. I learned that my faith in the Lord was not what I thought it was. I had believed all my life, but I never really gave God full control of my life until I read your book. Praise God for leading me to your ministry!

After I read the book about eight times, a friend I met in a prayer room had her sister email me as she also was going through a separation. I knew the Lord was asking me to give her encouragement. I asked for her address and sent her my book. I pray that the Lord leads her as He did me.

The only resource I had was the Restore book, but I am sure your other resources are excellent; I just haven't had the opportunity to get them.

Praise my Lord Jesus, His Word is the Truth! He will never forsake His children. God worked in me and then worked in my husband. I give all the glory to the Lord! Although our separation only lasted about three and a half months, it felt like an eternity. This is my testimony...

We had been married four years, but I had been with my husband for the past thirteen years. When he looked at me and said he didn't love me any more, I was devastated. He told me our marriage was over and, no matter how much I begged, he wasn't coming back.

When we spoke and I told him I was praying for him, his response was, "Not even your prayers are going to bring me back." I read the Word, prayed, and cried to the Lord. I knew He answered me when I felt a warm sense of peace come over me. The Lord was telling me I would be okay. I knew I could not fight this fight.

I had to let God take control and lead me. Two months separated, I was reading my Bible before church. It was early and I thought it strange for the phone to ring. The Lord had taken control—it was my husband! He asked if we could get together to talk. He told me he had not slept all night; a voice kept telling him he needed to call me.

God is awesome! We went to church together and spent a few hours talking. I felt as if all my troubles were over. My husband wanted to take time talking before coming home too quickly. I agreed, trusting the Lord to do His work.

Well, the enemy wasn't going to give up so easily. I found out that my husband was with the OW on two occasions. Once again, I felt like I was being slapped in the face. The more I cried, the more I prayed. Now the most important prayer was for the Lord to give me the strength and forgiveness I needed to deal with this news.

It was hard, but with prayer and time, it got easier. Yes, the devil tried many times to step back in, and there was one time that my husband was ready to walk out again. However, this time my fight was against Satan. I let my husband know that I was not going to give up on our marriage.

It's been over six months since my husband returned, and together we thank God for loving us enough to save us from the enemy. Thank you, Erin and Dan, for your wonderful ministry, and for your encouragement. God bless you.

Lord, I give You all the praise and glory! I did nothing except believe and trust in You.

Drugs, Alcohol, Another Woman, Pregnancy, Yet Restoration!

My husband left home unexpectedly, breaking my heart. I was desperately searching the Internet for books or anything to help me understand what was happening and to give me hope that God would bring my husband home. I found Restore Ministries and read your resources for three months, being encouraged before I ordered my own material.

I received Restore's materials on our anniversary and it turned out that my husband came over that day. He was dropped off and asked me if I wanted to get something to eat. I had read the first chapter of *How God Can and Will Restore Your Marriage* and it helped me through the dinner. That was the first bit of hope I had since he left April 1! God worked from then on, changing me and helping me to be kind and truly forgive. It was a miracle in my heart.

I learned about biblical submission and about trusting God no matter what the situation looks like. I learned to be thankful for very small things, knowing God is faithful to provide what we need when we need it. I learned that ALL things do work together for good for those who love God and are called according to His purpose.

I learned that God won't give me more than I can bear and yet it may be more than I thought I could take. I think I learned to love God above all else. I pray God will give me as many trials as I need to keep me humble and depending on Him—I mean that. Doing it our own way is not peaceful or joyful and He knows it!

The resources that I would recommend included:

How God Can and Will Restore Your Marriage—helped me so much to learn to control my mouth!

The Wise Woman workbook—so much help and hope!

The "Be Encouraged!" tapes—SENT STRAIGHT FROM GOD AND JUST WHAT I NEEDED!!! I did wait to listen until doing the entire workbook, too. I think God blessed me for my obedience.

The workbook and tapes were the most helpful resources.

God helped me repent of my selfishness in our marriage and in general. He helped me to see myself as I was and was there with His mercy for my broken heartedness. I became alive in my faith as never before, even though I had always been excited that He had saved me.

It was different to have Him sustaining me like that, as I was learning so much. I did not diet or exercise, but lost a lot of weight and felt better than I had in a long time. I fasted for the first time and discovered a deeper kind of praying than I had known.

Praise the Lord, for He has done it! I was married for seven years when my husband left. I found out he was involved with another woman, drinking excessively, and using drugs. We had attended church together the last few years and he professed to be saved, which he now says was just an emotional experience.

We do not have children and the OW became pregnant. She had a miscarriage just before my husband left and it was more than he could handle. He planned to leave me and build a family with her. God used the situation to completely break me. I lost all interest in everything, but clung to God who held me closely.

He gave me a song and hope when it was so dark and painful that I could not see. God gave me compassion and mercy for my husband and helped me to love him. That was not me. I can't even believe how God changed me!

I had been so selfish and was not the wife that God wanted me to be. I had been through disappointment before, but nothing had ever gotten to me like this. It was God's timing. He knew I needed to experience this to change more into the likeness of Christ.

My husband did not talk much to me for the first six months as God continued His faithfulness to help me not give up. He used Restore Ministries to encourage me; I could not have made it without you. I read and read and read and listened to tape after tape. I was so dependent on God, and although I had a lot of grief, I knew He was sustaining me and that was incredible.

God started to give me opportunities to spend time with my husband after six months. Extreme testing followed because he told everyone he would never get back with me because we were miserable together. He kept telling me how far apart we had grown and that I could not see it.

However, I just agreed, although it hurt. My husband shared things I did not want to know about the OW and I did pray for her, but it was killing me to hear the hold she had on him. I know that I am not better than she is and God knows that is true.

Around Christmas, my husband called crying as he was in a terrible state. He couldn't understand how I could ever forgive him or how he could have done this to me. He came over that night and slept, but left the next morning. Then he called New Year's Eve (he was alone—PTL!), and we made plans to meet the next day.

We went to lunch and he wound up asking me for a divorce! I did not know how to respond. I ignored him and then gently disagreed for a half hour and then God brought to my mind to agree with him. So I did. And it NEVER came up again! What a test!

My husband continued to run from God for another month or so, but then God, in His perfect timing, saved my husband. He came home in April—we had been apart exactly one year! What a year!

We have worked on our marriage since he came home, but I struggle now more than when he was gone. I see that clearly. I am so thankful though, and I give God glory every chance I can. I get down on myself and forget about grace sometimes, that it is by His power and Spirit that I overcame and will continue to overcome.

I am learning to this day how to respect my husband (thereby obeying God), which I had never done before because no one ever taught me or corrected me before this trial. Now when I see that behavior in other women I try to correct them gently.

I hurt my husband so much. I know now that he is ordained by God to get my respect—no question. I want to grow in that way. My husband does not drink anymore, and we go to church. He wants me to be happy and he tries to encourage me. He stopped seeing the OW before he came home (God's mercy on me).

My husband is growing and I cannot believe what has happened. God is so good. I am not sorry any of this happened and I expect God to get every drop of glory. Praise God for things just as they are, trusting our Father to do the work as we humbly obey!

Another Restoration Miracle of the Lord!

I found Restore Ministries online when I was searching for a support group for people who wanted their marriages restored.

The Lord showed me that He was indeed using the trials in my life to draw me back to Him. During the time I was away from the Lord, my life felt hopeless and meaningless, and, even though I had a relationship with my husband, I felt lonelier than I ever had.

I soon became a contentious wife, constantly nagging and treating my husband more like a child than the leader of our home. I became prideful and resentful. I was completely blinded to everything until my husband was removed from our home and I began to seek God. He showed me that I had been wrong. He also opened my eyes to see that the battle was not against flesh and blood, but against Satan.

God gave me a new perspective on my circumstances and taught me how to love my husband the way He does. God became my support, encouragement, Comforter, and Friend. He taught me that all things are possible with Him, and if I remain in Him and His words remain in me, He will give me the desires of my heart. He developed in me a deep love for His Word and for spending time with Him. He also opened my eyes to all the people around me who are hurting because they are lost and need to know the love of Jesus.

Even before I found Restore Ministries, I was certain God wanted me to believe for our marriage. I knew I had messed up in many ways. I wanted my husband to come home, but I was also terrified that he would. I was terrified because I didn't know how to be different. I was filled with fear that I would go back to being the contentious, nagging wife because I knew that when he came home he wouldn't be perfect.

But, through the resources of Restore Ministries and God's Word, I learned that reconciliation and forgiveness are always God's desire. I learned that I could claim that for myself and not doubt it. I learned what the Bible says about the role of a godly woman and wife in the home. I learned that other women were going through exactly what I was going through, and they were seeing God fulfill His promises to them through miraculously restored marriages! God led me to Restore Ministries, which provided the encouragement I needed at exactly the time I needed it.

I have the *Restore Your Marriage* book, the *Wise Woman* workbook, the Q&A books, the Testimony book, the "Be Encouraged!" videos, two Q&A videos, and Dan and Erin's testimony on CD. I had very little money, but I prayed that God would provide to buy the resources that would encourage me, and He did so faithfully! All of the resources helped me. They gave me encouragement, hope, and a sense of peace.

I especially recommend the *Wise Woman* workbook. It helped me learn how to be a godly wife. So many of the principles can be applied not only in a marriage relationship but in all of our relationships! I recommend it to anyone who is married or ever wants to be married. Many of the Biblical principles in it were new to me because I had been so diluted by the ways of the world.

Lord, I praise You for changing my heart and for molding me into the woman You created me to be! Thank You that You have worked all things together for the good. Even circumstances that seemed so horrible at the time—You used them to increase my faith and draw me closer to You. You have taught me the power of prayer and the importance of abiding in You.

Thank You for bringing my husband home, but, most of all, for giving him a love for You and a desire to seek Your ways. You have done more than I even hoped for, and You are not finished yet! I praise You for You are wonderful, wise, and omniscient! I love You!

You deserve all the glory, honor, and praise. Please use our lives as a testimony to our families of Your love, forgiveness, and power!

God Shines on Another Marriage in Illinois!

It was by divine intervention that I found Restore Ministries. I was so down spiritually and emotionally that I was surfing the Internet looking for help and hope, and I found you!

God filled all the voids with His sweet presence in my life. I have been filled with His Holy Spirit, and I enjoy just being in His presence. God always reminds me of that when I try to blame my spouse or others. I've grown confident in the fact that Jesus loves me no matter what and that makes the difference for me! It is easier to be free when I let go and let God.

I learned to shut my mouth, which was very hard because I had always been a people person. However, I now tell God all my concerns as I journal and seek Him for every situation in my life. My life is in God's hands.

In addition, I have learned to cast down imaginations and every high thing that exalts itself against the knowledge of God; I've finally learned that (as Dan and Erin say) the battle is going to be lost or won in the mind.

Oh, the joy that floods my soul! Even if God never did anything else for me, He has already done so much more than I imagined.

My favorite resources are the Women's Workbook and the "Be Encouraged!" video series. I have had them for almost two years and I still return to them from time to time. I have shared them with so many people who have had their marriages restored, too!

The thing that I like best about the materials is that they are straight from the Word of God, and you cannot go wrong following His Word! I know that this ministry is straight from God.

Please get the cassettes. Erin's voice will put you to sleep on those lonely nights when your soul can't find any peace. She soothes the soul with all the hope she offers through her testimonies. She shares the times she was out of God's will and how she got back on track.

Abba Father, Creator of everything and everyone, it is with sincere devotion and adoration that I praise Your holy name! Thank You, O God, for being the lifter of my bowed down head, my bowed down heart, and my heavy load.

My praise is long overdue. You, O God, had already restored our marriage, but I was being rebellious by not praising You even before I received the victory. Your Word says, "Don't wait until the battle's been won; shout now! Hallelujah! Hallelujah!"

When I finally stopped fighting in the flesh and went into spiritual warfare, God stepped in and took over everything. I can't stop praising Him for every trial and tribulation because He has been with me every step of the way. Thank You, Lord, for this ministry, for Your anointing of it, for the fellowship, for the friendship, and for the love that's shown here. I will bless the Lord at all times; His praise shall continually be in my mouth!

Hang in there, my brother; hang in there, my sister! Your season of harvest is about to come forth. God bless us all.

God Restores Another Marriage!

Praise the Lord—I have to give God all the praise and glory He so richly deserves! My husband has moved back home after being gone for four months. We have had problems for almost two years. I could not have survived the past two years without the Lord giving me strength and wisdom.

Thank you for your website and encouragement—it has truly blessed me. When I found your site, I immediately knew I was going to believe in God for a miracle in our marriage. The journey has not been easy or pain free—it was extremely difficult! I would not wish it to happen to anyone. At the same time, it has been a growing experience in my spiritual life that I would not trade for anything!

God has been so faithful and patient with me, even when I was not with Him. He has continually answered prayer, and has burdened people to pray and fast for me. I will never cease to give the Lord the praise and glory for what He has done. He asked so very little on my part. All the Lord asked was that I believe in Him, and wait on Him. That does not sound like much, does it?

At times, I made those two things a lot harder than they needed to be. I have had days when I was impatient and doubted God, but He never gave up on me! He kept picking me up, and continued loving me. There were times when things looked impossible in the flesh. Remember, WITH GOD, NOTHING IS IMPOSSIBLE!

I know if He could soften my husband's heart, He could do the same for anyone else who would believe. You do not have to DO anything (on your own). You just have to trust God and believe—it's very simple!

I discovered from your ministry's resources that I was not the great wife I thought I was. Can you believe that? I have been so judgmental of things my husband did or said. I nagged him, and was NEVER submissive. NO, not me! Boy, have I been deceived! I know now just how wrong I have been. Coming to that understanding has made the biggest change in me.

My husband came home because I changed! God changed me; my husband saw those changes and wanted to come home! He has told friends that he respects how my spiritual life has grown, and how I have matured in the Lord. I appreciate that comment more than anything he could have told me, including "I love you" (which he has not said in two years)! But he will!

The night before my husband moved back, the phone rang. It was the pastor of a church he visited with his best friend. His friend told the pastor that the house my husband was renting would soon be available.

The pastor called to ask my husband about renting the house. Afterward, my husband told me he had asked God for a sign that he was doing the right thing, and would not regret coming back. What a sign God has shown both of us!

When things look their worst, please don't give up—you are on the verge of a breakthrough! In the last few weeks, I have been under numerous attacks, but look where the Lord has brought me now. PRAISE THE LORD!

God is so good and worthy of our praise! I pray that God will continue to bless Erin, Dan and your ministry to further the good work to encourage others in our situation. All your materials are true!

The part of your book about having a quiet and gentle spirit might as well have been written directly to me. I thank God for changing that in me! My husband thanks you too! Amen!

Life after Miracle Restoration Will Never Be the Same!

I was referred to Restore Ministries by a man who answered a posted prayer on the Guidepost prayer site last November or December.

Within two weeks, God led me to several ministries that pray for healed marriages. I heard a voice that woke me up one Sunday telling me to go to church (when I thought I was alone). I thought I was alone but learned quickly that I was NOT!

My heart became forgiving and I sought and hungered for the Word. I constantly read about God and His promises. (Before that, I HATED to read!) I had complete faith and trust in God to heal my family and sanctify them all through me. I was armed with the weapons of God and was NOT afraid to use them.

I hate what Satan likes and refuse to allow him into my life or the lives of those around me. Through the trials (and there have been MANY—fires, floods, three lawsuits, one of our children placed in a youth camp for stealing, etc.), God gave me comfort and peace! It is amazing and exciting to be a part of everything. My life will NEVER be the same!

Most importantly, I learned to love and forgive just as Jesus did; when I thought I could not, I asked for help in doing so! It sounds too easy, but it is the truth! And, I learned to worship and praise and pray, no matter what! Even when you don't feel like it, force it and soon it comes naturally. I even recorded prayers so that Satan did not win any skirmishes! I played them when I did not want to say them.

Your resources that helped the most were *How God Can and Will Restore Your Marriage*, the workbooks and the "Allure" tape.

I DO praise God for the changes HE has made in my life. I praise Him for the changes in my husband and children. A year ago, I wanted to be ANYONE else and now I cannot wait to see the person that God will make of me. I like who I am now and cannot wait to serve Him and be a testimony of His great love and grace!

Restoration in California!

God has brought my husband home and He has made a new godly man of him! My husband is a blessed man of God and I am a new wife!

I found your ministry because I was in need of sound and very spiritual marriage healing advice and I began to search for anything from God. He led me to your website and I loved it from the first! I will continue to read the blessings and count mine daily. I needed to know of some up-close and personal restored marriages, which I found on your site.

I was blessed when I found Restore Ministries and started reading the testimonies. I was blessed, encouraged and impressed by the directions from others who had "made it through." I was also blessed by another friend whom I met through your ministry who gave me a lot of the literature that I now treasure.

God began to show me that one day I would be glad that He was taking me through my storm and that it was a growing process for just a season! He promised never to leave me nor to forsake me! He always carried me in my down and up days!

What I learned through all of this was that He told me to just trust Him, and if He would take me to it, He would take me through it! I had to learn to depend on Him only and put Him first in my life—no matter what! He taught me that nothing was too big or too small for Him! He taught me to hold on to His promises and that He would never fail me! He showed me that nothing was impossible for Him!

I have some of your literature and it is something to behold!!! I especially found "Facing Divorce" very helpful—I loved the prayer at the end that included everything in those five pages that I needed to pray about. I am still using those prayers daily! Let me say that the inspiration of God and the real-life stories will definitely cover what you are going through right then! You can just put your name in at any given moment! Please read and be encouraged about what God wants you to have and that is a restored marriage. Read Restore Ministries' books and do just what God has led them to share with you!

So many times when I felt low, I would read some of my books and just stand up and say "Thank You, Lord, for these encouraging books!" Believe it and receive it! The stories are right in your lap and you just get so happy to know what God can turn around for your good! Read them and it will help you to believe for your marriage no matter what it looks like to your carnal eyes!

God's Word does not return void! He will do just what He said He would do! So, enjoy the journey reading Restore Ministries' books and the many testimonies and believe that you will soon see your miracle story!

I can only offer up praise to God! He is the sustainer of my faith! I rejoice daily in what He takes me through! He orders my footsteps daily! I trust Him! He loves us so much, and believe me, every teardrop is being softly touched by Him! He knows every hair on our heads and that lets us know that we can cast our burdens on Him because He cares for us!

He loves us so much! He also loves your spouse who is gone more than you do. Seek ye first the kingdom of heaven and all else will be added unto you! I have been in prayer for my marriage since August 1, 2002! My husband and I have been together for 30 years! God gave me unconditional love for him! I had to see him through God's eyes!

I stayed in prayer so much of the time. I had to fall on my face before God! I asked Him to forgive me if I had ever put anything or anyone before Him! I had to learn that God was taking me through this for a reason and that even though I was saved, He wanted me to get closer to Him! I did and it has been such an awesome experience.

He told me to be still and know that He is God! He began to give me the peace that surpassed all of my understanding! He told me that I was to depend on Him and that He was taking care of my husband! He loves him more than I do and he is His child, too!

I would always ask God to let me get a glimpse of Him and He did each time! When that started happening, God began to really show Himself to me! I prayed daily for my husband and our marriage to be always blessed and covered by the blood of Jesus. I then began to thank God for bringing my husband home.

I would pray the prayers of thanksgiving and worship to God! The more that I gave to God, the more He gave to me! One Sunday when I least expected it, I came home to my husband mowing the lawn, which I had asked him to do many times before. I began to praise Him with all that I had!

My husband told me that this was now between God and him. I told him that I respected his thoughts, while at the same time in my mind and heart I was praising God for bringing him home! Well, all praises to God! The following Tuesday he came to my job and said that he needed the key to our home!!!

During my prayer times at home, I would always tell God what I wanted to see in our home and He blessed that very Friday night with just what I had petitioned in my prayers. Once again, my husband is a blessed man of God! God has brought my husband home and He has made a new godly man of him! I am a new wife!

It seems that the restoration process really begins when your spouse walks through the door! Satan will try to destroy your faith, but know that God is still in CONTROL! We serve a big God! He is faithful to His Word! He will do just what He said He will do! Trust Him no matter what it looks like!

God bless Restore Ministries and all of you continue to P.U.S.H. (Pray Until Something Happens)! God is real!

Virgie, RESTORED in California

Restored in Ghana!

I desperately looked everywhere for help and surfed through the web like crazy looking for godly guidance to restore my marriage. After I went through several sites and posted my problem on one site with a request for prayer, someone sent me an email with the web address for Restore Ministries; that was about three years ago.

God showed me that I needed to forgive my husband for all the pain and humiliation he had taken me through. He convicted me of my contentiousness and argumentative spirit and led me to repent. It was only at that point that I felt peace.

I wanted to draw closer to God and feed more on His Word. From time to time, I blew it, but God in His mercies sustained me throughout this difficult period. Our children and I hardly saw or heard from my husband for several months, and I wondered how (on earth) he would see the changes in me. However, I remembered from the RMI materials that it was because I was not ready. Many times I got distracted, but God never let me down.

My parents and his parents were supportive and encouraged me not to give up. Although they didn't know the details of most of what was happening, they continued to pray with me. My brothers were divided; there were those who felt I should call it off, but two of them stood with me in prayer. One of my colleagues who happened to know about my situation also stood with me and was an encouragement partner.

I cannot thank God enough for His unfailing mercies and for restoring our marriage after five years of marital troubles and separation! After I searched frantically and desperately for help, someone finally introduced me to Restore Ministries. That was such a godsend!

I was on the website every day for encouragement from the Questions and Answers section, the Praise Reports and Testimonies of Restored Marriages. I ordered the restoration materials and pored over them like crazy. God convicted me through Erin's materials of my contentiousness and I asked God for forgiveness. I wanted more of God and prayed like never before. It was a difficult walk and I messed up sometimes, but God gave me the strength to hold on.

With time, God was changing me but at that time I still didn't see much of my husband. My children wanted to know why Daddy was never at home and I told them Daddy loved them, but he had a lot of work to do outside and would be with them soon.

Their friends were curious and so were my friends and neighbors who always asked where he was, and of course I had to find some reason so they would not know about my situation.

We went through really tough times and I cried just about every tear in me, but God was always merciful. My husband threatened me with divorce many times, though he never actually filed. He gave everybody the impression that he had filed for divorce, but then I found out that he never did.

As I got into the materials and God was changing me, I could feel and see the anger and hate walls coming down and he stopped talking about divorce (although he made no plans of restoration).

The Lord has taught me through all of this the power of forgiveness. I have learned to trust Him more and depend on Him for all my needs instead of putting my trust in man. I have learned about the danger of being a contentious woman with an argumentative spirit.

The Lord has taught me to make my speech sweet and gentle, winning without a word. I have learned to let go and let God, and to stop pursuing. There are countless things that I have learned!

I believe it was reading your books and listening to the tapes over and over again that encouraged me to hold on and believe that no matter how terrible my situation was, God would restore our marriage. I would highly recommend *How God Can and Will Restore Your Marriage*, *A Wise Woman*, the "Be Encouraged!" series, the "Be Radiant" tape, volume 1, and the Holy Bible on cassette. I needed to allow Him to make the changes He required in me, and to teach me the biblical principles for a successful marriage and walk with Him. I found all these materials useful in making those changes!

After seeing the changes in me, my husband started to change. He held me and told me that he was sorry for all that had happened, that he loved me and always had despite everything. He said I was a virtuous woman and the best woman that ever came into his life, and that he wanted us to get together again and make sure that we never got back into this mess.

Then things started improving a lot faster. He was getting in touch more often and he told me he cared, but I was careful not to show too much enthusiasm. I saw him more often and he started talking about us as a family again. I tried not to push him.

Then, he started calling me "honey" sometimes and being nice and pleasant. After what seemed like an endless, almost five-year battle, I began to see many changes in my husband toward me. The anger and hate walls had come down completely. My husband asked me to forgive him for all that had happened and wanted us to get together again and make things work.

He's being so lovely now and I'm just amazed at God's goodness! It all happened so fast that it seemed as if I were living a movie, so much so that I kept wondering if it was real! Many things have happened after that and I give God all the glory!

He said he could not explain how it all happened and that it should never have come to that. He said that instead of using all the precious time we lost fighting each other we could have worked on our marriage to make things better. He said we needed to talk it all out and forgive and repair all the damage that had been done.

But this was unbelievable! Soon after he said all this, all kinds of thoughts came into my mind, playing back all the pain and humiliation, and I started wondering if I wanted him back. But I knew where that came from! So I asked God to forgive me because I had prayed for a miracle and when the miracle came, the enemy came to steal my peace and my miracle.

It has been marvelous since then, and for the first time in years, he led the family in prayer, thanking God for His mercies and asking for forgiveness and sustaining power for what lies ahead.

It is still like a dream to me when I think about it all. But I give God all the glory and pray that He guides us in the future. There are still many areas to work on, but I know God will give us the strength to pull though.

I'd like to encourage everyone to hold firm and see the salvation of our Lord. Believe me, it is impossible for me to give you the details of all that I've been through. It certainly looked like the most impossible of situations, but God in His mercies has restored our marriage. He will do the same for you if you don't give up. Praise the Lord!

Lina, RESTORED Ghana

God Restores Another Marriage!

I believe the Lord prepared me for my difficult circumstances when He specifically told me in January that He would not leave nor forsake me. In March, things got very bad, but by then I had heard of marriage restoration and found a website. However, even during my growth in the Lord, I kept hungering after more information.

By April, a week before I was hit with the "bomb," I had found Restore Ministries through a search engine looking for something else entirely. So in retrospect, I don't recall how I came to read your page the first time. Nevertheless, it was no coincidence!

From the beginning, this was a mighty battle for me to trust God and learn submissiveness. I had never put my husband first; I served myself. The Lord dealt with me and taught me humility. Many times He surprised me by tenderly comforting me in my circumstances.

I found it especially true when I messed up and fought in the flesh. God would send me a word, a friend, or even a hug from my husband (grudgingly given) exclaiming, "Don't ask me why I'm hugging you; I don't know why, I just have to."

I learned time and time again how harmful it was when I blocked the Lord by trying my own hand in this battle. I would make things worse every time. I am now reaping the things I sowed in the flesh two months ago.

I am a slow learner—I am amazed the Lord hasn't lost patience with me! I have learned to lean on and trust Him completely, especially when things look hopeless. I learned that God wants me completely, not my leftovers of thought or time.

I have the *RYM* book, the workbook, the Q&A books, and *Workers at Home*. Each and every resource helped me mightily to see where my place is in the Lord and my family. As a European, I was not brought up to be submissive or even nice. Tact has never been my strong point.

I believe that that is the reason so few Germans have a true relationship with Jesus. We are taught from early childhood on that we need no one but ourselves and that distorted view makes us extremely contentious. I am so grateful God used Erin to show me the Truth. And her resources helped to change me!

Don't ask me how God uses these resources, but every time I applied the principles explained in the book, believing them to be true and God-honoring, I was always rewarded in a big way for my obedience. But in the same way, I saw that God will not be fooled by halfhearted attempts at obedience to satisfy the flesh and look saintly or spiritual.

Please buy *How God Can and Will Restore Your Marriage*. It will not only open the heart and eyes of any woman who is truly searching, but it will also help you to focus on Jesus. That is the whole reason our relationships failed in the first place, because our relationship with Jesus has to be restored first!

Lord, I just praise and thank You from the bottom of my heart that You love me so much, that I am saved and that Your faithfulness to my family and to me seems to be truly endless. Just as Your Word says, You don't lie and You don't tease.

I truly believe that any person who You tell his or her marriage is restored, it is restored already—we just have to hold on to Your promises and let go of our circumstances to focus on You. The battle has always been Yours! I wish I would have seen that much sooner. I could have spared my family and myself much pain.

Help me to always look to You, trust You, and keep my hand out of Your fight to change my husband and our circumstances. Please mold me into the person You want me to be, every day a little more. I give You glory. If You can change me and turn my hard heart, You can certainly do anything!

A year and a half ago I was still searching. I still wanted to live as I wanted to without a thought to You or my family. I am so happy You found me and brought me back to You. Even if it's difficult sometimes, I never want to tread the wide road again.

Thank You that my husband says again that he loves me. Thank You that he never moved out even though he had rented an apartment and had the keys. I thank You that the OW is out of the country for good. Thank you that we are now speaking of our future again. Lord, I thank You for sparing our daughter pain during this summer; having her daddy home was a mighty blessing!

I thank You that my husband wants to stay with me! Even when we are both attacked with fear and anxiety, I praise You that there is always hope in You. Lord, I thank You and give You glory for allowing my husband to be in the home and for healing us. I thank You that I am allowed to serve and spend time with him, and that he once again talks to me about his dreams and hopes.

I give You praise, Lord, that my husband prays alone and with us again! Glory to God! I know that You will save him and bring him back to You. Thank You for everything You have done for us, everything You are doing right now, and everything You are going to do!

And thank You for showing me where to turn when things looked hopeless! Time and time again, You helped me through RMI's website and through people who would pray for me.

I have been really blessed by finding Erin and Dan's website and their testimony. They are being used by the Lord in a mighty way, reaching out to help so many in troubled marriages like ours was. They pointed me to Jesus—only He is able to save and restore! God's Word is true. It works. It was designed to make us live in harmony with each other and God, and I have seen some amazing things happen when God steps in for the rescue. Glory to God!

Marriage Restored Before Twentieth Anniversary!

In January 2002, I found out that my husband was having a relationship with the OW and that it had been going on for over a year. I was devastated, as I had trusted my husband implicitly. I screamed, cried, and begged, but to no avail. He never left our home during this entire stand but he did leave our marriage bed in September 2001. When I questioned him there were accusations and counter-attacks but there were no answers to my questions—just quarreling. (I later found, via Erin's tapes, what was happening and how wrong I was to argue as I was trying to argue with Satan without the help of GOD!)

Although he continued to live in the house, my husband made no secret that he was calling and occasionally seeing the OW. I got on my knees, determined to fight for our marriage.

For Christmas 2001, my Christian daughter-in-law gave me a book, which opened my eyes to my faults as his wife. This led me back to my church for the first time in eight years. I was so moved when I went back to the church that, although I knew few who were there, I went forward to rededicate myself to the Lord. God was there for me that day and immediately provided a woman at the altar call to minister to me. With her guidance, I was introduced to RMI's website, and I followed all the principles being taught. She told me that she volunteered because she felt moved to do so. How wonderful is OUR LORD!! To me that was the first step God took to restore our marriage. However, I firmly believe that He allowed Satan to come in against my marriage so that HE could again reclaim this "lost sheep."

The tapes from Dan and Erin Thiele's ministry and my now well-worn Bible helped me through the dark days that were ahead, as I struggled with the awful realization that our marriage was in shambles and my husband had turned to another woman. After listening to the tapes over and over again (the "Be Encouraged" tapes) I realized how many mistakes I had made and how God wanted to mold me into the image of His Son. That is what I concentrated on—letting GOD change me!

I also learned from God to forgive not only my husband but also the OW, and I began praying for her too because I had faith that GOD would restore our marriage. BUT (ladies, this is a VERY IMPORTANT point from Erin's books and tapes) UNTIL I let go COMPLETELY—not checking on my husband's comings and goings and giving EVERYTHING over to GOD and concentrating only on my LORD and Savior—our marriage was not healed!

I prayed to God that He would restore our marriage by our twentieth anniversary on October 1. I left everything in His hands. My husband said all along he wanted to come home. He wanted to see me accomplish a few things. I tried to be obedient, and I was able to do so with the help of my e-partner. If it had not been for her, I think I would have given up. Praise God—I did not! On September 1, our marriage was completely restored!!

The happy conclusion... God again answered my every prayer from the early days of my spiritual battle for our marriage! I had asked, "Please, if it be Thy will, heal this marriage before our 20th anniversary." My husband "came home all the way" on September 1! Our anniversary is October 1st!! GOD IS FAITHFUL and ANSWERS ALL PRAYERS. PRAISE GOD!! TO HIM BELONGS THE GLORY!

Without Him, our marriage would not have survived. I praise God and give Him all of the glory for our restored marriage! Amen!

Restored and Praising Him Forever!

My marriage is restored. My husband left me in July. When he left, I prayed that God would change and return him to me, but the good Lord began to reveal my REAL SELF to me. As I was, my husband would have nothing to do with me. I needed to change!

As I continued to pray for my husband, the Lord told me not to speak to anyone about him. Did I listen? Therapy taught me to let it out, talk about it, or you stand the chance of falling and going back to drugs and alcohol. My past life was so dark that I could never chance that happening. Instead of trusting in and fearing God, I trusted and feared man.

As my situation worsened, the Lord told me to stay close to home. Did I? No way! I began to go out almost every day after work with our youngest daughter to shop. My husband had never come home to a hot meal or his God-given companion. He came home to an empty house, cold, hungry, and lonely, so why wouldn't he leave?

As God revealed what I needed to do, I turned to those who I relied on as my backbone—but they would put me down, telling me I was crazy. They said that God did not put me in a marriage to be miserable and that I should get out and leave him. They mocked me (Christians of many different denominations, devoted and very religious), saying things like, "How come God doesn't talk to us the way He talks to you?"

Of course, I didn't know the answer to that question at the time, so it went unanswered and I began to think I was crazy. I am no good, so why would "good" talk to me? However, the one conviction that the good Lord placed in my heart as a child that remains to this day was that I never, ever believed in divorce.

When my neighbor and I began to talk, she would listen and tell me she would pray. The day my husband told me he was leaving, I looked for a lawyer and in my search I stopped at a Barnes & Noble. When I came out of the restroom and looked for an exit sign, the wall was full of spiritual books.

Here the Lord stood once again. In the midst of my trouble, He saved me! I began to read cover after cover. The books were titled *Save Your Marriage, The Power of a Praying Wife, The Power of a Praying Husband, The Power of a Praying Parent,* etc. Guess what I did? I bought them all!

I never did find the lawyer I was looking for, so I went home immediately to read. As I read *The Power of a Praying Wife,* the Lord began to soften my heart toward my husband and revealed to me the evil of my ways. Yet, the message was not complete. I still didn't know how to become the wife, mother, daughter, sister, and woman that God created me to be.

The Lord never left my side. I began to read, pray, and fast on my own with few results. In His greatness, He sent the resources that would put me on the path of reconciliation!

The first resource was my neighbor who repeatedly listened to my cries. One day she introduced me to her friend, a minister, teacher, and believer. In January, we began to meet weekly for prayer, and I was given simple yet direct steps and measures that began to change me.

Some nights I would cry so hard as God gave me a front row seat to the showing of my life, the choices I had made, the sins that I had never repented of, and the ones I didn't know I was committing (that is until He led me to your ministry and I read your books).

In February, my husband agreed to meet to discuss our relationship. That is when I became aware of your ministry. A friend told me to get your book *Facing Divorce,* telling me to read it, study it, and read it again; however, I was never told how or where I could purchase it. Then I went to restoreministries.net. Reading your "Welcome Page," I knew it was none other than God's divine intervention!

Your ministry informed me that it would take anywhere from five to eight business days for delivery of the materials I wanted. That was a problem, as my husband and I were to meet in four days. Your representative put me on hold and came back to the phone. Once again with the intervention of the Lord, your ministry sent me the electronic version of *How God Can and Will Restore Your Marriage.* I finished it in three days before I met with my husband! PRAISE THE LORD!

When I started reading your book, God got a hold of me right away. It was automatic! I was on my knees reading, and I could not get up. I was sobbing as I never had before. Looking at myself in that way was the hardest thing I had ever had to do! "Change me," I prayed. "Come into my heart and change me."

The first thing I had to do after seeking forgiveness from God was to seek it of my husband, our children, and all those who had listened to me about our marital problems. Through His grace, mercy, strength, and power I was able to do it.

My change has been slow and not without pain. When receiving promptings from the Lord, I would argue and resist. Then I would bargain—"Okay, I'll do it," but instead of approaching a situation the way God wanted me to, I would go backwards and approach things my way, failing every time. God never gave up on me, so I never gave up.

Finally, I would get it right and do things God's way. In October, when I tried to speak to my husband, my approach was an altered version of my prompting, leaving me feeling hopeless and wounded. Then I did it God's way and, though my husband was not very receptive, it was a beginning. Even though I cried and hurt, God was there the whole time.

I told my husband that I was sorry for everything I did to make him leave. As I turned to leave, he suddenly wanted to speak. I listened for the first time from the heart, the heart of Jesus. That was the beginning of the end of my self-righteousness! I left our meeting crying tears of joy, hope, and faith that God would complete the work He had begun!

When I met with my husband the second time in February, he did all of the talking. I only spoke when prompted, saying very little. When I left, my husband made reference to "the next time we meet." That was only by the GRACE of GOD!

The next time was March. After I prayed and fasted regarding our tax returns, my husband said he would file separately. After reading your book and learning about submission, my burning prompting was to hold off filing. Then I read a testimony on your website about another couple who had a similar situation, and the wife gave her husband the full return.

Next, I called my friend to pray and fast with me. I was instructed that the Bible says that the husband is head of the house. After more praying and fasting (my friend and neighbor fasted and prayed with me), I called my husband and told him he could pick up the tax documents whenever he was ready.

A miracle happened! He asked how I was and began to speak to me on a personal level! Then he said he would file our taxes together and asked that I make the appointment and call him back with the day and time! I did just as he requested.

That night my friend called to tell me that there had been a prompting to seek God's power through prayer and fasting—that God was ready to make a big move in our marriage. He said to have everyone pray that the meeting would turn into a date. After our taxes were filed, my husband took me to my father's house (we had not spoken for three years). God, through my husband, began reconciliation in another broken relationship. Then my husband took me to New York for dinner, to a place with good memories!!

With the scriptural principles that I learned and applied through RMI and God, great things were beginning to happen. In early March another miracle happened. My husband accepted an invitation to dinner and we got along so well from that moment on as the Lord continued to change me. As I read your materials, the more I fasted, prayed, and applied what I was being taught, the more I witnessed the power and presence of our Savior.

He changed me, and my husband commented on those changes. The more I read your materials, shared my testimony, and handed out your ministry cards, the more I witnessed the miracles that God and only God could perform in my husband, my children, and me.

By March, my husband began to come home three days a week. It wasn't until April that he spent a night. As we dated and got to know one another, we became real friends. Even though we had grown up together, we never had a relationship like this! I no longer judged him or depended on him for things that only my Lord and Savior could provide.

By May, my husband was home every night, only returning to his rented room to pick up his mail and clothing. In June, he told me he was coming home! In July, exactly one year to the date, God returned my husband to me. The good Lord was faithful—my strength and light in a dark situation.

Two weeks ago, my husband agreed to start meeting with a male friend! He is now being taught the same principles I learned! He commented that he now looks forward to coming home! In addition, the Lord continually uses the resources of your ministry to restore all of my family relationships. Praise GOD!

The following Scriptures were critical during my spiritual trial:

Confirming my belief in everlasting marriage — Romans 8:28; Matthew 21:21, 19:5; Psalm 23, 119:113; Proverbs 7:11; Malachi 2:16; 2 Corinthians 10:5; John 10:10; James 1:5, 7, 8; Revelation 7:2

Learning to depend on and fear the Lord — Psalm 1:1, 60:11, 108:12; Proverbs 12:4; Matthew 19:26; 2 Corinthians 16:9

Serving Him – Luke 11:9; Isaiah 9:6; James 1:17

Searching His Word – Psalm 46:10; Proverbs 16:33, 5:18; Matthew 7:7, 12:36; 1 John 5:4; Romans 6:16; 1 Corinthians 13:7; Galatians 5:17

Changing my behavior – Proverbs 31:11, 26, 20:3, 18:1, 16:28, 17:9, 14, 28, 15:1; Matthew 23:12, 5:25, 29-30, 12:37; Romans 3:31, 6:2; James 2:14, 18; Psalm 101:5

The change (the new heart given me in Jesus) – Psalm 34:5; 1 Timothy 1:18; Luke 14:11, 18:14; Matthew 18:22; Proverbs 16:24, 17:22, 18:14; Hebrews 12:11; 2 Corinthians 10:3; 1 Peter 5:8

All these passages are in your materials, and this isn't even the tip of the iceberg of what your books hold. The scriptural references in your materials are unlimited and touched every area that the Lord revealed to me that needed changing!

After reading *How God Can and Will Restore Your Marriage* and *Facing Divorce*, I ordered every resource you suggested for women, along with additional materials. To date, I have exhausted all of my Hope Cards and tracts and recently gave my sister my copies of *How God Can and Will Restore Your Marriage* and *Facing Divorce*

Your resources gave me HOPE and helped to restore my faith. You let me know that I wasn't crazy; as a matter of fact, now I know that when the world thinks I'm crazy, I can be certain I'm heading in the right direction. You cannot serve two gods, and the opposing one will try to convince you that you're crazy.

Your ministry let me know that I wasn't alone, that we do not fight against flesh. As long as I seek God's kingdom, ask for faith and strength, and knock on the door of knowledge and power, He will let the bad in my life turn to good. Praise God that all things happen to glorify His name!

If you are newly separated or heading in that direction, start with *How God Can and Will Restore Your Marriage* and *Facing Divorce*, then go directly to *A Wise Woman*. They are where I learned how to change the contentious behavior that marked my life. Then, continue through all the materials offered through Restore Ministries.

God is GREAT! When everything I trusted in failed me, He never did. Through it all, He was there. Praise His name! He has turned my pain into joy, my tears into laughter. He has changed me to a VIRTUOUS woman and enabled me to endure!

He revealed my filthy rags and clothed me in His righteousness. He has taken me from darkness and shone His countenance upon me. Give Him the power, the glory; sing praises to Him all the days of your life, for He is here to stay! I am the Lord's! Take and mold me as You will. AMEN!

Praising Him to Restoration!

I found RMI about a week after my husband left. I was so excited to have someone confirm what I felt God was leading me to do. It helped me to know that I was NOT in denial as many tried to tell me. Praise God for His mercy!

God changed my situation one night when I was contemplating death only four days after my husband left. I sat in the dark alone, believing that no one would care if I died. But God spoke to me and led me to my Bible.

I opened it to Matthew 19:3 and read through verse 12. We had read that passage at our wedding almost ten years before. That was when I reached out for the hem of His garment and struggled to never let go. I came to my computer to look for prayer—I didn't know what else to do.

That was when I found RMI. I wanted so badly to join the fellowship, but the money scared me. I signed up and hoped that I would be able to come up with the money when I needed it. (I didn't know then that God would provide for my every need.)

I continued to search His Word and hold on tight. I learned a lot about myself, but it still seemed so very difficult to hold onto my hope. Then one day, a friend that I had prayed with online sent me a copy of *How God Can and Will Restore Your Marriage*. I was riveted by the book.

It was telling me everything that I already knew in my heart! Praise God! But now it was being confirmed. I really wasn't making this up as I was going along—someone else trusted God, and He was faithful. It was then that I learned that He is not a respecter of persons.

I began reading the book all the time, cross-referencing with my Bible and praying Scriptures. PTL, I also had the small bit of money that I needed to purchase the membership. In time I was able to purchase many of the other resources RMI provides and was blessed by every one of them!

The most important principle I learned through God's Word was that He really loves and cares about my family and me. I also learned that trusting Him is the most important thing I can choose to do in my life. I must admit that sometimes it is hard to kill the flesh and to trust, but I have seen the rewards, and He is so faithful!

I learned about what I thought was my own righteousness and how filthy it was to Him. I saw everything that I did to bring about the breakup of our marriage. It no longer mattered what my husband was doing, and the OW was no longer a huge thorn in my side; she was still a thorn, but He made it bearable.

Through His grace and love, I was able to focus on what He wanted to do in me. Once I surrendered that to Him, everything that followed became easier to surrender. Yes, there were times that because of my flesh, I thought I would die because of the pain, but He brought my family through! I have learned to seek God first in EVERYTHING, not just my trials, but also my choices and my happiness.

The resources that I have from RMI are *How God Can and Will Restore Your Marriage, A Wise Woman, Facing Divorce, Questions & Answers,* all of the "Be Encouraged!" videos, the "Queen Esther" video, the "Facing and Avoiding Remarriage" video, and the "Being Obedient and Alluring" video.

I already knew in my heart that God was calling me to not give up on our marriage but to trust in Him. Each one of these resources spoke to me in a very personal way and confirmed for me what I already knew in my heart. They helped me so much when I was up against those who said I needed to move on with my life, find someone new, and get over it! They helped me learn that I did not need to "get over it," but I needed to get THROUGH it with God leading me—and how worthwhile it is!

Praise God that every single one of them blessed me in one way or another! If I could only pick one to recommend, it would be the *Wise Woman* workbook. Through my trial, I have had the opportunity to recommend your book to many, many people, and I believe that Erin followed God's will in writing it.

Sometimes she may come off as a bit abrupt, and it seemed as if I came to those parts when I wanted to be coddled. However, she still spoke the truth, and I have been so very blessed because of it! I pray many blessings for Dan and Erin, and thank God for leading me to your website!

My husband was gone for just under six months! I am praising the Lord and have, quite literally, gotten on my face many times to praise Him! In the beginning I struggled with my flesh, though I was able to follow His guidance more times than not. I rejoiced when I saw things that seemed bad in the flesh. I rejoiced when I saw changes in my husband and myself.

About a month ago, I REALLY began to see changes, and I just KNEW that my husband was coming home. I stopped praying for God to please do it, and thanked Him that He had done it! I received that oh-so precious assurance. I continued to pray and fast, but my focus was no longer on just returning what the enemy had stolen, but on others in my life, and other things that God was leading me to do.

I went through the fire, just as Erin described in the "Be Encouraged!" videos. It was so hot that I was sure the pain at the end was much worse than the pain in the beginning. And it was frustrating because there was nothing that happened in the flesh to cause me that pain. But I continued to praise God and tell Him, "Lord, I don't know why I feel this way, but I know You are working, and I praise You and thank You!" The enemy was working hard at trying to get me to give up, but praise Jesus, the only thing I knew to do was to turn to Him for comfort.

Quite SUDDENLY, two weekends ago, my husband and I were intimate for the first time since he left. I had been praying, based on what I had learned from Erin's "Allure" video, and God was faithful.

It was the week that followed that my husband told me he wanted to come home, and the following weekend when he returned! PRAISE GOD!

I am so thankful that God truly has put forgiveness in my heart. I can honestly say that I have no anger toward my husband, and I am so thankful for what God has done for us! I look at my husband and I am filled with love! I am so thankful for all of the changes that God made in me and look forward to everything that He will continue to do!

Thank You, Lord Jesus! And thank you, Dan and Erin, for your obedience!

Trustworthy Teaching Restored My Marriage!

A friend who has been working toward her own marriage restoration introduced me to Restore Ministries' principles. She would tell me about the radical concepts she was learning, and I was skeptical. Of course, MY marriage was SO solid....

My friend came to my rescue and reminded me that I already knew the principles in the book. God showed me what a proud, contentious, manipulative and selfish person I had been. When I looked in the mirror, I could find no evidence of Jesus in me.

I fell into the arms of the Lord and begged Him to forgive and change me. I dedicated myself to total obedience, fasting for seven days and praying the Lord's will to be done in my life. I allowed Him to empty me and refine me COMPLETELY. There were immediate and drastic changes.

God created a new heart in me in just DAYS! My husband saw the changes and said he wouldn't leave me! The Lord turned his heart back to me and away from her! He now sees our future together again. He is more affectionate than ever before!

I was able to forgive RIGHT AWAY! That amazed me! I prayed for God to help me keep my eyes off the battle and on Him. I LET GO OF EVERYTHING AND GAVE IT TO THE LORD! I learned that surrender, complete and radical obedience, humility, prayer and trusting in the Lord bring favor, love and FAITH into your life. I trusted Him to restore my marriage; now I trust Him in EVERY area of my life.

The restoration book is something I will study the rest of my life—I would recommend it to everybody. I haven't even finished the workbook yet since I have spent so much time in the restoration book and the Bible. The fact that everything is based on and backed up by Scripture makes Restore's program completely trustworthy. It has opened the door to many other areas of my life to be changed.

Glory to God on high! I thank Him for loving me enough to correct and refine me, not just for His glory, but because He loves me and wants to give me the desires of my heart. He took me aside, put His arms around me, and made a special project out of ME! He is the most loving Person we could ever imagine! I feel like I've been given my own set of keys to the kingdom!

Thank God and RMI for everything!

Laura, RESTORED in Georgia

Sweet Alabama Restoration—Husband Home!

Praise God for His many blessings! Abba Father, thank You for Your love! Your love, Abba, amazes me. Thank You for not giving up on me! So many years I have wandered away from You, so lost.

Thank You for bringing me to the point of facing my emptiness. Thank You for filling me with Your joy, Your hope, and Your wondrous love. Thank You and praise Your name!

This morning my heart sang as God revealed a truth to me. He showed how He has protected me from certain knowledge. He also revealed this knowledge at the right time. It made my heart thrill!

My husband lives at home. Praise God, he has been home for six weeks with no weekends away! It began with two, maybe three days at home. Then weekdays at home. And now, almost seven weeks at home!

Praise God! This morning my dear husband told me how much I have changed and that I've been doing so well! He said I no longer rant and rave. Praise God, who has molded me and continues to make me brand new!

My husband explained that about a year ago he made a promise to the OW to marry her! I had no idea! He explained that he loves me and that he has no intention of leaving me and that he loves our relationship!!! Praise to God!

So much more was said. After our conversation, I went to the bathroom and just shook, realizing God's wondrous power and love. HE TURNED my husband's heart to me! HE kept me in the home! He guided and lifted me up when I fell and loved me through the pain of change.

He changed me and He continues to change me! Thank You, Abba! I love You so much, Abba! You are wondrous!! Thank You, Abba, for RMI and the Thieles. Thank You for my prayer partners. Thank You for Your wisdom.

Thank You that Your love NEVER FAILS! My dear sisters and brothers who have claimed God's promise for a restored marriage, please seek His face. He is there, always! Hallelujah!!!

She Found the True Meaning of Life!

I praise the Lord God Almighty for what He has done in my life. He took my life, broke it down to nothing, and built in it the most beautiful piece of artwork you could possibly imagine! Best of all is that He has not stopped there—more is still to come!!

I found your ministry through putting my name up for prayer on a prayer website. Someone contacted me and referred me to your site. I went to have a look and fell instantly "in love" because you spoke right to my heart! I kept coming back for support and encouragement.

As I sought the Lord, He helped me to deal with all of the hurt, bitterness, and unforgiveness that I was feeling. He helped me to control the angry outbursts that I was having toward my children. He molded and changed me from being a very contentious person into a woman with a quiet and submissive spirit, which is precious in His sight.

The more I started following God's principles, the more my former husband's heart was drawn toward our children and me. I noticed that the relationship with the OW became as bitter as wormwood and my former husband was returning more and more to us. God was definitely at work in his heart.

I think the principle from God's Word that I appreciate most is that we must never repay evil with evil, but cover evil over with good. I think that had a big impact on my relationship with my former husband. Also, of course, is the fact that we must not be contentious, nagging wives. If we want to turn our husband's heart, it must be done without a word through prayer. These principals stood out to me because I saw results as I applied them.

The *How God Can and Will Restore Your Marriage* book was a revelation, something I needed to read and hear and feel. It opened my eyes and heart in a way that I can never explain. It felt like God was talking directly to me in a unique and special way. I recommend this book to anyone who is married or who intends to get married—even if your marriage is not in trouble. Through this book, you will learn how to be the wife God wants you to be. I also recommend the testimony tape or CD of Dan and Erin's restoration.

Praise you, Jesus! This trial has been the biggest blessing. I did not lose anything but GAINED LIFE!! Through the Lord and this ministry, I found the true meaning of LIFE; and for that I can never, never give enough thanks to God. I will be forever grateful. Jesus, You are truly LORD OF ALL!!!!

God Restores What the Locusts Have Eaten!

I feel a mixture of emotions today as I write to tell you of another restored marriage—MINE! I am overwhelmed with joy that God has been gracious to restore our marriage, and I am humbled at the same time. I know that I am the least deserving of it.

My husband came home last night and told me that he loved me and would never leave me again. He also said that he needed to be taken down "several notches" to realize that his sins were as great as mine. I told him that I was sorry for all the things that I had done and he said that he did not want to hear it because I had already said it before.

I found Restore Ministries when I typed in "marriage restoration ministries" one day on my computer and found your website along with many others. I found that there are other ministries out there, but the Holy Spirit led me to become a member of yours.

The first time my husband said he was leaving (but didn't) was in September of 1991. I begged, pleaded, tried to appease—you name it! He stayed but did not want to.

But this time I "won him without a word," with my behavior. I got into the Word and told no one of my situation except one friend and my mother. They both stood by me.

I prayed and went on an extended fast. I asked God to continually change me, and HE DID! I learned to keep focused on God and keep my mouth shut, only opening it to say or ask my husband something after prayerful consideration.

I had the *God Can and Will Restore Your Marriage* book on tape, the "Be Encouraged" videos, and the book *Facing Divorce*. Erin backed up what she had to say with Scripture and her experiences—and nothing speaks like experience! I would especially recommend *God Can and Will Restore Your Marriage* by Erin. I liked the tapes because I have a long commute to work, so I was able to listen to them over and over.

In just one evening, God has "restored what the locusts have eaten"! I don't have the words to truly express what I feel—only to say PRAISE GOD!!!!

Restored in Pennsylvania!

Praise God for restoring my marriage! My husband filed for divorce but never signed the papers! He moved back home seven months ago! In April, four months ago, his lawyer wrote him to finalize the papers so he could file with the courts, but my husband never answered.

God is indeed powerful and can protect marriages. I praise Him because He forgave me and protected us! I cannot describe how awesome He is.

It was with God's help that I met a woman in a church I was visiting. I opened up and told her how needy I was for God to intervene while I waited for my husband to come home. She, in turn, introduced me to other women who were in the same situation. God worked in all of our lives. It was these women who told me about your ministry and website. We have all been meeting every other week just to praise God, to learn to let Him work through us, to thank Him for "everything" and just put our focus on Him and our relationship with Him since that's what really counts!!

I began realizing that God wanted to have fellowship with me. My whole being is His temple; therefore, I need Him to help me build His temple in me. I need to concentrate on and be mindful of what He is doing in and through me. That's when I knew for sure that it was not about me, but Him; even my marriage is not mine, but His. It's incredible what He started to build and I just thank and praise Him that He even bothers with me and takes the time out to teach me and help me work with Him!

It was God who gave me His faith to trust and obey Him because I can't do it unless He does it through me! During my restoration process, I was so dependent on Him to do everything for me and He did! I just prayed for His strength in me to trust Him and He did! I also prayed that He would change my heart, my priorities and my focus, and He certainly accomplished it!

Praise God for what He has done and what He is doing and what He is going to do in my life! This relationship with my precious Lord is all I ever needed and it is the only permanent and lasting relationship! Every other relationship is only temporary, but this one is eternal. Thank you, Lord.

Once I realized all this and lived it, He brought my husband back!! Now that's how He works!! He is perfect in every way! I can't wait to see the rest of the changes He brings into our lives, but even if I don't see him working, I KNOW He is!!! I just have to pray for Him to give me His faith to trust Him and He will. I am a sinner saved by grace and more grace!!

Restored and More in Virginia!

I am sorry I haven't given a praise report in so long. However, the Lord has been so good to me that I guess I have been preoccupied with my blessings and I haven't taken the time to give one. I am certainly not going to give any lame excuses, so here goes.

When I began my search for the truth of God's plan for marriage restoration, I went to bookstores and searched the Internet for anything on marriage I could get my hands on. A chat group from another marriage ministry led me to Restore Ministries and its wonderful resources. I feel that out of all the marriage ministries I looked into, this ministry is the most closely aligned with the Holy Scriptures and has spoken to my heart the loudest!

One area in particular that spoke to me was regarding church attendance. I was attending church alone for a while when I began reading in Erin's books about not going without your spouse when he lives at home. It says in Erin's *Wise Woman* workbook that God's word is clear in 1 Corinthians 11:3: "But I want you to understand that Christ is the head of every man, and the man is the head of woman, and God is the head of Christ." Ephesians 5:22-24 makes it clear that God has put ALL husbands in the leadership role of the home. It says, "Wives be subject to your own husbands, as to the Lord...to their husbands in everything."

Every church and every other ministry I've found did not agree with this at all. Every time I would get sidetracked and rethink this, I felt the Holy Spirit telling me not to go without my husband. It was almost as if I didn't feel right about it. Everyone else told me I was being disobedient to God. However, I began feeling in my heart that if I DID go I was being disobedient to God! No one understood what I was doing, even other Christians and other marriage ministries.

NOW, by my following this principle, not only has my marriage been restored for a little while, but also my husband has been on fire (and I mean on fire) for the Lord! I had prayed for God to speak to my husband and send us to church as a family. The Lord is so faithful that He has done that and much more! My husband has been going to Bible study on Wednesday nights, getting involved with the church, developing friendships with the local body, studying the Word, and devouring anything he can get his hands on about becoming closer to our Lord and Savior Jesus Christ!

He is also thinking about ways that he can be in ministry. Believe me, this is more than I could have ever asked of the Lord and I feel so blessed! PTL! More than anything, I am so grateful that the Lord has used our marriage crisis to bring my husband to Jesus!

Then, I have a brother and sister-in-law who were in the process of getting divorced. A couple weeks ago, the OW was out of the picture and my brother and sister-in-law are back together, trying to work things out. Just last weekend, they came down to visit and I noticed that they both had their wedding bands on—PTL!

My husband asked me if I wanted to be baptized together and renew our wedding vows in the church since we did not get married in a church before! I was thrilled because I had prayed for that, too!

The resources at Restore Ministries are wonderful. I would recommend all of the tapes and books and any other resources that Dan and Erin decide to make available. I also like the fact that they make the ePartners available for us so that we do have the support we need when we are going through a difficult time in our lives.

Please don't give up no matter what the enemy tries to do or tell you. Fight the good fight to the end. I know without a doubt that the Lord will deliver you and your family, and you will be victorious! I want to thank God for Dan and Erin for being such a great inspiration to us all! God bless both of you and your whole family!

To let you all know the greatness of what God has done in bringing about my restoration and the incredible change in my husband, let me "briefly" share where I was when I came to this ministry. About two or two and a half years ago, my husband was having an affair with a colleague at work. I suspected something for a while, but I tried to believe that it wasn't happening. I guess when I first really knew about it, I sensed that God began dealing with me then, but I turned to everything except God. I had God in my life on and off for years, but never had a personal relationship with God until I began crying out to Him to help me get through what I was going through. I almost decided to have an affair myself, right before God really got a hold of me, but something stopped me from going through with it. I realize now that it was the Holy Spirit!

Believe it or not, I think God really got my attention when I went to a psychic, of all places, to find an answer to save my marriage. I looked around and saw candles of Jesus' image all around the room. I asked the psychic what she planned to do to help me, and she said that she was going to light candles and say special prayers on my behalf. Then it hit me, and I think it was the Holy Spirit, that I was to leave there immediately. I started to think that if she could pray for me and charge me all of that money, then why couldn't I pray for me?!? It was almost as if the Holy Spirit was whispering to me that God is a free gift to all, that I needed to go to HIM personally, and best of all, HE IS FREE!!

Strange but true—this was my first realization of my need to get back to God. I then went to bookstores and searched the Internet for anything on marriage I could get my hands on. I found a web site that talked about marriage restoration. This was different from Restore Ministries, but I got on a chat group and there someone referred me to RMI! (That was how I found this wonderful ministry!) Not only had I discovered this ministry, but many others as well. Many have similar beliefs; however, I do believe that out of all of them, Erin's beliefs are the closest to the Holy Scriptures and, as I mentioned before, they have spoken to my heart the loudest.

God showed me many areas about myself that needed to change. I began to understand why the affair happened, because God showed me that I had been unfaithful to my husband in other areas as a wife. God had me confess to my husband many things and began to change me in many areas (and He is still changing me, PTL!).

The affair ended almost two years ago, and it was my husband's decision. I believe this was when the Lord first started getting a hold of my husband (because I've asked him when he first felt led by God and he said that it was about a year and a half ago). We still went through many trials, and I still go through trials sometimes with my husband home, but I know that God is using it for the good of us both.

I did go through two ePartners and both of them were wonderful! I still occasionally contact them by email or phone, but not on a regular basis. I got the feeling from both of them that they thought I was more spiritually mature than they were. I do not want to boast about that. I was glad that I was there to help them, and they also helped me in many ways, especially when I needed encouragement. Unlike my ePartners, I was very blessed to have my husband home the entire time; he never left the home, though he threatened to several times.

God bless you and your family and I will keep you all in my prayers as well as the other members of Restore Ministries and the rest of the staff. I want to see others' marriages restored, and I get teary eyed when I read the praise reports—keep them coming, Lord!

*Sharon**

God Does Do the Impossible!

I want to thank my Lord and Savior for opening my eyes. Thank you, Dan and Erin, for being faithful to tell the truth about how to restore marriages God's way. I was doing and saying things to try to change my husband. I was told to follow the "tough love" tactic and I saw that it only made things worse. It pushed him to the OW.

I found your ministry while looking for Christian marriage restoration on the Internet. I was really blessed by the *Restore Your Marriage* book and all of the Bible verses it contains. The Lord showed me so many verses in the Bible and I have really grown closer to God through this.

I also had *Facing Divorce*, as well as Dan and Erin's testimony on tape. They showed me how to seek restoration God's way instead of the world's way.

I really needed to change. When I began to seek the Lord, it was then I saw Him working in my life. When my husband left again, he said he wanted a divorce; he said he would never be home and it was over and there was no chance of him coming home again.

Then I read the *Restore Your Marriage* book twice! Easter morning, I asked my husband to forgive me for the mean things I have said to him. After I asked for his forgiveness, I had such peace. I did not have that peace when I was being mean and trying to change things in the flesh.

God has done a mighty work in me. I am no longer that negative and sarcastic person. I gave it ALL to God and stopped doing things in the flesh. I fell in love with Jesus. I showed my husband love when I had a chance to see him. I had total faith in God that He was going to restore our marriage.

I fasted and prayed. I quoted Scriptures daily: "What God has joined together, let no man separate," and other Scriptures in the *Restore Your Marriage* book. I knew it wasn't God's will that this marriage be over.

One Sunday afternoon, my husband stopped by to drop something off and I could see the battle and turmoil in him; he looked sad. I fasted and prayed on Monday because I knew it was a spiritual battle. Well, at 1:30 a.m. Tuesday, my husband called and asked if he could stop by to talk to me. He told me he was tired of running and ready to come home. He felt so ashamed. He said he loved me and missed me.

He did move home. I thought my marriage was restored and even submitted a praise report saying so! However, he was only home for a couple of days, then he left again to move into an apartment with the OW. I was devastated!

THEN GOD CHANGED THINGS IN AN INSTANT!!!

The kids and I went to visit my parents for vacation. While we were gone, my husband went on a canoeing trip with the OW and the whole time he thought of me and that he should be there with me! My son was in children's church just this past Sunday at my parents' church and he requested prayer for his daddy, that God would bring his family back together again. All the kids and the children's church leader laid hands on him and prayed. While I was in church that morning, during praise and worship, the worship leader told my mom to look at me and say, "Joy is coming in the morning!" Mom said she has never done that before.

When we got back from vacation, my husband had tears in his eyes and said he missed us. We talked and he said he couldn't see himself growing old with anybody else but me! He cried and said how sorry he was for everything and that he loves me. PRAISE GOD!!!! The divorce proceedings had been scheduled for this Friday!!!

Thank you, Jesus!!! I know that this was all for good. God is a miracle worker! My husband said he would never be back home!! But, God does the impossible!! If you are seeking restoration and you've heard words like "I will NEVER be home," know that they are lies from the devil to get you to give up.

I never gave up. I prayed and lots of other people have been praying, too. THANK YOU, JESUS!! Thank you, Dan and Erin, for this blessed ministry. GOD BLESS ALL OF YOU!! I will continue to pray for all of you seeking marriage restoration.

Miracle Restoration in Louisiana after Three Years!

Mine is another victory for the kingdom! I want to first thank God for my Savior, Jesus Christ! Thank You, Lord! I have moved back home with my husband and our marriage is restored!!!

It has been three years this month. I moved out in July and moved home three years later! I want you all to know this was and is a journey. I had no idea that it was in God's plan to change ME. When

God first began His work in me, I was so ashamed when I realized that I did not know how to love people through God's eyes. God did a great work on my mouth, my controlling spirit, and my pride!

I found out about your ministry through a co-worker who is now my prayer partner. When I came to your ministry, I was in the midst of deciding about a divorce because I believed that I had married the wrong person. However, it was I who had the problem because I did not know how to love someone in the right way or look at a person the way I do now. When someone does me wrong, I now feel differently—I trust God! And then God began to WORK ON MY MOUTH, MY CONTROLLING SPIRIT, and MY BIG HEAD!

I started to see who was behind all that was going wrong, not my husband but Satan. Then I saw God changing my husband little by little. One big change was my husband's drinking. My husband and his family are drinkers. Then one day he just stopped drinking hard liquor and beer. He became aware of what he was doing to me! Would you believe that I did not even notice the change until I talked to my prayer partner on the phone?!

My husband's heart is turning back toward me constantly even though I mess up; the Lord has shown me mercy. He is a Restorer and keeps all promises. I still try to watch what I say or how I react, but victory comes from prayer and focusing on Jesus.

Thank you, Dan and Erin, for writing such a wonderful book and leading us to the Truth. I would like to tell everyone to read the book over and over—it will help restore your marriage! I also want to thank my sister in Christ and friend for putting up with me. Do not give up!!!

Remarried but Resentful, Then God Changed Me!

I praise the Lord for loving me and my wife and allowing us to learn how to love each other through the love of our gracious heavenly Father and His Son Jesus Christ. I found Restore Ministries through a friend at a Bible study.

My wife and I divorced 28 years ago. We had a horrible relationship during and after our divorce. My wife later remarried a neighbor who had posed as my friend but later I discovered he was involved with my wife behind my back.

I worked all the time and thought I was doing the right things by making money for my family. We had three beautiful girls. I had put my wife up on a pedestal before the divorce and worshipped my three girls. After my wife's new marriage she moved out of state where it became difficult to see my girls.

Her moving, along with her new marriage, caused me to hate my ex-wife. I felt destroyed and humiliated. After five years my ex-wife's marriage ended in divorce and she wanted to come back to me. However, I had no love for her and refused at first. But, through the advice of a Christian friend, I decided to give it a try so I remarried her.

We remarried but I still had resentment and the marriage was only held together because of our three girls. I would often think to myself that when the girls were grown there would be no reason for me to stay married to someone that I did not respect. Now, this is where I was dead wrong.

The Holy Spirit nudged me and my wife to start a Bible study, and through this study the Lord started talking to and teaching us about His will for me and my wife. We learned first to love the Lord and through His love for us we reached a level of love and respect for each other that we had never thought possible.

We chose to forgive each other without any thought of the past and enter into true "agape love." It was God who allowed us to achieve this. Today we still have our differences but we have the Lord as our referee and through His guidance we find a resolution of our differences—it works! We are now living a happy life filled with the joy of loving and respect for each other, AND we are best friends!!

The Lord taught me the principle of putting my faith in the Lord Jesus and constantly staying in his Word. He also taught both of us to seek His guidance through praying and consulting the Holy Spirit before we make any choices.

I recommend using the resources from your ministry (a Christ-centered resource) as a refuge to unload the baggage of guilt, hate, or disrespect. Then learn how to forgive as our gracious Lord forgave us.

Carl

Remarried in Ohio!

PRAISE GOD! My former husband and I remarried on Friday! I can honestly say that although this has been the most painful time of my life, it has also taught me not only the power and love of God, but also His faithfulness.

I cannot express how grateful I am to my God for putting our marriage back together. The changes He has made in me are extraordinary! I have learned to totally depend on God for everything and to pray for everything. There is still much work for my Lord to do in the lives of our children, but I know He can change their hearts, too. The most important thing I discovered is that God loves ME! I know people say that all the time, but this is different. I know on a different level His love for me. Praise God and thank you all for praying! His love endures forever.

As far as learning of your ministry, I had placed a prayer request on another site about my divorce. I had no idea that God could or would want to restore my marriage. A person read my email and sent me your book. That is how it all began. God led me each step. I cannot explain it, but I can look back now and see how God placed each person and even your book in my path to lead me!

The most helpful book I read was *How God Can and Will Restore Your Marriage*. That was the basis for the beginning of my belief for my marriage. To be honest though, the Bible has been my greatest help. I read the Psalms every day and cried them out to God. My minister did not want to encourage me in believing for our marriage, as he was afraid I would be disappointed, so that's why I looked to other ministries for help.

My friends, family, and children were against the idea of restoring our marriage, so I was pretty much alone except for one good friend and my Bible. God showed me how even though I thought I was doing what was right, I was blinded in so many areas of my life, and Satan just stepped right in.

As I said before, there is still much to do, but I know that God will take care of it. The days I thought I couldn't breathe or take one more step, He took me through moment by moment. He taught me how to really pray and trust. I have learned much through the experience.

I ask everyone to please pray that God will watch over and protect us and that we will build our marriage on the solid rock of Jesus.

Although you may not know from day to day what each day will bring, just hold on to God to take you through. And remember one thing: Always put on the whole armor of God each day to protect you in this fierce battle. The Lord has given us mighty weapons and I never really understood that until now. Read the Psalms every day and cry them out to God as your sword of the Spirit!

What a Wonderful God We Serve!

Thank you, Dan and Erin, for your encouragement and dedication to praying for marriages. Praise the living Lord—my husband is home! He is a mighty man for Jesus, and he guides, guards, and governs us in God's Word.

My husband left me for another woman who was pregnant with his child (I did not know this when he moved out). He swore he was never coming home. He told our children every time they went to visit that he would never come home, that he did not love me, and to get over it. But, our wonderful God had a different plan!

My husband returned home a broken man and very sorry toward God and us. He now serves the Lord. The Lord has chosen to remove this other woman and child. She became bitter and resentful (prophecy fulfilled about the adulterous woman!) and moved away. God's ways and thoughts are much higher than our own. I pray for God to bless her and this child for His kingdom. I am grateful that the Lord chose to get hold of my attitude toward my husband before I learned of the other woman and child. It was months after he moved out that I found out.

But, along with the devastation that he saw my children experiencing, my husband said it was my forgiveness toward him that drew him back home, and that God had to be responsible for my change. Bitterness and unforgiveness are not building blocks for the house that God builds. Love (as described in 1Cor. 13) is.

I posted a prayer request on a prayer board in December almost two years ago and a gentleman responded with a link to your website. Through the principles of your workbook for women, I learned that my ways were contentious and unforgiving. I also learned that God was in control and I needed to put Him first in my life. I also learned the importance of spiritual weapons (Scripture, faith, trust in God, and love). My husband and I stopped arguing because I stopped nagging! He remained cold toward me for a while, but he was still attracted to my change.

God taught me to be thankful for all things; He taught me that the battle was not mine. He showed me that He did want my marriage restored and that I should trust Him to restore it with my mouth shut. So I shut it!

Your *How God Can and Will Restore Your Marriage* book and the Workbook for Women were packed full of a Godly walk. I have shared these principles with many hurting women. I also received the "Be Encouraged" tapes. What a blessing! (I have since sent them on to my ePartner, who could not afford them.)

All resources from your ministry are good, but, as you suggested, I spent most of my time memorizing Scripture from many places in the Bible so that I would be armed for the battle in my mind (taking my thoughts captive). God was fighting on my behalf and I saturated my mind with His living Word!!!

We are still healing, and God is so faithful to guide us every day. My husband and I pray for broken marriages. He is not yet comfortable with us sharing our story with people who did not know about his affair, but he is an avid encourager of my prayer partners who are awaiting restoration. He prays for marriages!!

My husband spent 12 years trying to divorce me, and now he prays for marriages to stay together!!

He also says that he barely has a memory of last year when he was gone. What a wonderful God we serve!!

There are many verses that held me afloat (from your *Restore Your Marriage* and Workbook for Women) and without the prayers of my encouragement partner, I would have been devastated! She sent an SOS prayer request to your website last summer after I found out about the baby and was distraught, and you had a lady send me an encouragement email! After I read it, I realized that God had not brought me that far to drop me on my head!

God has surely used your ministry in all stages of restoration to get His message across. This is all for His glory and His kingdom. I am blessed to serve our Father with my life! Thanks for all you do!!!

Sarah,* RESTORED in Texas

Miracle Restoration in Ohio!

Praise God! He has restored our marriage! He stopped the divorce and brought my husband home! I asked Him to restore our marriage by April 16, before our son's wedding on May 3, and He did!

On Good Friday, I received a letter from his attorney, dated April 16, stating that my husband had asked for a dismissal of the divorce. If I agreed, I need only sign the enclosed papers. I could not stop crying when I saw the date on that letter!

I realized my Lord God cared about the smallest detail of my prayers. When I received a copy of the date-stamped court order dismissing the case, the date on the attorney's letter to me was June 5, our 27th wedding anniversary!

From the time I asked God for the April 16 date for restoration of our marriage, He continually confirmed that date. I work in an office where we deal with birth dates, and that date continually came up. The most amazing confirmation came when my son showed me his wedding announcements—the date on the RSVP card for his wedding was April 16!

Be encouraged to be specific in your prayers. Continue to pray, waiting patiently while you believe you have what you asked for, and leave the results in God's hands. He is able to do immeasurably more than you can ever ask or imagine. Pray His Word and His promises back to Him for your situation and circumstances. He loves to hear His Word spoken from your lips!

I do not want to forget mentioning that throughout my wait "until my change came," God changed my heart as well as my husband's. I was willing to be molded to whatever He desired for me. It is truly the miraculous work of God! Praise God! He is worthy.

Restored in Utah!

I have been disobedient by not sending in my praise report sooner. In March, my husband had me bring our children up to where he was working during spring break. He was working in the Denver area when they experienced their worst snow in forty years.

We were snowed in at his apartment in the forest for four days. Glory be to God! It was wonderful!!! We got to be together as a family!

I have other praises, too. My husband was home this weekend from his out-of-state job. He no longer sends me away when he comes home and says he feels comfortable being here with and around me. He calls almost every day to talk and sounds concerned when he cannot reach me. It is so wonderful from where we started two and a half years ago! Glory be to God!

This weekend was special as he took us shopping and to the movies, and then we enjoyed dinner as a family at home!!! Praise God—He is so wonderful! When I took my husband to the airport, he asked me if I needed anything! I told him I was having a hard time deciding which college to attend. (I feel a calling to teach and begin a private Christian school.) After I explained, he guided me where I should go.

That was an answer to prayer as I was struggling. Then my husband said not to worry about the tuition because he would pay for everything! (We are restored, but he still keeps some of our finances separate.) Praise God again and again as this was a prayer answered, too!

God is so good. He loves us all even though we are not worthy. I have a confession though—I have not been appreciating all the little things the Lord does every single day. Since being restored, it has been easy to be lax in praising and seeing all those little (and big) things the Lord does. I need to keep steady with my praises, appreciation, and warfare.

Dan and Erin, thank you, and all the dedicated people who help you, for all your devotion to the ministry. Your perseverance and faith are such an inspiration. I have enjoyed the weekly letters from Erin and Michelle. Thanks again and God bless.

Husband Comes Home in North Carolina!

Praise the Lord! My husband and I had been separated for two years. He lived outside the country for the last twelve months, and now he is home!

Although I am still praying for his salvation and for his heart to turn toward me, the Lord has answered two of my prayers! One was that he would return home and the other was that his heart would be turned toward our daughter and her heart to him.

Not only does our daughter remember her father (she was only one and a half when he left), but she also adores him! It is amazing that the bond between them is as though he never left. Praise the Lord!

When you are in the midst of a trial and hurting so badly, it is often easy to overlook what God has done. I just want to openly praise Him for what He has done and what He is going to do! Hallelujah!

I give praise to my Lord and Savior Jesus Christ! I was a foolish woman and left my husband (with the blessing of my parents/pastor) two years ago. I never wanted a divorce, but I was tired of hurting and wanted to "help" God create a crisis in his life. I thought that leaving him was just the crisis he needed.

He tried to reconcile with me, but due to my hard heart and stubbornness, I rejected him. At that time, he wasn't changed the way that I thought he should be, so I didn't want to take him back until I saw what I wanted. Little did I know that I was the one who needed changing!

A year ago, my husband left the United States to return to the country where he was born. It was only supposed to be for three months, but he kept delaying his return. I am not surprised because our conversations were argumentative and I was still a self-righteous Pharisee.

However, after he had been gone about six months, the Lord began dealing with me about leaving. He actually began to show me that I was wrong. Up until that time, I thought I was right. Even so, I would pray occasionally that IF there was a slight possibility that I was wrong, would He please show me.

He did begin doing that! First, He showed me that I needed to forgive my husband. I asked Him to help me do that, and He did! However, I still did not come to face my own sin until I found Restore Ministries. I was getting desperate because I had been praying for my husband for so long but wasn't seeing anything.

When I ordered *How God Can and Will Restore Your Marriage,* it was as if I was reading about myself. I had to pause every couple of pages and repent of all my sins. In that book, God revealed things to me that He had been trying to tell me all along. God used Erin to speak directly to me!

Immediately, there was a change in me. I could not see my husband's faults, but only my own. I begged for God's mercy and asked Him to forgive me for being so foolish. Once I finished the book, I thought I knew how I needed to change, and that would be that. I had no intention of joining the fellowship or ordering the other materials. However, as time went on, I knew I needed more, so I ordered the *Wise Woman* workbook.

Again, God convicted me of more sin and opened my eyes to the woman and wife He wants me to be. Before then, almost every conversation I had with my husband was stressful and argumentative. It had been that way for nearly four years. But, the contentious woman died and a new woman was born! Hallelujah!

Regardless of what my husband said to me on the phone, I stopped arguing and striving. I no longer felt the need to make my point or prove him wrong. I was determined to be that woman with a quiet and gentle spirit. I also stopped fretting over when he was returning. I used to cry trying to persuade him to come back, but then I stopped. I realized that had he returned earlier, I would have blown it big time because I was not changed. That alone taught me to trust in the Lord's timing.

A month ago, I overheard him telling our two and a half-year-old daughter that he was coming home next month. I knew he could change his mind as he had done before, but I wanted to prepare as though he were coming. Praise the Lord—he did come home last week!

I am so thankful to God that my husband is here. I also thank the Lord for taking this former contentious, self-righteous Pharisee and turning her into a peaceable woman with a quiet and gentle spirit. I thank God for Restore Ministries because you have truly changed my life! Even though I was a committed Christian, I was not living the Word of God in my marriage. I also thank God for my encouragement partner who is still there for me.

Praise the Lord that we are now in the first phase of restoration. I am praying for my husband's salvation and for his heart to continue turning toward me. I am also praying that God will give me wisdom as I finally have the opportunity to win my husband without words. The Lord is truly my beloved, and I am forever His.

I can't tell you how your ministry blessed me. I heard about another marriage ministry a long time ago, and went back to their site about one and a half years after I left my husband. Their website linked to Restore Ministries. For some reason, I felt drawn to your ministry. I never ordered a tape, book or anything from the other ministry, but yours was different. I now know that to be God.

At first, I saw the book *How God Can and Will Restore Your Marriage*. The word "restore" caught my attention because a few months prior, a guest minister at our church had called me by name and told me that God was going to restore for me (he hadn't known my name, or that I was the pastor's daughter). Instead of ordering the book, I tried to find it in the local Christian bookstore. When I didn't find it, the next day I went back to your website and ordered it. I felt such a sense of urgency and desperation. I could not wait to get the book. God had been gradually showing me that I was wrong for leaving, among other things. However, it wasn't until I got your book that I realized what a fool I was.

Erin, after every other page I was repenting. I could not believe what I was reading. I grew up in a spirit-filled church, and know that people say things like "this isn't a mistake that you are reading/listening to this." However, I am a skeptic of Christians. This time, what I read was true. God used your ministry to change my life in a way that He had been trying to all along!

When I found you, my husband was out of the country (sold his business and went back to his homeland). It was only supposed to be for three months, but he kept delaying his return. I would argue and cry with him about it over the phone, but it only made matters worse. My family knew I was standing for our marriage, but were encouraging me to move on. I knew that wasn't what God wanted me to do; I just couldn't find anyone who would stand in faith with me. So I stood alone. Anyway, my husband missed our daughter's second birthday, Christmas, and a planned vacation to Florida. HOWEVER, I know it was God. Had he returned nine months ago as he was supposed to, I would have destroyed things again because I wasn't changed!

I do have an encouragement partner. As I mentioned earlier, I had no intentions initially of joining the fellowship. I thought the book was all I needed. However, I began to realize I needed more help, so I ordered the workbook. After that, I decided to join because I became hungry for every resource available to help me hope for a restored marriage. I wasn't talking to family and friends, but I did have a wonderful ePartner and we still keep in touch.

While going through the workbook for women, I realized that I needed more. I proceeded to order the workbook on audiotape, the "Be Encouraged" series, the Queen Esther video, and the "Alluring and Unconditional Love" video. I knew I needed to submerge myself in God's Word, prayer, and the resources of this ministry. Every morning, at the conclusion of my prayer time, I would read another section of the workbook. At night, I would put on headphones and listen to at least one tape before going to bed. I told my ePartner that I felt like I was in "marriage restoration school"! I looked forward to prayer and reading my Bible so much that I actually started getting up two hours earlier just to have time with God and to study His Word!

The best recommendation that I have for those who are praying for restored marriages is to make sure they study the Word diligently, even as they are going through Restore Ministries' resources. Also, now that my husband is home, I realized how right you were on your "Be Encouraged" tapes—I have faced the biggest battle since his return. It has been absolutely painful, but God has prepared me. Women want their husbands to return, but sometimes they don't have any idea what they will be faced with when he does. They had better take heed and allow God to pour into them as much as possible so that they can stand firm in His Word when their husbands return home.

The one thing that I keep remembering is how you said you felt when Dan first came home. I never expected it, but I have battled more feelings of hopelessness and defeat since my husband's return. Actually, things have appeared to be more hopeless now than when he was away. I know that is not true, but it's amazing how the enemy does not want to let up. Anyway, I have won those mind battles through prayer. This first phase is really hard, yet I know God has equipped me.

I want you to know that I have no words to express my gratitude to God and to this ministry! The fact that I am changed is a miracle that

I still can't believe. We CAN win this war on divorce, one marriage at a time!

I Am Happy and Blessed of God!

I will bless the Lord at all times! His praises shall continually be in my mouth! I am rejoicing in the Lord for the restoration of my marriage. My husband has come back to me—he is back home!

God has turned my husband's heart back to Him, me and our son and away from the OW whom he was with for six months. Any feeling he had for her has waxed cold! In Jesus' name, that relationship has been put to death. That is one of the prayers I prayed and God answered!

I'm reminiscing about one of our conversations from the past week when he said, "I came to myself one day and thought, what am I doing?" Though living with her and sleeping in the same bed with her, he said he couldn't keep his mind off me. He went to bed and woke up every day desiring to be back home! He said he was lonely, but pride and shame kept him from coming home.

One day over a month ago, he boldly told the OW that he couldn't continue in the relationship and that he was moving back home to make things right with his wife and son. PRAISE GOD! He said he left immediately and does not want to look back. He cut off all communication with her and declared that no one will ever come between us again! God is so good!

Since my husband's return, he is attending church with me and has given his life to the Lord! Praise God, he came home to me broken before the Lord. I told my mom that he behaves as if a ten-foot angel came to him and sat on the foot of his bed! He cannot say he is sorry enough for the things that happened. He says he was foolish. He told me that he was not even worthy of a second chance and thanks me for giving him one every chance he gets.

I thank God for the changes He made in my husband and in me. Through this crisis, my husband and I have been molded and shaped into the persons God desires us to be. I thank God for helping me to see that my first ministry is to my husband. I thank God for loving me enough to show me my shortcomings. I thank God for showing me that I was a contentious and controlling woman and that my behavior contributed to pushing my husband into the arms of another woman. Even so, he takes full blame for the adultery.

I thank God for showing me how to be a lady, to keep silent and to pray and let Him deal with my husband. I thank You, Jesus, for my husband who has been (without coaching from me) leading his son and me in prayer each time we come together. Praise God! My husband says that he realizes that he can do nothing without God. His cry to God is "Help!" God is truly helping us on the road to recovery.

I encourage everyone who is believing God for their marriage to not give up and to apply the biblical principles from Erin and Dan's books and their audio and video tapes. Especially follow the principle that informs us not to pursue our spouses—it works!

I am so happy for my husband. At one time, he didn't want to see me, but now he makes excuses or begs to see me. At one time, he only wanted to communicate through email, but now we talk...talk...talk...and chat on the phone like teenagers! At one time, he just wanted to be friends, but now he says he loves being my husband, my best friend and my lover!

God is so good!

Thank you, Dan and Erin, for Restore Ministries.

God Has Restored in New York!

Praise our holy Father! I give Him all the glory for He has answered my prayers! My husband did not intend to return to our marriage; he did not feel the same toward me as I felt toward him.

Once I received Erin's book, I learned a lot about myself and how I needed to change, starting with trusting God for everything. My husband had been gone about one week and I was very distraught. I was already a Christian, but I was not trusting the Lord completely. For the first time in our relationship, my husband told me he did not love me any more. (We had been together for thirteen years.) Your book encouraged me daily, and once I let God take full control, He began to change me, as well as my husband's heart.

I found your ministry when a man from a prayer request group I had searched for sent me an email suggesting your ministry and your book. (He had the man's version of the book.)

I ordered your book *How God Can and Will Restore Your Marriage*. It showed me how I needed to change first before God would work with my husband. It helped me to believe that God wants to restore all marriages, and it taught me how to fight the spiritual battle. I felt strengthened knowing God was in full control, once I allowed Him to take over. Most importantly, I learned how to trust God completely with all of my trials, especially our marriage. I highly recommend your book to anyone who is praying for a restored marriage. It was the best twelve dollars I ever spent!!

Once I had complete trust and faith that only the Lord could change my situation, I began to pray several times a day, talking to God and giving Him total control. I felt peace inside when I prayed at the lowest times of my day. God gave me strength to avoid calling my husband. I was tempted several times. God's Word kept me going. I knew that if I had faith, He could change ANY situation. God also changed ME. As I found out, I was a CONTENTIOUS WIFE, and I used bad language.

We had been separated for exactly two months when my husband called me and said he needed to talk. He told me that he had a feeling that God was talking to him. Praise the Lord!

Thank you, Erin and Dan, for your ministry, and God bless you! Love in Christ!

Restored in United Arab Emirates!!

Remember Jesus! All glory to our merciful Savior. After nearly six months of waiting, crying and praying, I received a call from my husband. He is coming home shortly! All glory to our merciful Savior who cherishes us close to His heart.

I know how much it hurts for you to be where you are today. I have had days when I never wanted to face the world, when my future looked uncertain and it was difficult to trust in the Almighty. My reasoning was, if He is the merciful, compassionate Lord, why does He not deliver me?

Remember—He has a purpose for you and He has plans for your life, plans not to harm you, but to give you a bright future. I love Jesus more than anything in this world; never give up on Him. He will make you new and set you free from all your pain.

It Is Finished! Restoration in Virginia!

The Lord has worked miracles! We have been back together for almost a month! My husband has returned over twenty times in the last two years. Each time I knew it was to be short-lived, that he was only home because "they" were fighting. However, this time, I knew the Lord was working!

About three months ago, I heard "It is finished" when I asked Him to please restore our marriage and heal our family. With complete faith, my prayers changed. I claimed that I knew it was finished, and asked the Lord to please finish changing me so that I would be ready. One morning, I cried out to Him, "Lord, my family is hurting—do WHATEVER it takes and make me ready."

Without details, I will tell you "ask and you shall receive." Big things happened to separate my husband and the OW, things that could have only come from the Lord. I am praising and worshiping Him, knowing that I have seen the Lord move mountains!

Thank you for your ministry and the knowledge and wisdom you have shared with me, for teaching me to be a godly wife and helping me to deal with my husband's needs. I know I will be walking this course for the rest of my life. I know that God will always be my Comforter and Supporter!

Never, ever give up on God. He didn't give up on my husband and me, and He won't give up on you, either!

Restored in New Jersey! Praise for God's Continued Refining!

All praise to His Holy One that my husband has been home for nine months after a three-year separation! What a miracle! Right now, though, I want to praise my dearest Lord for refining me each day my husband has been home!

I have finally reached the point where I place in God's hands ALL my trust, love and peace. I am not deceived into believing that I have to learn to trust my husband since it is my almighty Maker who is to be trusted with all things—my marriage and TOTAL restoration included!

Brothers and sisters, please remember—it is living in this truth that makes ALL the difference in the total restoration of our marriages after our spouses' return. When I feel (God's truths are not "feelings") afraid (God did not give us a spirit of fear) and begin to mistrust my husband, I go to prayer and reaffirm the trust I have in Him. Amen!

All my prayers are in agreement with your prayers for the restoration of your ultimate relationship—the one with God—and for your marriages.

Thank you, Erin! God is truly so very awesome! It makes we wonder how I could have left Him out of my life for so very long indeed...

From Gloom to Glory in California in Three Months!

Thank my Father in heaven. Praise His holy name! This is the third time I have started this praise report. There is no way I could express enough glory, honor, thanks, and praise to my Lord for the restoration of our marriage!

My husband and I separated on February 3. The Lord led me to Restore Ministries two days later. How's that for God's work? Your ministry opened my eyes to everything I was doing wrong. I found Restore Ministries through a web site called marriagebuilders.com. Someone on one of the message boards asked if anyone knew a web site that had Christian-based support. They had your link there, and I never went back. The Lord's timing is perfect. After reading the book and doing the study, I realized quickly what a mess I had made of my marriage and how I, with my own hands, had torn down my house!

In that short time I had already done so many things wrong. There was so much tension in the house. I was so desperate to make my husband love me again. Almost every other day I would get in his face and tell him how we could make this work. I forced him to make a decision that he wasn't ready to make and he chose divorce. Although at times he would tell me he would always love me—praise the Lord!—he said he just couldn't see us putting our lives back together again.

I told him I forgave him for his sins, but probably mostly out of my own self-righteousness. I even preached to him, which he hated the most. I had already slandered his name and he knew it. I stripped my husband of his place as head of our home. I denied him the right to the pleasure of my body whenever he wanted it. We even tried marriage counseling. The world was telling me I couldn't save my marriage by myself. By the time I found RM I was losing hope fast.

MY sin was ever before me and I no longer dwelled on his sins. Forgiveness and repentance soon followed. I continue to pray that my husband will someday be able to forgive me for all the hurt I've caused him. The Lord is my strength and my Deliverer.

When I found RMI, it was like I regained all the hope I had lost. I cried as I read the introduction because it sounded just like me. Everything you said was exactly what I was feeling. That same day I ordered the book and the study guide with the tapes. As I read the book, my Lord so convicted my heart. I had never understood what "a peace that surpasses all understanding" meant. Now I have it!! God is so good to me. As I read through the book and study guide, I had such a renewed hope, peace, and even joy. I had an understanding of the Bible that I hadn't had before!

Psalm 23 took on a new meaning for me. I knew I had truly forgiven my husband because MY sins were EVER before me. I'd never had such an intimate relationship with God, and I certainly had never fasted before. I started to pray before I did anything. I just wanted the Lord to change me into a godly wife, mother, and woman. I prayed that the Lord would help me with my son, and to keep my house in order.

The "Be Encouraged" videos were tremendous support for me. They either validated what I was already doing or caused me to do something I hadn't thought of. "I can do all things through Christ who strengthens me." THANK YOU, FATHER IN HEAVEN!

I lost 20 pounds and began to dress differently. I focused my attention on those things I had lost sight of and let go, especially my Lord and Savior. I never talked with my husband about our marital situation unless he brought it up. Otherwise we spoke about our son, the house, or work. Every time after my husband left, I would pray and praise the Lord that He brought him home even for a little while.

God is so good. Though we were separated, my son and I saw my husband often. We continued to be intimate, praise the Lord. Ladies, if it is at all possible, make yourselves available to your husbands—ALWAYS. This was ONE of my sins. My husband continued to meet our financial needs. I paid all our bills together and he always called to make sure things were okay with the house, even coming over to mow the lawn. I have much to be thankful for.

My ePartner was a great encouragement. It was wonderful to have someone to keep me on the path. We would lift each other up during the bad times—when the day was especially tough, or the time I fell. My husband and I had a birthday party for our son. We started talking after everyone left. Of course I spoke too much. We both got angry. Needless to say, I fell on my knees after he left. My partner just picked me up and dusted me off, reminding me that we WILL fall but that it is important to seek the Lord when we do. It was important to me to have someone to believe in my marriage with me.

When my husband asked if he could come back home, I was sort of shocked. I almost felt like I wasn't ready to have him back only because I felt that the LORD's work in me was not done. But HIS timing is always perfect; He restored our marriage suddenly. He knows best. On April 14 my husband asked to come home, and he officially came back on April 30. Thank You, Jesus!!!

Because we (my husband and I) are definitely going through a period of adjustment and there are times when I get that sick feeling in the pit of my stomach, I'm so glad to be getting a new ePartner from the Restored group to keep me on track during this new phase.

Now my focus is that I am standing in the gap for my husband, praying that he would come to a saving knowledge of the Lord. I will not go to church without him; I will wait until he asks me to go with him. The hard thing for me now is carving out time for my Lord and me.

Erin and Dan, I praise the Lord for the calling He placed on your lives. I was blind but now I see!

Husband Comes Home in Nebraska!

I want to thank my Lord and Savior for opening my eyes. Thank you, Dan and Erin, for being faithful to tell the truth about how to restore marriages God's way. I was doing and saying things to try to change my husband. I was told to follow the "tough love" tactic and I saw that it only made things worse. It pushed him to the OW.

Then I read the Restore Your Marriage book twice! Easter morning, I asked my husband to forgive me for the mean things I have said to him. After I asked for his forgiveness, I had such peace. I did not have that peace when I was being mean and trying to change things in the flesh.

God has done a mighty work in me. I am no longer that negative and sarcastic person. I gave it ALL to God and stopped doing things in the flesh. I fell in love with Jesus. I showed my husband love when I had a chance to see him. I had total faith in God that He was going to restore our marriage.

I fasted and prayed. I quoted Scriptures daily: "what God has joined together, let no man separate," and other Scriptures in the Restore Your Marriage book. I knew it wasn't God's will that this marriage be over.

Sunday afternoon, he stopped by to drop something off and I could see the battle and turmoil in him; he looked sad. I fasted and prayed on Monday because I knew it was a spiritual battle. Well, at 1:30 a.m. Tuesday, my husband called and asked if he could stop by to talk to me. He told me he was tired of running and ready to come home. He felt so ashamed. He said he loves me and misses me. He is moving back home today!!!

God can and will change things in an instant. Thank You, Jesus. Thank you, Erin and Dan, for speaking the truth and being faithful to God. May God bless you and your children. For others out there, hang on to Jesus and have faith that He will restore what the devil has taken.

Restored Marriage and a New Baby in Mississippi!

I am rejoicing in the Lord! In my last praise report (see below), I announced the birth of our child and how my husband unexpectedly came to the hospital. After that, praise God, he moved out of the apartment he was renting from the OW and back with his mom.

After that, he called to apologize for what he has done. A few days later, he moved back, declaring that he wanted my son and me back in his life, even if it took the rest of his life to prove it. I thank God for delivering him out of bondage, out of the adulterous relationship with the OW.

During our crisis, we lost our home, so he is living with his mom and I am still at my mom's. We decided that we would begin talking and working through things during his visitations with our son, but God had a different plan. Exactly three weeks after he moved home, we were visiting with the baby. I invited him to my graduation from a 12-week class I had taken at my church called "Purity with a Purpose." He was glad to be there and was even fifteen minutes early. He looked very, very nice.

He was touched during the ceremony; I actually saw tears falling from his eyes. He asked if it was OK if he asked our pastor to pray with our baby, him and me. He said that maybe prayer would help us to move forward in the reconciliation of our marriage. What a wonderful surprise!

I asked him if he was sure and he answered, "YES." We went into the pastor's study, and my pastor and his wife were there. They ministered to him about the importance of family. My husband was so receptive that he was in tears. He admitted that his pride had kept him from coming home, even though he wanted to badly.

Other issues were discussed, and then my pastor asked if he was ready to devote his life to his family. He said "Yes," and then the pastor asked if we really wanted to reconcile our marriage. We looked into each other's eyes and said, "Yes."

My family was not pleased that he returned and were advising me that I should put distance between us. They wanted me to make him suffer for leaving me before accepting him back, but that is not what I've been praying for or what I am led to do.

My pastor advised us to begin the process of reconciliation that day. He told us we needed to get away and rekindle our relationship. We've made plans, to my family's dismay, but as my pastor said, this is my life, my marriage, and my husband.

Thank God for the reconciliation of my marriage. Thank you, Dan and Erin, for Restore Ministries.

God is Merciful and Good!

I am overjoyed as I write as I gave birth to our first son on March 28. He weighed five pounds, twelve ounces. Three weeks before his birth my husband had cut off all communication. I could not get him off my mind, so I began to ask the Lord to put the baby and me on his mind and cause him to contact us. And praise God! My husband called the following morning after three weeks of silence. I was floored—look at God!

We had a wonderful conversation. He asked if he could take me out for dinner and I said, "Yes!" I was modest about it, but I was bursting with joy inside. He told me that it would be two weeks before our date because he was short on cash, but that he was starting a new job.

He told me that he had been thinking about me and wanted to hear my voice. He said that he wanted to reconcile our marriage, but wanted to work and save money so that he would have something to offer when he comes back. He also said that he still considered himself my husband and wanted to work things out if I wanted. He gave me a number to reach him in case of an emergency!

I was in awe of the humility from a man who had walked out on me five months before, disappearing without a trace. Then, he wrote me a heartbreaking email two weeks later to tell me that he didn't want to come back, that he was confused about what he wanted in life and that he was moving closer to his job (the OW). HOWEVER, GOD TURNED his heart back to his son and me which was one of my petitions before the Lord. I thank God for answered prayer!

That week I prayed that my husband would not be satisfied with the other woman and that she would not be satisfied with him. I prayed a hedge of protection around him and that he and the OW would not be able to live peaceably with one another. I prayed, in the name of Jesus, that the OW would become as bitter as wormwood and that she would drive him away. I prayed that something would happen to cause him to move back home with his mom and dad.

God began to answer prayer! With my husband's desire to reconcile our marriage, I sensed that his relationship with the OW was failing. A week went by and I heard nothing, yet I knew that God was working.

While I waited for our date, I prayed that God would give me the words to say that would compel him to come home and that my husband would see the changes God was making in me. As the week rolled on, God was working behind the scenes! It turned out that my husband and I wouldn't have to wait three weeks to see one another.

I went in for a prenatal appointment and my blood pressure was very high. My doctor checked to see if I was in pre-term labor. After it was determined that I had not dilated, my doctor sent me to the hospital to monitor my blood pressure. I was told that if it did not stabilize I could have toxemia. After a few hours of monitoring, my blood pressure had not regulated and it was expected I would deliver the next day.

My mom called my husband's grandmother to tell her I was in the hospital. Later, my husband's mother called. I informed her that I could be giving birth the next day and she asked if I wanted her to contact my husband. I told her to wait until I knew for sure that the doctor was going to induce labor because I did not want him to make an unnecessary trip. She said that she was calling. I did not expect her to find him or him to come, but I was awakened by the squeaking of a door as my husband walked in. I was in shock! He wanted to be with me and make sure I was going to be OK. He stayed the night and the next day. I was induced at 3:13 p.m. with my husband by my side.

He carried our baby to the nursery and then brought him back to recovery to be with me. He told me that I did a good job and that he was proud of me. He stayed two more nights and left to go to work. He confessed many things he had done wrong to my mother. He kept expressing how sorry he was for all the wrong he had done to me. He told me he wanted to make things right and be there for the baby and me if I would have him back. I accepted his apology and told him yes, but that we had to take things slowly as we have a lot of healing to do.

He told me that today he moved in with his mom and dad! Thank You, Lord, that he no longer lives with the OW. I asked him what happened and he said he would explain this weekend. Thank God for my husband's deliverance from the other woman!

Thank God for turning my husband's heart back to his child and me. Lord, turn his heart toward You, also! Thank God for Erin and Dan and for Restore Ministries. The biblical principles you have shared really are effective. God bless you and your family.

Restored for Good in Pennsylvania!

Praise the Lord—my husband has come home! My husband, who was living with an OW, came into our house unexpectedly last week and said, "Hello," and then asked, "Would you come and help me get my things out of the car?"

When God moves, He moves suddenly! We have not talked about what happened, but it does not matter. What matters is that God did it. He brought my husband home!

Although I am undeserving, God has shown His infinite grace and mercy to me. I would not say we are completely restored just yet, but my husband is home. I know God will continue to work toward full restoration.

God is so good! All praise and glory goes to the Lord!

Three weeks later...

My husband has been home for three weeks now. Praise the Lord. I waited a while to write again to make sure his stay was permanent. In the last two years, he has left three times for the OW.

This time is different, though. I know this is it. My husband is home for good! He has been so kind and loving toward me. He talks about our future together. Just last night he said something about our future children. He was at our family Easter dinner and it was like he never left. He joked with my family just like old times.

He refinanced our house and has worked on getting us almost completely out of debt. He also mentioned that he wanted to learn more about repairing and doing home improvement.

God is so wonderful! I used to worry about everything, but not anymore. After what I have seen the Lord do, how could I ever worry again? I know that He will take care of everything. All I have to do is trust and obey. All praise and glory go to the Lord. I never again want to live without Him!

Restored in Florida!

I just moved into our new home with my husband after being separated for one year! I cannot begin to explain all of the wonderful miracles God has given me over the past twelve months. Every single prayer that I brought before God was answered above and beyond what I could ever ask or imagine!

The most current miracles are that my husband asked just yesterday where his Bible was! He has been constantly telling me how beautiful I am and how much he appreciates me! We are expecting our first child and he has shown concern and affection as I have never seen from him. I mean when God answers prayers, He really answers prayers (smile).

I would also like to apologize to you who are still believing for your marriages for not giving my praise report earlier. I know how encouraging it was for me to come to the website and read the praise reports of restored marriages. They always increased my faith in God and gave me hope that one day I would be writing my praise report of a restored marriage.

Keep on praying until you get your breakthrough. To God be ALL the glory!

Another Canada Restoration! Isn't God Amazing!

I must praise my Jesus! He is so faithful! My husband is home now! He has not once mentioned the OW or leaving again!

I know my God is faithful! I am so happy to have my hubby home! Things are not perfect and we have lots to work on, but I know God will help us and get us through!! I am believing for complete healing and restoration of our marriage and home! As I continue to stand on God's promises, I know He will see us through. God bless all of you, and do not give up!!

I am writing to report that God has miraculously restored my marriage!!! All praise, glory and honor to Him! I am working on the whole story and I will send it in very soon.

What would you do if your pastor were counseling your close friend NOT to do all the things you have been taught from the Word? And what would you do if she started to apply the biblical principles anyway and had her marriage restored, and then left the church at her husband's request? What would you do if that man were YOUR husband? Well, I can and will answer all of those questions. I have seen the mighty hand of God, and He has brought two others to me to tutor as I am learning to walk in radical obedience!

I have pored over all the resources and am hearing God's call to minister to incarcerated women. God can do ANYTHING!

A Hopeless Marriage Restored in North Carolina by Jesus!

My situation looked hopeless. After six years of marriage, my wife had finally given up on our marriage. She said she didn't love me any more, nor did she want to be married to me any longer. Her thoughts were that she had gotten married too early.

She left me and rented an apartment and simply moved on. I heard through a friend about Restore Ministries and I got the books and studied God's promises. I had several friends praying for my wife and me. Within three weeks, God softened my wife's heart and she came back home!

We are building a new marriage now—not like before. I have decided to follow God's Word and treat her as a wife should be treated. She is already responding with joy.

God's Word truly stands the test of time. The question is, will we do it God's way or ours? I just praise the Lord for His eternal truths and promises that we can stand on in a world where everything changes except God and His Word! Thank You, Jesus!

Restored in Canada! All Praise, Glory and Honor to Him!

I am writing to report that God has miraculously restored my marriage!!! All praise, glory and honor to Him! I am working on the whole story and I will send it in very soon.

What would you do if your pastor was counseling your close friend to NOT do all the things you have been taught from the Word and that we ARE to do to have God restore our marriages? And what would you do if she started to apply the biblical principles anyway and had her marriage restored, and then left the church at her husband's request?

What would you do if that man was YOUR husband? Well, I can and will answer all of those questions. I have seen the mighty hand of God, and He has brought two others to me to tutor as I am learning to walk in radical obedience!

God can do ANYTHING! I have pored over all the resources, as you know from your records, and am hearing God's call to minister to incarcerated women.

A Reason to Never Give Up!!! Incredible Restoration in Ohio!

I received a card Sunday from my wife. After two and a half years of separation and divorce, and after almost two years of restoration, we can now speak of her salvation and her finally growing in our Lord. It made all of the pain and tears worth it.

I, like most, at one time or another wanted to give up, find someone else and get on with my life. If I had done those things, I would not be witnessing my wife grow to love Jesus. We would not be going to church and studying the book A Purpose-Driven Life together at our church.

Read the words from her card. I realize it could be to another person, but it was not. It was from a loving, formerly wayward wife to her loving, believing husband. First are the words from the author of the card:

"I Believe in Love Because of You"
Love can come along just when we least expect it to,
And turn an ordinary life into something sweet and new.
Love can light a candle where the sadness used to be,
And heal the broken parts of us with trust and honesty.
Love can give us wings to fly above the world we know,
And lead us on adventures where we never dreamed we'd go.
Love can lift us to our feet and teach us how to dance,
Dare us to believe again and take another chance.

Author—Emily Matthews

These are my loving wife's words:

You gave me back something I thought I'd lost—
Feelings I thought I'd never feel again.

Somehow, you saw through all the walls
I'd built around my heart,
And helped me to trust enough to let love in.

And I just want to say thank you for being so patient
And good to me in every way—
For all the things you do that make me feel like the
Most special person in the world—
For being you, and for helping me believe in love again.

All my love,
Your wife

Our God is Amazing! Restored in Ohio!

God truly is amazing! What a journey He has taken me on to show me His love and truth. Briefly, about nine short weeks ago, my husband told me that he was not happy in our marriage, had not loved me for a long time, and needed a change. I discovered that there was another woman.

Initially, that sent me into a spiral of revenge and vindictiveness. Upon hearing the gory details from the OW's husband, I shamed my husband in the worst possible way—I told one of his coworkers, his family, several of my friends, and even the jeweler where my husband had bought jewelry for me over the years! I cleaned out the safety deposit box and savings account, took all financial records, and sought the best lawyer money could buy.

After I came to your website and ordered some materials, God COMPLETELY changed MY heart. I saw how my sins had caused strife in our marriage. God showed me what I had to do—repent and ask forgiveness, starting with my husband.

I asked my husband to forgive me for my contentiousness and for my slandering mouth as well as other sins I had committed to destroy our marriage. I apologized to all parties I had told, emphasizing my sins in dishonoring my husband. I also released my lawyer, gave back all financial records, and then didn't put another thought into how my children and I would manage financially (it is in God's powerful hands, not mine).

I apologized to my husband for slandering the OW to my friends and prayed for blessings for her, for my husband, and for my husband's family and acquaintances. I spent hours in prayer, fasting, and meditation, asking God to change, mold, and shape me according to His will.

My husband still proceeded down the path of separation. He secured an apartment and bought all new furnishings. We even refinanced the house so he could afford his new place. The more cruel and distant he became, the more I clung to God.

Last Friday, my husband moved out. I can only describe what I experienced as the supernatural peace one can receive only from God. At the time in my life that I should have been most despondent, I felt utterly content and joyful because I knew that no matter what happened, God was with me. I have NEVER felt such peace!

My husband called over the weekend; in the course of the conversation, I "released" him, as I gave my future to God. On Monday night, he came to see the children and to put them to bed. In the morning, I found a letter from him apologizing for what he has put me through!

Yesterday, he called from work and asked to work things out! He is moving out of his apartment today (a four-day stay was enough!) and will be coming home tonight! God changed his heart—it is true!

God has transformed me and has turned the heart of my husband. It is true that when one hands over one's life to God, life is so much easier and more enjoyable! God has the eyes to see our future. I am so glad that I placed my life in His hands. What an awesome God!

Restored in West Virginia—Never Give Up!

Don't give up on your marriage! No matter how hard things seem, God is working and testing you to see if you are ready. There were a few times I failed the tests, but I always asked for forgiveness and did not give up.

I just praise God for all that He has done in my life and for taking my husband away for a short while. It made me appreciate my husband more and learn more about my Lord and myself.

My husband has been home since December, and we are expecting our first child in two days! Previously, my pregnancies (three of them) ended in miscarriages. I praise the Lord for this child and pray that he is a healthy baby.

How God Can and Will Restore Your Marriage was so wonderful. That book is what started changing my life and getting me closer to God. I learned so much. The second book I ordered was the workbook for women, which interested me in the child discipline area. As I said, I am pregnant and due in two days and I never knew how or if I was going to discipline my child. This will be my first child born and I praise God for that. My three miscarriages occurred when my husband and I were just dating. I still wonder sometimes if that was the reason I miscarried. Anyway, the most recent book I ordered was "Workers at Home," which is helping me in my household. I still have some work to do in that area!

I have seen so many changes in my husband since God began changing me (it took a little while). He is more loving and kind, and we have had no arguments! When I feel that Satan is trying to make me doubt and not trust my husband (which he will), I just pray.

I pray for all of you who come to Restore Ministries, that you not give up, no matter what the circumstances, no matter how poorly you think your spouse is treating you, and no matter what everyone else says. PRAISE THE LORD IN EVERYTHING!!!! I am telling you not to give up; it is all worth it in the end!

Thank you for this site and thank God for my husband!

Restored in Kansas!

My husband came home last October so my testimony is about our restoration. We are getting ready to build our home about fifteen miles from where we live currently. We came across land to bid on that is in the country but close to a small town.

I was getting anxious about the land as the people hadn't contacted us about it for three weeks. Then, I was reading what Erin said about not being anxious and letting God work. I felt at peace and said that if we are meant to have it, we will.

The next day the lady called and said the land was ours! I am so thankful for all that God has done for my family and me, and for all that He continues to do. Thank You!!!

Arizona Restoration!

My husband is home! God orchestrated circumstances to bring it all about. The OW is still in contact. Please agree with me for God's intervention and pray that I can be silent and let God be God!

Georgia Restoration!

Hallelujah to the Lamb of God! My husband returned home Sunday after packing his clothes and moving to his brother's house five weeks ago! He spent many nights with me, including all last week, but he finally brought his clothes home!

I can see the Lord working mightily in my husband's life. Friday night, he asked me to make a list of the things that I wanted to see changed so that he could decide if it would be possible. Among the items on my list were that we pray and read the Bible together daily, develop more hobbies together, and share responsibilities in the home.

After reading my list, he marked each one as impossible. Yet he returned home, indicating that he is willing to try! This from a man who never thought HE had any flaws and who constantly told me that he would never change!

I believe that through prayer, fasting, crying out to the Lord, and remaining faithful to Erin's teachings, the Lord is working in my husband. Yesterday, we put his clothes away and spent several hours thoroughly cleaning house (TOGETHER). Before, it was always my job to do those chores alone.

He has been helpful doing little things in the home without being asked, and he has shown more courtesy to our sons! Even though he said that my list was impossible, he has already begun to change. I give credit entirely to our awesome God through the power of the Holy Spirit!

We haven't begun to pray and read the Word together yet, but I believe the promises of God who said in Philippians 1:6, "Being confident of this very thing, that He which hath begun a good work in you will perform it until the day of Jesus Christ."

Restored Marriage in Georgia!

I wanted to share my praise report. My husband left the OW and came home—suddenly!!!! He was out of the house since September and came home in March! He put his wedding band on just tonight and surprised me by showing it to me and saying, "We are going to make it through this." He had not thrown it away during our separation. He knew right where it was!

My husband came home because the relationship with the OW was over and he missed the children. He even says he never stopped loving, thinking about or missing me. Praise God he's home and God will complete what He has started. It sure is easier to keep your mouth shut when you see him only once a week! =) I definitely will sign up for a new ePartner, because I definitely need support during this time. Now, I really have to keep on my toes and in faith, because it seems as if he rises and falls according to the level of faith that I'm walking in.

We are taking it slowly, but God is doing things quickly. I am keeping my spiritual walls up through prayer. While this is a great victory, the war is not over and I'm not going to sit back and let the devil steal what God has brought back from captivity. Fear is under my feet.

I found your website while searching for help dealing with adultery. I was only searching Christian sites but still found garbage, garbage, garbage! I ran into a few articles explaining the truth about divorce and remarriage and then I found your website! Your explanation of "one flesh" and the verses about divorce and remarriage not being an option just because of adultery were what made me keep reading. I'd never heard this teaching before. I had no intention of divorce. I was going to watch God do a miracle. My husband and I have been through a lot in nine years, and I knew if I clung to God and obeyed, He'd lead me to restoration.

You also described what love was—NO ARGUING, NO MATTER WHAT—but agreeing!! And learning about using NO "tough love"—oh, that is what made my husband come home to me when the other relationship went sour!!! He could have stayed living by himself—but he came right home because he had no doubt that I loved him and would take him back—no questions asked or nagging or whining or any of that!!

Because I loved him the way you taught, even though my husband several times mentioned foreclosing, selling the house, giving me 2/3 less money, etc., I agreed with everything he said and NOT ONCE did he give me less than his WHOLE paycheck!!!! He, for seven months, paid for his apartment, truck payment and "entertainment" on side jobs. Not only did he give me his entire paycheck, but also when extras came up he'd pay for those, too—and most of those times, he just saw the need and asked if I needed help. God supplied everything!

Not pursuing my spouse was the hardest, since there was never a hate wall up and because he always treated us well (our three boys and me). But I'm learning this one over, too, since he's been home and he needs his space. I just meet his needs and do not pry and wait.

My husband has said that I always treated him well no matter what, and if I did say something not nice, I was very quick to call him and apologize. I never even knew if he was listening when I did that. He'd just say "Yeah, OK, whatever." The OW became sour and contentious and I stayed quiet. Now that he's home it's harder to stay quiet—and I'm having to remind myself of all your teachings on kindness and not being contentious.

I never missed a day of reading the praise reports on your website. When I was down, I could see all the other believers rejoicing over the littlest things and it'd make me look and see all the praises I had to give!

There are so many more awesome details that I could share but I would be up all night typing! God took care of my children and me wonderfully during our time of separation. God had such mercy on my husband and me. For God to forgive me daily when I would mess up and run my mouth is amazing. He was so merciful to forgive and pick me up. DESPITE my failings, God knew my heart and loved me and HE restored my marriage. He doesn't lie!

Thank you for your ministry's support. As I said earlier, there was not a day during my crisis that I did not read the daily praise reports. Those were such a blessing each day to encourage me to never give up and to see the blessings each day in my own life. Thank you for sowing into my life and marriage. May you reap a great reward from the Lord.

I praise God and give Him all the glory for what He's doing in my life and other believers' lives, and what He's done in your life. I recommend your website and materials to any/every woman who I come across going through an attack in her marriage.

Thank you. You have made a real difference in my life. I knew I was going to do this with God and get the victory, but finding your material really got me going in the right direction from the start, without wasting time asking advice from people and searching for materials that "might" work. You had THE WORD of GOD written out and explained every situation I was facing—and I devoured the Word and went forward and never looked back. Praise God. He is so good!!!

Glory to God!! Restored in Louisiana after Only Twenty-Two Days!

God moved suddenly. I just wanted to give thanks to God for bringing my husband back into my life. After a twenty-two day separation with a divorce filing pending, God gave me another chance. He broke me down and rebuilt me into someone more like Him!

My husband cannot believe the person I have become. And it is all because I found God. I cannot imagine life without Him. Thank you, Dan and Erin, for showing me the way to God.

I would like to encourage all women and men who are having trouble in their marriages to find THE LORD first and He will change you and then your husband. There is no other way and even if there was I am so glad I chose His path to restoring my marriage.

My marriage is better now than the first day we got married because I have Jesus in my life showing me the way. I have never been as happy and fulfilled as I am now. I praise God for choosing me to give this blessing to. GLORY TO GOD!

My husband left on Valentine's Day, got an apartment, contacted his lawyer, and phoned to tell me that the paperwork was going to be started. I was in shambles. I didn't know which way to turn or what to do next.

Three days later I started searching the Internet to see what was involved in the divorce process. I stumbled upon a divorce chat room and the first message I got was www.restoreministries.net. I had no idea what it was about.

I was desperate and decided to check it out. I was truly amazed at God's work. I started reading all the testimonies of the restored marriages and decided I can do this. The next day, my husband came to get some things and brought me some boxes that we had in storage.

The first box I opened contained a Bible. I think God was trying to tell me something. The Bible belonged in our house, not put away in storage. I opened it and started reading for the first time in my life. All the answers I was looking for were right there before my eyes!

I ordered Erin's books and immediately started working on them and applying what I had learned. Every day I asked God to send more trials into my life so that I could become a better person. And believe me He did.

I devoted everything to His Word. Almost every day I had some sort of blessing from THE LORD. I could not believe I had lived the first thirty years of my life not knowing God and instead living by the world. I don't know how I made it this far without Him. He was truly calling out to me and I ignored His calling.

Within 22 days of finding God, I found myself being tested every day and I passed the test usually without thinking about it. God is wonderful! He has changed my life completely. I have never been as happy and fulfilled as I am now with God in my life. I let go of my husband, accepted Jesus into my life and asked Him to break and rebuild me into someone more like Him and He did!

When my husband asked to see me, he could not believe I was the same person he had left just a few weeks before. We enjoyed each other's company so much that he invited me over again and again!

My husband and I separated because we could not get along. We would constantly argue over everything. We hardly ever spoke to each other just to avoid arguing. We led completely separate lives and we were not one flesh.

I was probably the most contentious woman you have ever met. I had to be right about everything. God changed me completely. My husband started to see me the way God saw me. I was not the woman he left, but someone completely different. I am now someone he enjoys being around, talking to and laughing with. I have become more like the woman God intended me to be. Every day I change a little more. With every change, I feel so much better about myself. God is amazing!

God stopped the divorce because I was willing to give everything I had to be the woman He desired. I gave up everything to become completely devoted to God. Everything else came along with it.

I saw my husband on Sunday and he was wearing his wedding ring again. GLORY TO GOD!! We are making plans to buy a new home to start a new life together! The only thing different this time is that God will be in the center. I cannot imagine living my life without HIM.

I am so grateful for Restore Ministries and my friend from the chat room who directed me to the website, and I am so grateful that God chose to change me into someone more like HIM. I never felt alone, even when my husband was staying the night at the apartment, because I had God in my life and He will never abandon me.

I encourage all women to reach out to THE LORD and find true happiness with God. There is no other way to be complete. Believe for your marriage; listen to God and He will guide you in the right path. Keep your eyes on Him and everything else will fall into place. Remember, you have to wait for His timing, but it will happen. Have faith in God and all things are possible!

A Thirty-Two-Year-Old Marriage Miraculously Restored!

I want to praise God for all He has done, that He is my Beloved and I am His. Before this trial in our marriage, I never knew God as I know Him now. My husband and I were separated for sixteen months, and he is now home! Joel 2:25 is the truth—God is restoring all that the locusts stole and bringing it back better than it was before!

For 32 years, I was a contentious wife (in modern terms it's called being a feminist or having an equalitarian marriage). I was walking selfishly, always trying to control and get my piece of the pie. God has shown me and forgiven me and continues to mold and change me as I submit to His will for my life.

And what blessings He showers on me when I walk in submission to Him!! Friends, it has been so sweet watching our wonderful restoration unfold, and yet I must continue to be patient and not get ahead of what God wants to do in His timing.

Keeping quiet about my opinion is so hard, but when I do God blesses a million times! God's principles are the Truth, and I see it again and again. My husband has come home even though he is still "clinically depressed" and God continues to heal him.

I am watching every day. When he arrived he said, "I am not in a hurry to see anyone." But then last night, he called my mother, who loves him dearly and has prayed for him every day during the trial. He also gave me permission to tell others that he is home. When I told him of so many who love him he said, "Thank you. It's just that I cannot feel anything so I reject it."

Dear fellow believers, we can never hope to know another's pain! Only God can, but He commands us to love no matter what. So be encouraged, all of you who continue to wait. The pain is great and the wait seems like eternity, but God will be faithful because He promises in His Word that He will be. Cry out to Him because He will supply ALL your needs, even after your husband returns home!!

My husband asked me to divorce him many months ago, and after I responded with a letter saying that I was "letting go," there was a turning!!! God is an awesome God and loves each of us and wants to bless us. Just hold on to Him and watch Him battle for you. May God bless and restore all of your marriages and families!

To answer your questions about how your ministry helped me during this time, I must tell you about my friend's restoration as well. My marriage crumbled before hers by a few months. When I talked to my friend after Christmas she said, "I think we are going to be single together," but I had discovered your ministry and I replied, "No, we aren't!"

Together we ordered the "Be Encouraged" audio tapes, the "Restore" book and the women's workbook. We prayed, fasted, and studied God's Word together, sometimes praying four or five times a day as her restoration was very, very intense. Mine has been slower. All this time we have been supportive, helpful, and accountable to each other. Your materials pointed us both to God's Word. The tapes were so very helpful. We listened to them again and again, and each time we heard new truths from God's Word as our circumstances unfolded.

We both give God all the glory for what He is doing in our marriages and our families and are humbled by His grace!

Thank you for the sacrifice that you give for this ministry. It is desperately needed as so many (even Christians!) believe that once a spouse thinks it is over, nothing can be done, but the Truth of His Word says otherwise. May God bless, protect, and honor you for this work you do in His name!

Another Restoration in Texas!

I had been separated from my husband for almost three years. I would like to thank God and tell all who read the praise reports that my husband returned home!! I was not able to let go of the thought that we would be together again, so I prayed and asked the Lord for guidance.

We were back together in September, but that was short-lived. He left again after only two and a half months. The devil was trying to make him believe that he could not make it without the OW. When he was home in September, she would call and harass us constantly. He now sees that God and God alone is in control of the situation.

Now that he is home, there is such a calm over our household—it is unbelievable. The OW knows my phone number, but not one time has she called!! I know God has us in His hand.

When he came home before, she would call and say some of the most awful things. But glory be to God, for He has removed that obstacle from our lives and we are moving forward. Thank the Lord for all blessings.

One more Restoration in California!

A friend of mine shared Restore Ministries' website with me on January 3. I was very encouraged by reading the praise reports and added our names to the prayer list for restoring marriages. That very day my husband moved back home and said it was over with the OW! But two weeks after I found out about the OW, he moved out of the house.

In the 21 months since then, he has lived with his brother, had his own apartment and even moved back home for short while. For too long, he actually went back and forth between home and the OW's apartment! He has now been home for a wonderful 23 days!!!!

I truly believe that God has brought him home to stay this time. We are talking more and making long-term plans for our home; preparing to buy a new bedroom set, etc. He also calls me if he will be home late!!!

I have also been blessed because through it all, my husband continued to spend time with the kids. I believe it is because of this that they have stayed out of trouble and continued to be good students.

I know that our marriage still needs a lot of restoring, but I praise God for the big, huge, giant step of bringing my husband home! I trust God to bring him ALL the way home to Him! I pray that my testimony will encourage others to not give up before receiving their miracle! I praise God for the ways He has worked in my life and in my husband's life!

Don't give up! It may be a looong haul, but God can and does restore marriages. I am blessed with a praying friend who has been through the same thing and has encouraged me all along to love as God does.

Restored and Loving Him!

Praise God! Oh how excellent is His name! Bless His holy name! He is so worthy of all the praise! I am so thankful to God that He does hear and answer prayer.

I had been praying for my marriage to be restored. We have been married for 28 years when my husband left me during some serious family problems. He began living with another woman. I was so devastated, but prayerful. I could only stand and pray that God would bring my husband back home.

I knew that God gave him to me and I had no reason to doubt that God was giving us time apart for His own reasons. We needed to have a closer walk with Him. I did and he did! I also had so many faithful prayer partners from all over the USA. They all encouraged me to just continue praying and standing on the Word of God because His Word never changes.

My husband filed for divorce and I didn't have the money to respond. I just left the courtroom and said, "Well God, this is truly in Your hands." The papers never went anywhere! Only God! I praised God daily and I began to thank Him for bringing my husband home even before he came home.

God began to give me peace that I knew surpassed all of my understanding. I knew that God had my husband and I just had to do my part through His guidance. I even saw my husband together with the OW. I always asked for God to make me desirable to my husband and let me act accordingly at all times.

I thank God that He did just what He said He would do for me! He told me to trust Him! I did! He did! I thanked God for who He was in my life and I knew that He was so faithful to His Word. I began to read and let it totally get into my very soul.

My time alone with Him can never be replaced. I got an up close and intimate relationship with my Creator, Savior, Provider, Protector and my constant Guide. He is real!! Reading His Word and letting the seeds be planted gave me more strength each day. God let me know to believe, believe and believe.

Each day I thanked God for my husband's clothes being in the very closet where he had removed them. I thanked Him for my husband's work truck being in the driveway and for his car being in the garage. I also began to purchase some things that I knew my husband loved and put them in place at home.

I reaffirmed my total trust in God to bring this about in His appointed time. I give all of the glory to God; He brought my husband back home after months of being gone! I could never give up because God continued daily to give me more hope to endure and to pray and to depend on Him only.

I have learned that it is all in God's timing and not ours. I still thank God for him being home and with the mind of Christ! He loves the Lord! We now study our Sunday school lessons together. God is a good God and He lives within me!

I am able to share my testimony with other women who are now where I used to be. I can tell them with all assuredness that God is faithful to His Word! I tell them that God is on our side, Jesus is praying for us and the angels are encamped 'round and about us!

Our God is an awesome God! I thank Him everyday for each day that He made and I will rejoice and be glad in it. I pray daily that my life will be a blessing to someone else. God bless you and do not give up! No matter what it looks like, God is in control and He will bring you out! God has a blessing with your name on it! He is blessing me right now! Praise Him!!! Hallelujah!!! I just love Him so much!!!

Restoration *after* Remarriage!

Thank you Restore Ministries for your faithfulness in following the call of our Lord. You are spreading His message of love and healing to us all. I am praising and thanking the Lord for all He is doing in my life and the life of my husband.

Yesterday was my last day in physical therapy (last year I had both hips replaced), and this coming Monday I go back to work restored in body. The surgery and recovery went wonderfully, and because I was alone, my children came and took care of me. It was a wonderful healing time for our relationships—God restored those relationships and allowed me to share HIM with my children, parents and siblings!

When my husband filed for divorce back in October right before my first surgery, I followed all the things you suggested—no lawyer, no fighting about anything and no signing the papers. What you said was true, my husband continued to support me by paying all the bills, including my car payment! He also made sure that I was covered under his insurance, even though none of that was in the divorce decree!

Although there was no hate wall between us, after our divorce we had almost no contact. The Lord had already prepared me for what my husband had to tell me—that he married the OW because he thought that he was in love with her. However, the Lord had already given me total peace and had readied me for his confession.

Then one day my husband unexpectedly walked in the door! He said he never wanted to leave! Then he told me that they were having big troubles and that he could not believe that he traded the life he had had for the one he had now. We began by having a lot of time to talk and praise God!

I believed that the restoration of our marriage was close at hand even though it looked complicated and impossible, but nothing is impossible for the Lord! Because of what He is doing in my life, I have been able to share with women what the Lord has brought me through. Their marriages, too, are improving with wonderful healings and in their husbands! The message is spreading along with the Lord's healings. Wow!

We were financially stable and doing well, and now we are at the point of losing everything, but Praise the Lord, it is only stuff!! None of it compares to all the wonderful healings going on around and in me! The Lord has shown me that my security is in Him and I have nothing to worry about no matter what happens. A wonderful peace surrounds me and fills all my waking moments.

I am very grateful for all the Lord has done in my life and the lives of those around me. I am also thankful for my e-partners. My first one's marriage was restored and the one I have now helps me through her prayers and understanding because she, too, is walking this walk. May the Lord bless her and all of you for being faithful and following His call. Keep believing "for what seems impossible for man is possible for God!" Thank you all again.

Another Restoration Miracle in Wisconsin!

Praise the Lord! My husband has returned home after seven months! God is so faithful when we trust Him. I love Ephesians 3:20—"He is able to accomplish infinitely more than we would ever dare to ask or hope" (NLT).

I have learned so much about being the wife that God expects—with a gentle and quiet spirit. While I still struggle with images of my husband with the OW, God continually tells me to be patient and endure. God is showing me how to respond differently to the sins (the world would call them addictions) that plague my husband, to be loving and kind and not contentious.

His plan is so much greater than we can understand. I came to know the Lord only four and a half years ago at the age of 31. My husband still does not believe in God. But God continually shows me that He will use these circumstances for His glory. Who am I to question His plan?

We must continue to grow in our knowledge of Him, and in doing so, we will grow in wisdom as we apply that knowledge to our lives. I need to do more to demonstrate to God and my husband that I am fully committed to my marriage.

The Lord reminds me every day that I must trust Him and live by faith and not by sight. Psalm 40 is one of my favorite Psalms. Early in my desire to restore my marriage, I found comfort in knowing that God had heard my cry and was lifting me out of the pit of despair. I believed that "many will see what He has done and be astounded. They will put their trust in the Lord" (v. 3b).

Proverbs 23:26–35 is a wonderful piece of Scripture I used in prayer for my husband when he was caught in adultery and alcohol/drug abuse. This, combined with Ezekiel 36:26–27, is a regular part of my daily prayer for my husband, that he would give his heart to the Lord. God keeps showing me that my husband could and can be reached, but it was not and will not be through my words.

Erin, thank you so much for following God's plan for your life and helping others in need.

My Husband Moved Home Saturday!!

After one year away, my husband moved home last Saturday!!! I know God brought him home! The things he has shared with me confirm His work in my husband. I know we have a long way to go, but I also know that God is able to do all things!

It is very hard when he leaves for work in the morning because he works with the OW. I pray that he will quit his job. He always said before he came home that he knew "if" he came home, he would have to quit. He said it, and it will happen.

Our family has been called into a music ministry and my husband is aware of it. A few years ago the Lord gave him three visions of our ministry, but Satan has fought against our family in many different ways for many years. I know that we serve a big God who is able to do exactly what He has purposed.

I am still praying that my husband will come back to church and that his heart will get right with God. Our church family is GREAT and they have missed him so much. I know, because of the things he has said to me, that he came home out of fear of God. At first I was hurt because I wanted to think that he came home because he missed and loved me, but I now know that coming home out of fear of God is best!

God has worked wondrously in me, and I so want to be a godly wife and woman!! I love the Lord so much! He is truly my Everything! Praise God!!

Also, God has started bringing women into my life with marriage problems, so my prayer is that I will be able to minister to them. I have led all of them to Restore Ministries. One lady already reported after only two months that she and her husband are not divorcing! They are talking and things are getting much better! Praise God! He is so faithful!!

Erin and Dan, thank you a million times over for being obedient to God. Dan, thank you for coming home to your wife and family and for being a godly man. Erin, thank you for becoming my friend through your videos and books and for allowing God to use you.

I really don't know where I would be today if a friend had not told me about Restore Ministries! Through this ministry and God, I am a different woman today! All glory and honor go to God!!

Restored and Remarried in Washington!

I have a restored marriage!!! My husband divorced me in June after we had been married for nine and a half years. Then, on January 4th we were remarried in our home. I am praising God that He controls the heart.

Thank you Erin! I am so thankful for yours and Dan's ministry and the encouragement that you give in all your materials. I found out about you when I was in desperation. I had been with you for about

6 or 7 months before I got brave enough to get my ePartner. My partner has been wonderful and I still cherish her friendship and want so much for her marriage to be restored. I have contacted my ePartners (I was blessed with two) and have talked with them since my husband and I got remarried and he looks forward to traveling and meeting them, also!!

I would like to be of encouragement to others and to get back into Restore Miniseries' Fellowship. I want to help others by praying and sharing how important it is for us to keep covering our homes in prayer. I also have been learning why Erin stressed the importance of taking a year off to help heal and guard my marriage more than ever with prayer and God's word.

Since my remarriage, my hours at work have been cut by 32 hours. I believe it is due in part from the discrimination of my belief in my marriage. My fellow employees believe as the world does, that LOVING YOUR husband unconditionally is crazy.

What helped me most was the Word of God, my prayer closet and all your tapes and videos of which I went over and over until tears flowed where I needed to correct myself and to learn to shut my mouth and be quiet.

I, also, had a prayer partner close to work and we would meet and pray at lunchtime. The workbook for women on how to build your house on the Rock and to gird yourself in Scripture and let God be the leader is tremendous!!! I followed everything and even took the 3x5 Scripture cards with me to work to look at them anytime anxiety wanted to get my mind in turmoil.

I also learned to enjoy reading the Psalms and Proverbs. Just like in the book of Solomon and I can truthfully say with all my heart that I am my beloved's and that he is mine.

Love is a treasure to be cherished and it must be lifted up in prayer and the intimacy we share is so beautiful that God helps us grow to be more like Him. I love my husband more now than ever and I pray for others who need to watch their contentious, self-centered and narcissism attitudes. I praise God for convicting me in areas where I needed to change. He is still helping me to become a better wife and partner to my husband. I now know that submission is a beautiful fulfilling role of a woman and I am glad I am a woman who is becoming a flower but yet still needs to grow to reflect God's glory.

I know that with man this all seems impossible but with God nothing is impossible. We were apart for 15 months, which now seems like it never happened, but the growth I learned made it worth it. During all of this I lost my mother six months after my having to leave our home, I lost a cousin in April, and I lost our precious grandson in May. This all happened before my husband called in September.

My God is the lamp of my path and the light He sheds His wonderful!! He faithfully molds us into a servant for His glory.

I praise God for my miracle of my restored marriage and I tell my husband, every night, "I love you and thank you for loving me." I love him more now and we are closer because of the trial we went through. God is so faithful when we stay close to Him. I will send pictures soon. My husband and I are Catholic, like you were Erin, but we were married by an Assembly of God minister who my husband loves. He wants us to attend services there now. I don't know where our feet will land yet, but I do know that my husband is the head of our home and Christ is the head of him and He will direct my husband and I will praise him for my husband's leadership!!

I pray that more families will be restored and our nation will be stronger because those who believe in the restoration of our homes will prevail!! Praise God for Restore Ministries. God bless all of you who are waiting and believing for the restoration of your marriage—my prayers are with all of you.

Thank you for your ministry Erin and Dan.

Husband Comes Home in South Carolina!

Thank God for letting me find this website. Just last night, I prayed that He would send me some sort of encouragement. My husband is home after a 5-month separation! He was living with the OW.

Although he is now home, I feel that the hard work is just beginning. I feel so much more encouraged after reading some of the testimonies. I know that my prayers will not be in vain.

It seems sometimes that my husband will never let go of the OW and that is extremely hurtful. However, I now see that nothing is impossible with God, not even my husband's salvation!

My next step is to purchase the material suggested and get busy. I hope that the next time I send a praise report it is to say that my marriage is truly healed.

GOD BLESS ALL OF YOU!

Restored in North Dakota!

Praise God!! My husband moved back home last Saturday after being gone for one year!

First I want to thank my Lord and Savior, Jesus. He is my all in all! I could not have done this without Him! I can now say He is truly my Lord, not just my Savior!! Second, Erin, I want to say a big THANK YOU to you and Dan. First to you, Erin, for being a willing vessel, for being willing to go through the fire, and for letting God do His work in you! And then for being willing to share with all of us. And Dan, thank you for coming home and for getting your life right with God again. Because of you, Dan, I believe many other men are coming home!

It was 18 days short of one year, the day my husband moved home—a day I will remember as long as I live!! I wish I could say he came home broken and repentant and right with God, but it is not so. However, I do know that what God has started He will finish, and I know He brought my husband home. I now have to live out all I have learned over the past year, including "won without a word"!! Erin, please pray for me, that I will not blow it, and that I truly will be able to be all that God has taught me to be!

I am a member of Restore Ministries Fellowship. I joined your ministry just a little over one month after my husband left. I have two very good friends here, who believed in your ministry with me, believed in what I was doing, and stood behind me all the way! They never let me give up, and they always encouraged me to go on, even when I felt like I could not take another step!

I came to your ministry almost every day, to read testimonies, to pray for others, and to read the daily devotion. Because of finances, I was not able to get all of the encouragement series videos, but I did get a couple of them and the Esther video. The book and the workbook for women—I read them, and read them, and read them! I was broken and cried many times as I went through them, because that was me—prideful, contentious, arrogant! I know I drove my husband away! Then through your books and the videos, God was able to break me and begin to change me. He has healed me of so many things!

I would definitely recommend your book and workbook to all women, and I would also recommend that they get as many of the videos as possible. I now have the new workbook and video series for women and am teaching it to about four other women right now! I too promised God that if He would heal and restore my marriage, I would give my life to helping women to believe and follow His will for their marriages and homes!

I have one more exciting thing to tell you! In January, as I was crying out to God, I asked Him how much longer? He told me "soon," and two other women confirmed it; they called me and said that as they were praying for us, God told them "soon." About two weeks later, again I asked God, "When?" and He told me "soon." And then ten days later, on a Saturday, my husband moved home—I didn't even know he was coming home until he was here!!! I knew he was thinking about it because we had talked about it, but what a surprise to see him come driving into our yard with all his stuff!!

Oh Erin, praise God—He is so faithful!! More than I ever dreamed! What an awesome God we serve!! Love in Christ!

Miracle Restoration in Georgia!

Praise the almighty God who is faithful and compassionate! On Tuesday, after a 5-month separation, the Lord restored my marriage! It is all so clear now. Because I was very contentious and disobedient to God, He took my husband away for a time.

By bringing me to brokenness and teaching me obedience, God was faithful to restore our ordained marriage. My husband tells me that he loves my gentle and quiet spirit and that he will do anything for me! The first week was a little shaky at times because the enemy was desperate for God not to receive the glory, but I prayed every time an attack would come.

I want to share with all the ladies that God's Word is true and He IS faithful when we are faithful. For five months I prayed night and day and suffered the enemy's blows. God seemed to minister to my spirit many times that He would turn my husband's heart and bring him home. Then Satan would lie to me that it wasn't true. The thing is, we have to praise God when we are so down and weary that we can't stand.

My husband left last August and filed for divorce in October. For a time, things got much worse. Nevertheless, little by little I saw glimpses of light. Finally, a week before our court-ordered mediation, I shut the world completely out; no TV, family or friends. I wanted to focus totally on God and I felt He wanted me to get alone with Him.

Every morning I would read the daily Psalms. Personally, I like to read a section of Psalm 119 every day along with the other daily Psalm readings. Psalm 119 encourages me to love the Lord's precepts, which are very important. After work, I would spend time with the Lord in His Word and prayer.

On the Saturday before the mediation, while seeking the Lord through His Word and prayer, He put it on my heart to totally lay my marriage at His feet. So, I wrote at 1:10 p.m., my marriage and my husband were laid at the feet of Christ and that He is in control.

About fifteen minutes later, the enemy attacked fiercely. I became so weak and hopeless, I wasn't sure I was going to make it. The battle continued throughout the day, but by God's grace, I read, prayed and fasted. By Sunday, God had given me perfect peace. Tuesday, I got up early and just listened to the Lord and let Him love me. He gave me peace and I knew it was all in His hands.

At the mediation, my husband grinned at me every time our eyes met! I smiled back. When it was over, he asked me to take a ride in his new car and we went to lunch! My husband dismissed the divorce, praise God!!!! We never looked back and our marriage is the best it has ever been!

The day after we reconciled, my husband emailed me at work saying that when we got home he wanted to explain what turned him around so abruptly, what made him realize why he loved me so much and his desire to give our marriage another chance! I couldn't wait!!

At dinner that night, he said it was because I told him I was sorry at the hearing. However, I had said I was sorry a lot of times, so what was so different about that time? He said that God had softened his heart!! I prayed for that so many times and to hear my husband say those words. It just proves how awesome, powerful and faithful God is!

It is so important that we be as close to God as possible and listen to His voice. My marriage is blessed more and more every day! We pray together, read the Bible together and are in church.

Please understand, when we separated, my husband was very angry and turned his back on God. God is truly a miracle worker. I praise Him and give Him all the glory for being there for me and saving my husband's love and our marriage.

One night my husband came across my RM materials in a drawer and began to read. He was so impressed and happy that he was ready to submit a praise report to Restore Ministries! Thank you, Erin and Restore Ministries, for your wisdom, guidance and support. My encouragement partner was so perfect. It turned out that we are so similar and had much in common. Of course, I am continuing to stand with her in prayer for the restoration of her marriage, which I believe will be soon!

My marriage is absolutely awesome right now! God has truly worked a great miracle! I give Him all the glory and honor and praise! Thank you for allowing God to use you to help us understand how important submission to our husbands "as unto the Lord" is. It has truly brought peace, joy and harmony into our home!!!

Thank you and God bless!

Supernatural Marriage Restoration in New York!

PRAISE GOD with all of your hearts and souls for HE is GOOD! This report is long overdue!! I first came to this site for what seems like a long time ago, but in reality it was just last April, less than a year ago. At that time, I had separated from my wife (by her request) and was lost in a sea of despair.

Things got progressively worse in my marriage even as I drew closer to God. There was no talking to her, as all I ever got was anger and resentment. Things went from 'let's just take a break and see where it leads us' to her filing for custody of our girls, getting an order of protection against me and filing for support claiming I was not paying anything (when the whole time I had been giving her almost half of my paycheck every two weeks).

It forced me into the court system that many of you know causes much more harm then good. We had to see a counselor jointly, individually and as a part of groups.

The counseling was going nowhere and she was insistent that "this marriage was over." She only wanted to work out issues relating to our girls. Things got progressively worse as we were ordered to go to a court-ordered forensic evaluation to determine our status as parents.

With this news my wife filed for divorce on July 9. During all this, I kept drawing closer to the Lord and relying on Him for my strength. I used the *book How God Can and Will Restore Your Marriage* and *A Wise Woman* as my guides. I continued to pray and fast, giving my wife everything she asked for and more, if it was at all possible.

In the midst of it all, she and the girls went away for a vacation, and it was during that time that the Lord began working on her heart! We had several phone conversations, and while there seemed to be no movement on her part, it was more than we had talked in the past four months!

We ended up arranging the next appointment to discuss "separation" versus "divorce" and to talk about how we were going to handle the upcoming evaluation. (Certainly, God was beginning to move things in the right direction!)

My wife came back from vacation without the girls who where spending a week with their grandparents. God was using the time away from our girls to continue to work on her heart, to show her my heart and how my separation from our daughters and her had made me feel. At the same time He showed me her heart and how she had felt for so long in our marriage.

Instead of dwelling on what was happening and the upcoming evaluation, I just continued to attend three weekly church services and let the Lord lead me in whatever His will was for me.

Eventually, this led her to call me while I was at still at church. When I went, I went with the intention of asking for prayer for myself over the upcoming evaluation and I ended up laying hands on two brothers who where in similar marital crises. I was overcome with their grief, pain and sorrow. I was wiped out, but strangely filled with God's peace. I arrived home late to find a message to call my wife.

What happened next can only be explained as God's mighty hand at work! We ended up talking for over three hours, and all of it was good!!! Praise the Lord! The next evening our counseling session went so well that the therapist asked if he should say something controversial to provoke an argument as we were getting along so well. (Can you imagine?)

We both responded with an emphatic NO! Instead, we spent the next two hours eating and talking over a meal that I had prepared for us! When we got up to leave, my wife gave me a hug—the first one in over six months! Hallelujah! I was singing God's praises all the way home!!!

I arrived home to a ringing telephone and it was my wife! We talked for another three-plus hours! There were no harsh or angry words! The next day, she called in tears because she was not able to drop the order of protection. She was afraid that I would be angry and that it would cause us to lose the ground we were gaining.

I prayed for and with her and we agreed to meet for dinner. We enjoyed another two-hour dinner and a three-hour phone call. Friday evening we again talked for three hours and she invited me over to see our daughters. This was beyond anything I had hoped for because previously she had insisted on a strict two-week visitation schedule.

Saturday, I was surprised to be invited for dinner. Afterward, she asked me to come over and spend Sunday with them as a family to talk over the evaluation that was taking place the next morning. During the previous week my wife's greatest fear was this evaluation and the (remote) possibility that something terrible would come of it.

That fear lead to lots of prayer and Scripture reading for us together! Once again, GOD showed HIS GRACE and the evaluation went extremely well. So well that we went out as a family for dinner to celebrate! This led to us spending ever-increasing amounts of time together for GOD to work on healing wounds that had festered for years.

In September, we celebrated our fourteenth wedding anniversary by going away for three days (without the girls) and I moved back home!!! Hallelujah!!! It has been four months since then and we continue to draw closer to GOD and each other! We attended a "Family Life Weekend to Remember Conference" in November and we are teaching a seventh through ninth grade Sunday School Family Faith class! Awesome!!

I praise and thank the LORD every day! I continually look for ways to let my wife know how much I appreciate and love her. I bring home flowers, chocolates, make dinner, pack lunches in the morning and leave love notes for her when she comes home from her group late at night.

Dear ones do not despair, for if ever there was a hopeless situation it was mine. GOD can change the hardest heart and heal the most broken marriage! Trust in HIM, worship HIM, give HIM thanks in all things and let your JOY in knowing HIM as your LORD and personal Savior be your guiding light.

All my love in Christ!

Another Restoration! Isn't God Amazing?

I must praise my Jesus! He is so faithful! My husband is home and not once has he mentioned the OW or leaving again!

I know my God is faithful! I am so happy to have my husband home! Things are not perfect, and we have lots to work through, but I know God will help us and get us through!!

I am believing for complete healing and restoration of our marriage and home! As I continue to stand on God's promises, I know He will see us through. God bless all of you, and do not give up!!

Restoration in Australia!!

Last May 2002, God called me out of adultery to return to my husband at a point in my life where I had lost all respect and love for him. The man whom I was going to be with had four children, like me (and a wife), which meant the devastation would have been huge.

God called me out of it, convicting me through revelations He gave to my mother who was praying diligently for us. Within nine months, all praises to God, He changed my heart, helped me to let go of the OM and restored the love I lost for my husband.

God is so faithful and so gracious as He has poured out His Spirit on us both. Our individual walks with God are amazingly close, and we talk with each other on such a deep spiritual level, it is great!! During those nine months, not only has God supplied us with the STRENGTH to hold on and the FAITH to stay with each other (despite tremendous difficulties and emotional pain), HE led my husband to change law firms. He now works alongside other Christian lawyers!!

God has also called us to sell our home and start afresh, challenging us on so many aspects of our relationship and even our beliefs. We believe that God is set to shake our world so that only the things that are built on Him remain. God has given us a new beginning and a new hope and our children are thriving on the change they see in each of us!

We have the women's and the men's packets and they have been a great encouragement and help. We believe that God will use our experience to help others believe that God CAN restore marriages. In mid-March, I, along with a group of other women, are going to start a small group in our church for women to encourage and equip them to restore and enrich their marriages.

Divorce Dismissed! Marriage Restored!!

Praise God, my marriage is restored!! The circumstances seemed hopeless in the beginning. In September 2001, my husband filed for a divorce and put our house up for sale. A year prior to this event, my husband was "confused" and wasn't sure if he wanted to be married. We married young, and I have always been an overbearing and contentious wife, unaware of the damage I was doing to my husband and my marriage.

I spent weeks crying, begging and pleading for my husband to reconsider, but he would not. He was adamant that the divorce go through and said we could work on things afterwards. Fear overwhelmed me, with thoughts of him being with another woman and me having to see him in town with someone else. I fell into the devil's wicked scheme and moved hundreds of miles away to be near my friends and family for support and comfort during this trial.

Ladies, never leave your home like I did!! Satan uses this device to divide and conquer, and ultimately your husband will end up in adultery! Care enough for your husband's soul to never put him in that compromising position! After we were separated for three weeks, God got a hold of me and dispelled the myth that I "would find someone better" as so many of my Christian friends and co-workers believed.

I discovered Restore Ministries and immediately applied the principles. I dismissed my attorney, began fasting and praying, and began practicing the "gentle and quiet spirit" that is pleasing to God. The results were instant! I was able to spend Thanksgiving and Christmas with my husband! My husband gave me a beautiful pearl and diamond ring for Christmas, and to top it all off, I found a job that put me within an hour's drive of my husband!

In January 2002, the children and I moved back. It was scary, but I had faith and trust in God that He would work this all out! Everyone thought I was crazy for moving back so soon, and eventually I began to think I was crazy too, but as Erin says, if you are not being radical enough in believing for your marriage that people think you're crazy, then you must not be that serious!

I was serious!! I fasted twice a week, and as a result I lost 15 pounds!! With a slimmer figure, a quiet and gentle spirit, and improved cooking skills, I won my husband without a word! We visited each other about once or twice a week as our schedules permitted. We went on a date, and my husband revealed to me that his life was not the same without me! My husband still lived in our home, and when the children and I would visit him, it would be so dirty and trashed. My husband began to drink more, smoke more and never seemed to have peace.

As we began to see each other more and become more intimate, I became more comfortable and started praying less. I felt like my marriage was about to be restored and that my work had been done. Ladies, this is another trick of the enemy!!! Never, never, never give up praying! It doesn't matter how great things are looking with you and your husband, or even how bad things are looking! Never stop praying!! Satan will use this scheme of "arrogance" or "comfortableness" to attack you and your husband! He did it to me.

In April 2002, I lost my job. I was terrified! How could I support the children and me? I had followed the "don't pursue your spouse" principle perfectly, and my husband had responded by giving me child support faithfully, every two weeks without me asking, but that would not be enough to cover the bills. I panicked and cried out to the Lord, and the Lord delivered!! I received enough in child support and unemployment to adequately support my family!!

Then, in May 2002, I was hit with my worst fear! I came to our home to care for my husband after an accident (another warning, among many, to my husband that his life was not in the will of God), and I discovered my husband in adultery! I was devastated!! How could this happen?! As I said before, I thought my marriage was restored—surely there was no other woman in the picture, so I didn't have to pray as fervently, or so I thought. Satan used that ploy to get me off my stand, and it almost worked!

I cried out to the Lord for two days and asked Him to give me guidance in which direction I should go, and the Lord said to me "Keep believing—your miracle is around the corner." Scared, confused, angry, and hurt, I obeyed my Lord Jesus Christ and continue to believe.

In June 2002, after all these trials, we went on a family vacation. The trip was pleasant, and it was an answered prayer to have my relationship intact with my husband after discovering him in adultery. God had put it in my heart to forgive and to treat him as if nothing had happened. It was hard, and I failed a couple of times, but I ultimately renewed my heart and mind to my Lord, husband, marriage, and family.

During our family vacation, my husband told me what I had prayed for. He told me, "You can come home when your lease is up." Praise God!! He asked me to come home!! I finally had my testimony! We signed papers to have the divorce dismissed—I had a restored marriage! I told my friends and family and most were skeptical, but I knew that God would prove them all wrong!

My husband wears his wedding band again and treats me like a princess! I love my husband more now than I ever have before, and he truly loves me and appreciates all that I have done for our marriage, our family, and for him.

I thank Dan and Erin for sharing their testimony. It inspired me to continue to believe for my marriage. I thank my encouragement partner for making me strong when I was weak, for taming my wild thoughts about my husband and his intentions. It would have been so difficult, if not impossible, to keep trusting God for restoration without her.

Ladies, never give up! My world has been turned upside down, but I was faithful to God and His Word. Galatians 6:9 tells us to not grow weary when we are doing good, for at the proper time we will reap a harvest if we do not give up! For my obedience, God has blessed me with a faithful husband, a beautiful home, and a wonderful family!!

You see, it all worked out for my good, and it will work out for your good too, if you don't give up! You will receive double for your trouble!

God bless!

Ohio – My Husband Is Home!

After much prayer and the support of the SOS team, and many others, my husband is home! God is also bringing him out of the confusion that Satan tried to put on both of us. What an awesome response of a wonderful, miracle-working Father God! My situation looked hopeless, felt hopeless, and was a real mess. I waited for FIVE YEARS and prayed the Word of God.

In the "Be Encouraged" tapes, Erin said we do not know what God is doing behind the scenes. How true! I cried and cried and just kept praying the Word of God found at the back of the *How God Can and Will Restore Your Marriage* book.

Since my husband has been home I have been severely tested, but because of the tapes and book, I understand what is happening, and it has given me the strength to stand firm in my faith!! I would have never made it without Restore Ministries and the direction of Jesus Christ with the Scriptures He also gave me to stand on.

This praise report is a promise I made to Father God and Jesus Christ to give Him all of the glory, for He is faithful! Yes, many times I failed. Do not be discouraged if you stumble; just get back up, dust yourself off, and apply the principles again and again. God broke the adulterous relationship, too. He does not play games!

Satan cannot establish what God broke, and God is in control of the situation.

God does use for good what was meant for harm! I must admit I am having a difficult time now waiting for my husband to lead in the area of taking me to church. But, I KNOW it will happen eventually.

He REALLY loves the fact that he now has authority over the finances and I listen to his directions and instructions!! I believe allowing him to have that authority and not arguing anymore (which is a miracle in itself) were some of the major turning points in our marriage. He likes me being home and taking care of me. Isn't that a turn-around from what the world says about being a working woman to be fulfilled!! I like this a LOT better and he likes having clothes ironed for work, supper fixed and me just being home when he comes home from work! I like being submissive a lot better too! It has actually taken pressure off ME!

God will complete the work He started. Take care of yourselves, ladies. Be kind, sweet, and look as pretty as you can. Smile and build your husband up. Don't EVER tear him down. He needs to hear from you that he is wonderful!!

Thank you!

Restoration in Georgia!

I give God the glory and honor because He is so awesome! There is nothing too difficult for God to handle. God called me to believe for my marriage in 1999. I was separated from my husband for six months. During those months, God dealt with me through prayer.

When my husband returned, I stopped praying, and I did not forgive him in my heart for leaving me with an eight-month-old baby girl. I was going through the motions of being a wife who honored and respected her husband, but in my heart, I did not. Unfortunately, things did not change.

I struggled about 18 months trying to make my marriage work, but couldn't. We ended up separating again. This time, I gave my marriage and my heart to God completely. I also gave my husband to God and continued to pray for him. God dealt with me on forgiveness. I started looking at my husband the way Jesus looks at us. Jesus died for our sins that we may be reconciled to Him.

Now we have to "die" to our flesh and truly forgive our spouses for what they did or what they are doing. It is very hard to do, but with God, all things are possible.

The second time my husband left, it was for only one month. However, before he left, I told him that I forgave him and then asked God to cleanse my heart of the hurt and anger that I felt towards him and the OW. I praise God for giving me the desire to forgive and throw the past into the sea of forgetfulness.

Stand on God's Word and know that it cannot lie. He will restore your marriage. I know, because He restored mine. We are happy. My husband initiates all the "we" and "ours" now without me saying a word. But I had to ask God to help me truly forgive my husband and the OW.

Now that God has returned my husband to his home, I continue to pray and praise God for His gift of reconciliation. God is awesome and greatly to be praised. Forgive and "die" or "crucify" your flesh and let God reconcile your marriage.

Restored Miraculously in South Africa!

I have not posted a praise report for many months. I trusted God to restore my marriage for a year. I fasted, prayed, and cried out to God. Then I started to lose hope, since this is my second marriage, when it started to look as if nothing was happening, I decided just to quit.

Why would God give me another chance? I already messed up my first marriage. Nevertheless, I knew that God wanted to restore THIS marriage. I was constantly praying for it to happen. When I married my second husband, I didn't know that I was not allowed to remarry.

Although there were many things God did to keep the hope in my heart alive, I started to slip away from God and all the promises He had given me. I finally decided to give up about two months ago. I decided since it was unacceptable to marry again, I would move on with my life.

I knew in my heart that I was wrong. Then, I decided to visit my prayer partner (she is 1400 km from where I live). I asked my former husband to look after our house while I was gone. I was away only two days when he phoned me and asked me to come home and told me that he wanted to try again!

This was totally unexpected! He had just told me before I left for my trip that he didn't want a relationship with me. This same man told me just a week ago that he did not want a relationship with me, and now we have been together for four days already!

There is a lot of work to be done, and God has to rebuild our relationship, but God is faithful and will restore us in His time. Erin, you were right about EVERYTHING! God is so faithful, even when I gave up.

He came through for me, and this brought me closer to God and made me again realize how awesome and powerful our GOD is. I want to encourage all of you—DON'T GIVE UP! Believe me, my husband screamed that he would NEVER come back and that he didn't love me, and yet he just returned!

He even told me after he came home that even if it didn't look like it, he never stopped loving me! When you feel like giving up, that is when your breakthrough is near! I honor God and thank Him for giving me the desire of my heart.

Thanks, Dan and Erin, for what you believe. I believe God is going to restore the truths regarding biblical marriages in South Africa and I really want to be part of that.

God Is Always on Time!!! Restored in California!

HALLELUJAH! PTL!!!

God sent my husband home after seven months! We are still praying for total restoration, but our God is so awesome and He is so faithful to whatever He has promised!

I could never give up on my marriage because God continued to give me hope even when my husband would not communicate with me!!! However, in the twinkling of an eye, God turned it all around for good!

We are recovering everything the devil tried to take! God is so good!!!! Trust Him!!! Believe and receive!!!

I just kept posting my prayer request, knowing that people I had never even met were praying – God had them take time to pray for us! I used most of the resources from Restore Ministries along with many, many internet prayer partners, most of whom had been or were going through the same things.

I would try to stay positive and believe in what God has already promised in His Word. I took in no negative thoughts from well wishers who told me that I should go on with my life! Instead, I believed only in what God had told me in His Word. I just needed to wait for the victory!

God is replacing all that the enemy "thought" he had stolen. I am now, with God's guidance, helping others I meet who are where I was. I can easily tell them that God is so faithful to His promises and He will never fail us! We have to believe without doubting Him!

It was very hard but God continued to give me hope day by day. I had to finally say, "Okay, God it's You and me!" Then He began to give me that peace that surpasses all of my understanding. He also reassured me that He was working on both of us.

For a time I continued to send my husband love notes and many, many messages but he never read any of them! But then, when I let go and let God, my very last letter to him was just what God wanted me to say. Then I just stepped back and finally put it all in God's hands. This was so hard because I felt that my husband was going to forget about me.

But, God!!! Oh, but God!!! He is so awesome!!! He is so faithful!!! He is my everything!!! I just love Him so much!!!!! I know that He will do just what He said He would do!!! And He did!!!

I thank Him every day for saving me and for my husband. He had to do a work on both of us in order for us to remember who He is! He is in total control!!!

Thank you. Praise the Lord!!! Hallelujah!!! God is so good!!!!! He may not come when you want Him, but He is always on time!!!

Miracle Restoration in Canada!

With man this restoration would have been impossible, but with God all things are possible! He said, "I am the God of all flesh, is anything too hard for me?"

My girlfriend prayed for my husband and me last year faithfully, submitting our name on a weekly basis to your ministry's website. I believe it has been the power of prayer that has done this work in us. My girlfriend also lent me your book, *How God Can and Will Restore Your Marriage*.

I am a born-again believer, who, through my wounds and distress, committed adultery (I found out my husband opened himself up to pornography). However, God gave my husband a vision, and He is changing my heart and replacing it with love.

We have been apart for **five years**, and I gave up believing that God could restore! I couldn't believe for it any more, and I wasn't sure I even wanted it.

I want you to know that with God, all things are possible! I just gave my two months notice on my job and my apartment. I will be moving in with my hubby in our hometown! He is willing to have our marriage vows renewed, and he is coming to church with me! God has made us both willing!!!

Restoration is the road less traveled, but it is the heart of God and I, like so many others, fed on such deception. But a merciful God, a few good friends, a husband who was willing to forgive adultery, and a lot of people with your ministry praying, motivated God who started to heal my wounded heart and change it. He restored my love for my husband in my heart—love that I thought was dead.

God has made my husband willing to forgive and has softened his hardened heart toward me. Ladies, all I can say is God is faithful and His Word does not lie!

I look forward to even more praise reports on your site. Your book is truly a tool for "God's Kingdom girls" who believe their marriages are hopeless.

Make sure you stay away from "vision killers": people who don't have enough faith to believe with you or give you truth.

Erin, God has a mighty plan for this ministry. I have even had unsaved friends ask me for the website—that's God!! In His mercy, God bless you all.

Wife Is Home—Praise Him!

I have to give our Lord all the glory and praise; I have waited far too long to send my report. My wife of seventeen years divorced me in July of 2001 after only four months of separation (first time ever). That very weekend she began to show signs of wanting to work at rebuilding.

Since then, I have seen so many answered prayers that I cannot begin to list them all. With two children and twenty-two years of our lives together, I have finally let the Lord into my life in my darkest hour. HE has given me so much strength and patience to endure many trials and much pain.

I became a newborn Christian in early 2001, struggling with my faith. Each time I have doubts, I come to Restore Ministries to renew myself and lift the Lord up in my life.

I made so many mistakes in and out of my covenant with her that I have beat myself up repeatedly. I have seen the Lord change both of us in so many ways that you cannot imagine. We have violated His ways and each other so much that I had thought our life could NEVER come to what is happening now!

I held on to what the Lord had been telling me to do—"wait." Seeing the pain she was in was hurting me so badly that I had to let her go several times. The trials have been many and tough; still, we are inseparable to the end. When we talk, we both agree that the LORD is holding us together until the work is complete.

She has been home (by her choice) for three weeks after a year and a half of being divorced and 21 months apart; she is still having a hard time with it. I know the Lord is working on both of us, but the enemy is still trying to steal our lives as well. We get along much better than we have in many, many years. It seems our minds are working overtime with what the enemy is placing in them to again separate our family.

Please pray that Satan will be removed from our lives so that GOD'S WILL be done. I have come to Erin and Dan's site for nearly two years now and purchased the materials for others and myself. Each time I come here or re-read the materials, I gain new hope and encouragement. I found this site by chance when searching for knowledge on why our lives were falling apart and how to repair them.

I have long let my unforgiveness to the OM for the happenings in our lives linger. PLEASE join me; lift me up so that I can have genuine forgiveness and faith to let this take its course in GOD'S WAY AND TIME.

After all, HE has brought her and our daughter home to our son and me. Now my wife and I are in dire need to let go of the past so we can build a future. For some reason, the OM is haunting my mind as well as hers. Please pray for us as we take this journey that the LORD has planned for our children, to restore what has been taken from us and what we have taken from one another.

Thank You so much LORD . . . for giving all of us Erin and Dan to assist You in bringing families together after enduring such hard times. The praise goes to the LORD; many thanks and blessings to Restore Ministries and their family for the work they do to help deliver His word in ways that many can understand. In the world today it is so hard to stop and take hold of what the Lord has to offer each and every one of us.

Restored Two Days after My Mom's Funeral!

Just two days after my mother's funeral my marriage was restored!! I am sending this gift to thank you. It is the money that was left to me from my mom. Here is my testimony:

First, I'd like to thank you for your ministry. I cried out to God for help because when I went to my pastor and asked what I could do he just looked sad and said it was up to my husband. Before my husband even left I was looking on the Internet for prayers for marriages. I was sickened by all the marriages in trouble. Then one of the people who had asked for prayer asked for someone to write her. I did and that led us "by the Grace of God" to Restore Ministries. I found a prayer partner and her friend led us to meet others who led us to Restore Ministries.

Over a year ago, my husband of twenty-five years left me (and our five children, four who still lived at home). He did not leave to live with someone else, but he left with no thought of coming back. I, like you, went to my pastor and he said there was nothing I could do; it was "his will." I had my priorities wrong; I needed my husband and wanted God; now I need God and want my husband. Like many, I was desperately trying to hang on to our marriage while he wanted to leave. By the time he left he loathed me.

From the beginning the Holy Spirit told me to believe. I was going through tests for cancer and my husband was telling me he was not in love with me. In pride, I took off my wedding ring the night he left and told him when he was ready to be my husband he could put it back on my finger. I got your book that week but before I put the ring back on, my finger bruised where the ring was "supposed" to be. This was only the beginning of God's power and mercy.

Four months after my husband left, the Holy Spirit told me my husband would be home before the following Christmas. I just sobbed because there was no evidence seen. I don't know why; maybe God knew how weak I was and gave me that word so I could make it to the end and see my miracle. The enemy not only attacked us with my husband leaving, but also right after he left our oldest son got cancer.

I got your books. I read Psalms and Proverbs continually as you advise. I also bought your "Be Encouraged" videos. I had praise music going almost all the time just as you did and I still carry my Scripture cards with me—I love them!! I can only say it ALL helped to restore my marriage. As I look back now it was only the Grace of God that kept me going. The videos were very encouraging; being able to know someone whose marriage had been restored helped me so much. I followed whatever you said to do: I prayed constantly for God to guard my mouth as with a muzzle; I would cry out to God and He would help me through the day or night or through any situation I would face.

I can't tell you how many times I would be praying and singing praises to the Lord when my husband would call. I am so thankful for all that God showed me along the way. I didn't know anyone could hurt as badly as I did. However I am thankful because it led me to visit my mom more often before she died.

Six months after my husband left he asked me if I was praying. I was stunned, but said, "Yes." He said, "I want you to know I have been talking to my dad and if you will have me back I want to move back in the near future." It's amazing—I had been praying for this miracle and I sat there thinking, "Wow, he can feel me praying! What an awesome God!" At first I couldn't figure out why he wasn't coming back and then as time went on I knew God wasn't done yet. I remember feeling so much anger and saying to God, "You have to help me with this." But God spoke to me and said, "That's not anger; it's pain. Your husband can't heal you; only I can do that." For the next nine months my husband told me only twice that he loved me but said he would be moving back soon.

Only a couple of weeks before my husband came home my mom asked me when he was moving back home. I told her "soon" and she asked how I knew. I shared your Scripture: "They looked to Him and their faces are radiant and they shall never be ashamed."

Then my mom got sick and we had to take her to the hospital with a minor infection. But when they put her to sleep she died. This is why I am so thankful that while my husband was gone I had the opportunity to spend more time with my mom. God's ways are perfect and His timing is never late.

Erin, in our pain, God is so good to us. Two days after my mom's funeral, my husband moved back home.

Erin, I want to thank you for what you do to help marriages. I pray for you and Dan. I am so thankful that God has restored my marriage and as I continue to seek Him, I now think I know what you mean.... BE STILL AND KNOW THAT I AM GOD!! Thank you so much!! God bless you, your family and your ministry. In His Love...

Restored in Texas! God Is Able!!

Earlier this month God delivered my husband from the OW! The devil tried feverishly to stop the process. The OW didn't want him to leave and tried everything in her power to make him stay. While she was begging and pleading, I was praying and praising God.

My husband tried to leave about 4:00 that morning, but didn't make it to our home until 4:00 that afternoon. We live about thirty minutes away from each other. I just praise God for delivering him out of the hands of Satan.

I know it isn't going to be easy, but I will do all that God wants me to do. God is the only reason that my husband was restored. This is the same man who told me we would never be a couple again, that he hated me and that he wanted a divorce. God is able!

You must trust Him and believe what you pray. His Word will not come back void! He may not come when you want Him to, but He is definitely on time. PTL!

God Restores Another Marriage!

To all who are encouraged by Restore Ministries, by the Word of the Lord and by prayer, I am proclaiming that my marriage is finally restored!!

I want to tell you what my husband said after coming home (he mentioned it on three separate occasions to friends and to me): "As the nagging stopped, suddenly, I wanted to come home! I always missed you and the children, but when I thought about the quarrels, I didn't want to call again."

After reading Restore's website, I stopped nagging and asking him when he was coming. What a difference it made from when I thought I had to "express my feelings" and "win the war" as I lost peace for eight years!

Praise the Lord for His living Word!

My Husband Is Home! Hallelujah!

My husband is home! He arrived almost one year to the day after the Lord allowed him to leave. I was contentious, controlling, angry, suspicious, hurt, bitter, had committed adultery, and was ready to kill myself when he left.

I cried out to the Lord for three months, consulted witchcraft and screamed at the Lord until the day He came and told me why. "I allowed this because you spat upon my covenant!" I was self-righteous, a Pharisee and full of poisonous words, always correcting and criticizing. Yet all along I thought it was all everyone else's fault...if my children hadn't run away, if I just hadn't been fired from that great job, if his friends would have left us alone.

Like Mary when her brother died, I eventually got to the point where I said, "If you would have been here Lord..." When my husband left me I thought this was the last straw, the last bit of mercy He may have had left for me, but I cried to Him, begging Him to give me another chance and asking Him to help me to allow Him to change me (as I do now again and again).

As I allowed Him to change me, my husband saw the changes in me. After he came home he told me that he was watching me to see if the changes were real. Then he told me he liked falling asleep here as I opened our home to him (even though he slept on the couch); it felt to him like home.

Would you believe that now he keeps telling me how lucky he is to have married me and wants to "show me off" to his friends and family!! He even said that he "always wanted me; he just didn't know what happened."

My husband sent me "D" papers all filled out and he went back and forth over whether I should sign them. I kept repeating "all who call upon the Lord shall be saved."

My husband was not with another woman; he was with his family—first his mother, and then his father...all of whom he left to be joined to me and to be one flesh. I have been truly blessed to have not gone through that particular trial!

There have been so many trials. First, my daughter's friend was hit by a car after my car broke down when I was arranging a tow truck. Our finances were all going crazy at the bank over a lot of unauthorized charges, and one of my other daughters "appeared" to be missing for a couple of weeks!!

After my husband came home, our TV broke (an answer to prayer—Hallelujah!), my car broke down a couple of times, one of my daughters got sick (and is still sick) and my husband had a heck of a time finding a job. I also was injured at work and he was re-injured at work.

Things are not perfect, but my husband is home and he is ecstatic about it!!

God does not break His Promises; this I DO know!!!

I have prayed for opportunities to share this ministry with people. My husband's friend and his wife are separated and my husband was the one who gave them the little Restore Ministries "At Last There's Hope" tract!!! He even says he would like to get the Men's Manual when we have the extra money. Wow!

My two sisters are going through similar circumstances and I have shared a bit with them also.

Erin, I want to thank you so much for being so honest with all of us. Thank you for allowing the Lord to change you, and for allowing Him to help you spread the truth.

Husband Home in Wisconsin!!

I have a wonderful praise report to share! Two weeks ago, my husband asked if he could come back home!!! He broke the news to me on January 1 of this year that he no longer wanted to be married; he moved out on January 6. He moved back home immediately after finding out he was still welcome!

God has done wonderful works in both of us during our time apart. I am very much enjoying my "new" husband! I praise and thank the Lord each day!

May God bless each of you and give you peace in your heart during your times of hurting (and always)! Remember that the will of God will be accomplished in His timing!!

Restored in the UK!!

Dear people who are encouraged through this webpage, through the Word of the Lord, and through prayers—our marriage has been restored!

I wanted to tell you what my husband stated after coming back home, what he has said on three occasions to friends and to me: "I always missed you and the children, but when I thought about the quarrels, I didn't want to call again!" And, "The nagging stopped (my nagging!) and all of a sudden I wanted to come back home!!"

After reading this webpage, I stopped nagging at him and asking when he was coming. I only spoke to him to ask his advice. Once, when I asked his advice, he protected us from going to an area that shortly thereafter was flooded and many people who were there died!

What a difference than from before! When I thought I had to "express my feelings" and "win the war," I lost the peace!!! I lost the peace for eight years!!!

When I "met" Restore Ministries on the Internet, our marriage was in a crisis, tormented, full of quarrels, misunderstandings, separation, and old grief. We have been married for nine years and have two children. Right from the beginning, there were problems. I filed for divorce three times. I loved my husband but always nagged at him. I worshipped my own depressions, my ability to work hard, and also my intellect. I thought he was idle and unable, and told him so and tried all I could to change him.

In fact, changing him was the god that I worshipped every day. The results were separation every year, my husband leaving us regularly, and financial breakdown. Nothing progressed.

I found Restore Ministries while surfing the Internet, looking for positive words and expressions connected to marriage healing. Praise the Lord for His living Word!

Our heavenly Father taught me first to KEEP MY MOUTH CLOSED, to not pursue my husband, but to pray fervently for him and not talk negatively to others about him. God taught me to submit to him in everything. I started to find joy in my situation, to enjoy being a housewife, exploring what the children and I could do together. Before, I used to work, work, and work, and if I didn't work, I was exhausted. I had another woman looking after the children.

As I studied Restore Ministries' resources and started to read the Bible regularly, submit, shut my mouth, and pray and fast, our situation turned around within three months.

I learned the following:

We walk by faith, not by sight!

Delight yourself in the Lord, and He will give you the desires of your heart.

Submit yourself to your husband as unto the Lord; be subject to him in everything.

Reward evil with good.

God is not a respecter of persons.

Your fruits will show others Whom you believe in.

The Lord's ways are so much higher than our ways; His thoughts higher than our thoughts.

The Word of the Lord NEVER returns void.

My husband then announced he would be coming back home. After two more months, he returned, and we immediately moved away from the country we had lived in as my husband desired.

My husband took over all responsibilities, began to build his own company, started an education, and feels very satisfied here. The restoration process is progressing every day like the parable of the growing seed—it grows while we sleep. I have backslidden and made many mistakes along the way, but the Lord always forgives and allows me back into His presence.

The latest step along the way is that my husband has started to read his Bible and pray with us. PTL!

How God Can and Will Restore Your Marriage and the *Workbook for Women* were the resources that helped me to become obedient (and it was very difficult for me to accept some of the sayings—I rebelled in the beginning!). They have been a continuous support, encouragement, and means of breaking my resistance and disobedience, as they are very clear and demanding. I would recommend both of these resources.

Every time I read the praise reports, they lift my spirit. Now that my husband is home, I see changes in our marriage every day! The main thing is that God REALLY answers your prayers when you believe what you pray, and especially when it is according to His will!

Materially, we have lost everything, but spiritually, we have gained so much more than that. I pray that the beliefs and the message of Restore Ministries and God's Word will go out to hurting couples and accomplish more than anybody asks or imagines!

I cannot express enough all that the Lord has done for us! In fact, I feel that the main thing that has happened to me is learning to trust in the Lord and stop doing things on my own. The further we progress into restoration, the more clearly the Lord stops me from DOING. He has given us ALL we ever imagined and so much more.

He has turned curse to blessing, night to day, rain to sun, and storm to peaceful quiet! Praise His holy name! His mercy endureth forever!

I pray that all who believe and pray steadfastly for the restoration of their marriage will be strengthened by the Word of God—strengthened not to give up until the battle is won! And it will be won! It is already won!

All we have to do is to pray and believe! All praise be to God, to Jesus Christ, our Lord and Savior, the bright Morning Star!

California Restoration!

I was having problems in my marriage. My husband packed all his clothes and told our two children and me that he was leaving. I contacted the Lord and the saints at Restore Ministries, and they began to send up prayers when I could not do it.

At times, with tears in my eyes, I would get on my knees and cry out to God to heal me and my marriage; I asked Him to make me the wife in Proverbs 31 (she who builds her home). I asked Him to help me right the wrongs I had done to my husband, not forgiving him and not being honest with him.

Ladies, we have to be honest because it will catch up with us. It caused serious problems—lying about money, doing what I wanted, not pleasing my husband and not being submissive! But, when I realized that he was serious about leaving after eighteen years of marriage, the Lord opened my eyes. Thank You Jesus!

He allowed me to see where I had gone wrong. Don't get me wrong—my husband was not perfect, either, but I was far from perfect! I thought I was PERFECT, and he could not tell me otherwise! But God let me see my faults before going to divorce court and before my husband left! I asked God to forgive me of my faults, to give me a forgiving heart and heal my soul.

Then God started working on my husband and our marriage. Hallelujah! My husband never left! He put his clothes back and we are sleeping together, holding each other and talking! Yes, I'm still praising the Lord and shall never stop praising Him.

I know it was no one else but the Lord who gave me my miracle! Now, I treat my husband as God would have me. My husband is lord of our home (Sarah called Abraham lord), and he feels as if he is loved and respected. He left the Lord when this started and has not yet come back, but he WILL!!! Praise God!

But our home is finally "home" again, and Restore Ministries helped me see that it's not what I think or what the world thinks, BUT WHAT GOD WANTS ME TO THINK AND DO! Don't listen to people's opinions; go to God! Do what the Lord says and it will work!

Praise God! Thank You Jesus, and thank you Restore Ministries for the guidance to get myself in tune with God's will!! God can and will restore if we let Him! IF WE LET JESUS DO IT, HE WILL DO IT!! PRAISE GOD!! PRAISE GOD!!

Restored in Illinois!

One of my continual prayers during the time my husband was away from home was that this crisis would somehow be a positive, faith-building experience for my three daughters. Even though circumstances didn't leave much hope for reconciliation, I chose to fix my eyes on Jesus and ignore (as best I could) the raging storm.

And, like Peter, when I would take my eyes off Jesus and look at the waves, I would begin to sink. Praise God for His unchanging Word and Erin for her conviction to share God's message! Although our "itching ears" would like to hear something different, His Word remains true!

Major discussions began in January. My husband of thirteen and a half years moved out in early March, signed a year lease, and filed immediately for divorce. Through much anger, tears, and contentiousness, God was speaking to me from the start. I was heading in the right direction before I received Erin's materials, but they definitely challenged me to go "whole hog" and do things God's way.

It is true that God's people "perish for lack of understanding." There were many, many praises along the way! God was moving in incredible ways to change BOTH of our hearts. There was a major spiritual breakthrough for my husband in early July and reconciliation in late August. We celebrated with a weekend away at an "I Still Do Conference"; he moved home and we celebrated our fourteenth anniversary in September as a united family!

God has done more than I could ask or imagine, even making my husband the spiritual leader in our home. He is committed, faithful, loving, not perfect, but wanting to please God in all that he does. Amazing!

But, here's how God has used the whole experience with one of my daughters:

My twelve-year-old shared with me that her main goal in life is to bring others to know Jesus (hallelujah, especially since my husband and I only came to know Christ about four years ago). We recently made the decision to homeschool her, primarily to make up for lost time. We are focusing on character issues, biblical instruction, and how to study God's Word.

We have seen fabulous results in just the month and a half since "school" started, but she does miss her friends. She has days when she wishes she were at public school. So, when she said that she just wants to "be able to defend her faith," I jumped on that to reinforce why we are homeschooling. I said, "I know it's hard for you to believe now, but there will come a time when you may doubt; and when that happens, we want you to know where to go to search for answers."

With tears streaming down her face, she said, "I will NEVER doubt. Not after what I've been through. I've seen my family ripped apart, then put back together by God." By this time, I had tears in my eyes and I knew. I knew that every time I cried out to God, sobbing to Him that I just couldn't hang on, angry at Him for asking me to do what I didn't even want to do, awake in the darkest hours, praying that God would fulfill His promises—it was all worth it! Not just for me. Not just for my husband. It was also for our girls!

It was worth it for their faith, and for the countless others who will be influenced by their testimony over their lifetimes. IT IS WORTH IT! Hang on for all you've got and be RADICALLY obedient to Christ. Have faith, even when those around you have given up and are encouraging you to do the same.

For our God is an awesome God—He holds the "king's heart in His hands and directs it like channels of water." GOD will restore your marriage—He did ours, and I give ALL PRAISE AND GLORY AND HONOR TO HIM!

My Husband Is HOME!

My husband asked me if I wanted to get back together. I said, "Yes!" He moved home three days later and today, a week later, he is bringing the rest of his belongings home! Praise the Lord!

He asked me what I expected out of this relationship. My response was "to be able to love him as a wife should love her husband, and to respect and honor him until death do us part." He laughed and squeezed me tight. God is Faithful.

I trust the Lord with all my concerns that I may have yet for my family and I know that God is faithful and we will be better than we ever were!!

We were separated for only two months. I'm grateful that I did not have to hit rock bottom in order to seek the Lord. After being apart for only two weeks and my husband living with someone else, I sought the Lord with everything, turning everything over to Him.

The Lord has been my strength during this time, as I have had to face many difficult situations with the children by myself. Thank God, my husband is home and will also be here to support our family.

Praise the Lord! God is so Faithful!

God Has Brought My Husband Home in North Carolina!!

I am so in awe of what the Lord has so miraculously done in my life that I fear I won't be able to express all the joy I am feeling! All the PRAISE, GLORY, HONOR, and WORSHIP are due my precious Savior. God has brought my husband home!!

I am in such awe and in such a humbled state of contentment that words cannot express my feelings or the gratitude and thanks that I owe God. After years of a troubled marriage (and the past year being one of lovelessness and selfishness), my husband moved out over a year ago, to begin a relationship with another woman. They were living together, with her two children. My husband was absolutely certain that she "was the right one," certain that divorce was what he wanted. He just wanted to "get on with his life" with her and be happy.

God is so mighty, gracious, and wonderful! All the pain, the heartache and grief that I personally endured has been well worth it! Not only for the stronger relationship and deeper appreciation that my husband and I now share, but most importantly, THIS whole situation is what brought me to my relationship with God!! I had been running from Him and pushing Him away all my life.

I believed in Him, but I wanted nothing to do with Him. I certainly didn't believe that He would ever DO anything for me or in my life. The ripple effect that this restoration has had and will continue to have has brought so many blessings to so many people. I don't even realize and probably never will understand till we meet on the other side of heaven.

That was His purpose. Yes, it was painful, but God is so gracious and loving. So far, everyone has wanted "details": "What did your husband say?" "What changed his mind?" "Has he told you he loves you?" etc. There really is not much to tell by way of details. To put it simply, God answered my prayers—to the very letter! The hedge of thorns that I prayed every day around my husband and the other woman worked, and God simply did as so many have asked of Him in our situation. HE TURNED MY HUSBAND'S HEART BACK TO ME, OUR DAUGHTER, OUR FAMILY, OUR MARRIAGE, AND TO HIM!!

Praise You, Jesus! Erin, you were so very right saying that God gives us the grace to forgive TOTALLY. I imagined many times how I would react when my husband expressed his desire to return. I knew it would happen, I just didn't know when, and I was prepared (and EXPECTING) it to be a long wait.

I knew I would have issues with trust and self-consciousness, worrying about being intimate for the first time. I KNEW I would not be able to get past the hurt, pain, and rejection of my husband being with another woman emotionally and physically as well. God is so merciful—it was NOT an issue!

It is just another transgression that our Lord, in His infinite mercy, has fully buried and covered with His blood. It is as if it never happened. I could not do this or feel this way on my own. Please praise and thank God with me for all that He has done in our lives!

I ask that you agree in prayer with me for the salvation of the other woman and her husband so that God can heal and restore their marriage, too. They are one, just as my husband and I are. I know that God loves us all and desires to be one with all of us. I want God to bless them in the same way He has us.

I really don't even know what else to say other than THANK YOU, heavenly Father! I love You. I am Yours. Our marriage is Yours. ALL the Glory and honor go to You alone!

BE encouraged and take hope and strength from this testimony, for I tell you that ours was most definitely one of those marriages that looked totally and completely hopeless!! Faith and patience inherit the promises. God is faithful!

Restoration at Thanksgiving!

As my marriage is being restored with renewed vows around Thanksgiving, I can think of no better way to celebrate than to give praise to God! No big dinner, just reflect on God's love and His wonderful gift of my husband.

We are but filthy rags and saved by His grace and blood. We must continue to praise, pray and fast for our marriages and hold our spouses up in prayer. Satan is still a wolf, devouring and destroying lives, but he is defeated and our victory is in Jesus.

I thank God for my husband, and I knew all along that his emotional well being had been hit. He walked away because he didn't realize what was happening to him. All he knew was that his life seemed out of control. Hearing him say, "Thank you, honey, for not giving up," I cry tears of joy! It was God who placed unconditional love in my heart for my husband.

Thank you, Erin and Dan, and for all men or women who continue to believe for their marriages. The reaffirming we share with each other is wonderful. God bless all of you!

Pray Until Something Happens!

God is wonderfully in control of every area of our lives! How beautiful it is to know that all we really need to do is to lean not on our own understanding but in all our ways acknowledge Him and He will direct our paths! God is telling all of us that are waiting just to trust Him and to stand still and see the salvation of the Lord.

Praise God with every breath that He gives us. I thank God for this wonderful ministry that I've been visiting since December of 2001 when I was at my lowest. Erin and Dan, you have been like John the Baptist to me, pointing me to the direction of God, my first Love.

I had put my husband before God, and I now know that this was idolatry. I have a spirit-filled encouragement partner who prays and cries with me. She always points me back to our Lord and Savior. God is working in my situation by first changing me and speaking to my heart about forgiveness and new mercies every day. I was in the pit of hell, but God reached down and picked me up and turned my darkness into light, a beautiful soul-saving light!

My husband is home, PTL!! He is more affectionate and considerate, and he tells our family that we must put God first! God started a work in us that I know will be completed in His own time. I am so comfortable sitting back, resting in the Lord, knowing that I don't have to be in the driver's seat. The battle is not mine—it is the Lord's!

I can't help but cry tears of joy when I think about how far God has brought me and to know that God loves me even with all my shortcomings. Who wouldn't serve a God like this? Just P.U.S.H. (Pray Until Something Happens). Let's continue to believe that God can and God will restore all of our marriages! Hallelujah!

God Does Not Change!

TRUST IN GOD—HIS WORD STANDS FIRM. For those of you out there who are wondering if you need to apply all the Biblical principles that Erin suggests, JUST DO IT! My husband has been home now for a little over one month and has shared with me one story after another that confirms the wisdom of following God's way.

"Letting him go" allowed him to stop spending emotional energy on tension between us and, instead, caused him to spend his time examining his relationship with God.

"Letting go of my lawyer" diffused the battle between us over finances, and (in my husband's words) made him realize that "now the decision to divorce was all on his shoulders"! He had to deal with what he was about to do to his family, his daughters, and his legacy. After so many years of me subtly (and often not-so-subtly) telling him what I thought he should do about something, or being sure I communicated to him my dissatisfaction about our relationship, about discipline issues with the kids, about all kinds of things in the name of "communication," I finally learned how to be a 1 Peter 3 kind of wife and SHUT UP! (OK, so that's not the literal translation, but it sure gets the point across!)

After he began to say that God had convicted him that he needed to come home, he asked me if I had any ideas who we should talk with (a counselor, perhaps, or our pastor) to resolve any lingering issues. A few months ago, I not only had ideas, but I had written them down and shared them with his male prayer partners/small group members! Talk about trying to manipulate the situation and play junior Holy Spirit!

But, praise God, my only response this time was, "I'm sure that whatever you decide will be the right thing." And you know what? Although I had previously foolishly and unknowingly done my best to strip him of his God-given authority, my husband rose to the leader position that he deserves! Submitting to him, yet trusting in God, has been a key to restoring our relationship!

God is so good! Although my husband decided two months ago that he would definitely be coming home, he felt that God was in control of the timing and that there were some changes he still had to make before he could come home "for good." Perhaps by Thanksgiving, certainly by Christmas, he said. Well, I believe that by refraining from trying to "suggest" how we handle his "re-entry" to our home, God truly gave me the desire of my heart, and my husband came back much sooner!

My husband made all the arrangements for an entire weekend in downtown Chicago, complete with tickets for an "I Still Do" conference! Six months prior, the week that my husband moved out, I saw an advertisement for a "Marriage Covenant" certificate and wanted so badly for our relationship to be restored to the point where we re-committed ourselves to each other before God. God is SO GOOD! I never mentioned anything about it to my husband, and yet he chose the exact thing (the conference, our recommitting to each other through words/vows and on paper, an entire weekend to "reconnect") that completely fulfilled my heart's desire ... won without a word!

These past four weeks (since the conference), my husband has been staying here every night, yet he still has things (and a year-long lease) at an apartment. We spent last weekend packing up the last of the stuff and unloading the U-Haul. Although some might say that was when he "came home," I know that he came home first in his heart. His "stuff" was just a formality, but praise God that HE COMPLETES the good works that He starts!

God brought home to me A CHANGED MAN! Each day I marvel at the miracle God has wrought in our lives. What was dead (our marriage), God has resurrected! Not just to the same old mediocre state it was before, no, we are finally experiencing what "true" love is about, what it means to be "one flesh."

My husband has told me how sorry he is that he hurt me and our girls; he has asked for my forgiveness (which I had already given many times in my heart, with God's help). It is incredible how God changes us when we seek Him first. When we live to please God, not ourselves, that is when we experience joy. I praise God for loving us enough to allow this crisis in our lives. He knew what it would take to bring about the changes in each of us that would allow us to experience God's best!

I know I never would have believed that I'd be saying I was thankful that my husband left me, and yet I am closer to Jesus now in a way I had never known before. I KNOW beyond a doubt that my husband is home for good because, as Erin says, when God does it, it's complete and it's permanent. I thank God daily for all that we have gone through—AND for bringing people to me over and over again with whom I can share this testimony and give them hope.

I am convinced also, as Erin is, that "marriage crises" are not about the marriage but are actually "spiritual crises" in disguise. So, to all of you out there who have not experienced your marriage restoration yet, I say, "Hang on! Keep your eyes fixed on Jesus, not your circumstances. You are not the one case to which God's unchanging truth does not apply. Be encouraged!"

Restored for our Anniversary!

God is so good! My husband called me today, after talking with his mom, and he told me that he wants me to buy a one-way ticket to Jacksonville FL where he is! He said he wants to try and work on our marriage! I am sitting here and I don't know what I am feeling—I feel like I am dreaming this, but it's real!!! I am in shock because of how quickly it happened.

thought he wasn't working. I give Him all the praise and all the Glory! He wants me to come right away so we can spend our wedding anniversary together! PTL! God is so good!

Husband Is Back Home!

I am so moved by your reports, especially those who have been holding on for YEARS.

Now I want to report that my husband is back home! Praise the Lord! He's been gone for nine months! We have had an off and on marriage for eight years.

I have been a contentious, disobedient wife. I started to see this one and one half years ago. Then, three months ago, I found the Restore website. I started to learn to submit. There have been awesome changes in our marriage!

My husband is clearly taking the lead. I ask him for permission to do things. It is so new to me! I was brought up exactly the opposite way (a full women's libber). This is really the truth of the Word of our Lord! He said He would set our feet on the Rock, and He has!

I still need prayers to continue submitting to him and to give EVERYTHING to the Lord. Thank you for being there, for this ministry and all those who are walking in the ways our Lord wants us to walk.

Praise God from the Mountaintops!

It is time to shout from the mountaintop! How great and awesome is our Lord God! No one (no one of this world, that is) would have believed that my husband would come home! I made so many mistakes in the four and a half years he was with the OW (I didn't even know about her for the first three years). I drove him to her each time I was disobedient to God, until I got serious with Him.

For the first year and a half, my husband would stay out all night, or not come home for two days. I would yell and scream at him when he was at home. After a year and a half, our six-year-old son and I moved out of our wretched house away from that "horrible man"! FIRST HUGE mistake! With the anger wall up in him, we saw little of my husband. However, I was seeking the Lord.

Praise God, He did not allow the divorce my husband said he wanted. It gave me time to grow and to learn over these past years about Satan's little "circumstantial" schemes. I began recognizing them left and right. I guess the worst one was when my husband returned home (for the first time) and within two months was back with his long-term OW. He said she forgave him for his casual affair, while I had not.

The pain and despair were awful. I got to work with God quickly; the Holy Spirit woke me up at 6 a.m. one morning saying, "Trust Me, just trust Me." There was NO turning back. The Holy Spirit let me know that I had to seek the Lord with all my heart and ask God to sustain in me a spirit of obedience. Yes, I had to change! God would take care of my husband. I had to pray and allow the Lord to work through me.

Then one night I was going through the Spiritual Warfare Ministries website (the Holy Spirit had made clear to me that I was entering spiritual warfare in praying for my husband). I began searching for other sites and in my search a series of sites came up with the letter "f" even though I asked for an "s" search. Well there were about 100 sites and I scrolled down to find "First Jesus" and decided to click on that. I then saw "prayer requests," and I clicked on that. I began reading them and noticed there were some for marriages. For some reason (of course the H.S.) I decided to scroll back and look at requests made on my wedding anniversary; I found one on that date asking for prayer for her marriage. Since the email address was listed, I decided to write to this person and tell her I was praying for her and tell her about another marriage restoration site. She wrote me back telling me about Restore Ministries. WOW! When I went to RMI, I devoured the information and KNEW it was God telling me to take the next step—He doesn't overwhelm us and I was now ready to follow the principles and guidelines based on Scriptural principles. I got the *RYM* book and *A Wise Woman* too.

I began to see all my terrible mistakes, but, at the same time, I was also learning how to see through circumstantial illusion, a tactic so often successfully used by Satan. For the next eight months, I did the following:

I prayed unceasingly,

I sought God's will on everything,

I fired my attorney,

I gave back my husband's support checks,

I asked for his forgiveness,

I asked him for nothing,

I never again burdened my husband with my needs,

I gave him my tax return with the option of amending my return to file together,

I gave him space,

I didn't call (unless he called first),

I helped him through the terrible and tragic illness and death of his father,

I suggest he visit our son convenient to his schedule (as long as it didn't contradict what my husband had already offered to do), and

I opened our home as a place for him to move.

These steps began the process of tearing down his hate wall and helping him to trust me again. During the whole time, the Lord kept bringing more and more believers and prayer partners into my life! AWESOME!

Five months later, the Holy Spirit told me that my husband would be home suddenly and unsaved. I didn't know when, though. He came home suddenly and unsaved eight months from when I had made my changes. God allowed him to return in this way, unsaved, for a reason; I am still praying unceasingly and seeking His will for my life and the lives of my son and husband. I believe, just as I believed my husband would come home, that God will bring him to salvation! To believe anything else would contradict the laws at work.

You are right Erin, that RIGHT before your miracle, Satan tries to pull out all stops! When my father-in-law died, my husband sent our son and me away to "be alone." The pain was incredible—it "looked" like he would choose the OW since he was living with her since his dad died but that was God forcing them together (no respite at his dad's house, though, since it got hit by lightening—no electricity!!). God knew what he was doing when he went to live there with her. The woman who helped me through all this kept telling me that God was allowing these things—yes, I had to trust God. The lesson for me was about TRUST. Prayer changes everything, for God has called us to love deeply, no matter HOW MUCH it hurts!!! I will NEVER give to Satan my husband's soul!!

To the world, it looks like the law of the impossible, but to those who believe and trust in God, we know that it is the only Truth! NOTHING is impossible with God!

I praise You, sweet Lord, with ALL my being. Not because You brought my husband home, but because I love You. You changed me and made my life whole, meaningful, filled with love and compassion.

Our son is going to a Christian school and my husband is even paying the tuition! Our son will forever be a firm believer in his generation! He has seen the mighty power of the hand of God! He believed, prayed with me, and loves the Lord with all his heart.

God is truly so awesome! It makes we wonder how I could have left Him out of my life for so very long indeed....

Praise You, Lord Jesus Christ! Grace and peace to you, fellow brothers and sisters; keep believing, keep trusting, keep obeying! God is awesome!

God Restores Another Impossible Marriage!

My husband left in January with a very hostile and angry attitude. He was cold and seemed to hate me. It hurt like I never imagined I would hurt. I was a Christian, but was not as close to the Lord as I needed to be. Our marriage had been in trouble for a while. We were too far gone to recover, even though I wanted it with all my heart.

Lots of damage had been done. The next year proved to be the coldest of my life. He would not tell me his exact location, only the city where he was living. I had to call his mom if I wanted to talk to him. She would call and relay messages. He would take his time returning calls, all the while being as cold as ice.

This treatment continued for a year. He would come and visit, but was withdrawn, cold and bitter. He didn't seem at all as if he wanted things to work. After a year of torture and postponing the divorce, he decided (with persistence from me) that he would drop the divorce and come home. He still was distant, and things were very tense, not at all like a reunion or "making up" should be.

He continued to work two jobs (out of town) and only came home on Sunday afternoons. He would leave on Monday afternoons. I finally quit my job and moved to where he was, but it still wasn't the fairy tale ending I hoped and longed for. He became more and more bitter, hostile, cold and distant.

After a while, I started to piece things together. To make a long story short, I caught him with the other woman. He still didn't respond. He left me again. Only now, I had quit my job and left my friends and family to be with him. He would not have anything to do with me. He would not spend the night. This continued for over a month.

I prayed on the phone every night with my parents. Lots of others were praying. I was told by many people to just "give up", that I could not do anything and it was hopeless. Even Christians! I was raised in a Pentecostal church. My parents had engrained in us, "ask, and you shall receive." I believed with all my heart, and when it is your heart you can really believe.

I refused to believe that a God who did not condone divorce wanted me to divorce my husband. I believed more strongly than ever. I knew that God answers prayers and that He would answer mine. I knew I was not praying against His will. I knew that the situation was impossible, and my husband's heart was totally cold. Unless God did it, it would never happen.

I could be here all night if I told you all the details, but the cold treatment I received from this man was beyond my wildest imagination. I was devastated! Approximately one month ago, he came over for the night, and then two nights. The third night, he left and returned for his sunglasses. The OW left a message for me while he and I were out.

He listened to the message, went and got his clothes, and returned to spend the night! The next day, he came home with more clothes. By the end of that week, the OW quit the job they were working together. HE IS HOME!

We are working at restoring our marriage, and I give GOD ALL THE PRAISE FOR IT. IT WAS AN IMPOSSIBLE SITUATION! MY HUSBAND'S HEART OF STONE IS SOFTENING, AND I SEE EVERY DAY THE MIRACLE OF GOD! I REFUSED TO GIVE UP. ASK AND YOU SHALL RECEIVE. GOD IS IN THE MIRACLE-WORKING BUSINESS. THE SAME GOD WHO TURNED WATER INTO WINE, WALKED ON WATER AND RAISED DEAD PEOPLE, CAN STILL PERFORM MIRACLES TODAY.

I DO NOT UNDERSTAND WHY CHRISTIANS DON'T EARNESTLY SEEK AND ASK GOD FOR MORE MIRACLES. THE WORDS AND PAGES OF THIS COMPUTER CANNOT BEGIN TO EXPRESS OR HOLD THE JOY THAT MY ANSWERED PRAYER HAS BROUGHT ME. PRAISE GOD! HE IS AWESOME!

This testimony was submitted by a woman who was not a part of our ministry's fellowship; therefore, I contacted her because I was concerned that there were changes in her that needed to be made or she would soon jeopardize her restored marriage.

We are receiving many cries for help from women whose husbands have returned home but are leaving again or asking them to leave. This is a premature restoration. It shows that God WILL answer your prayers, but if you are not changed, then the same sins that beset you which caused your spouse to leave will be the cause of the restoration falling apart.

Your restoration date is on His calendar, ready or not. Make sure that you use your time wisely to give glory to God.

God Turns the Heart and Restoration Follows!

My precious sisters and brothers in Christ, we have an awesome God! He has changed and molded me so much since I started to believe for my marriage. It is unbelievable!

I am a full-time housewife now, enjoying making our home neat and preparing it to meet my darling husband when he returns home. I plan cooking extensively, and plan on his favorite dishes. Since I was brought up in the fire of the women's liberation movement, this was something I never thought I would be doing, much less talk of enjoying it.

My sweetest darling came home! I am rejoicing in his decision, and I thank our heavenly Father that He has restored our marriage (there is still a lot to do)! My husband has not confessed to the OW, and we have not cleared all the basics, but I know that will happen in God's time.

Thanks for this ministry and this website and all the praise reports. They have strengthened me so much in the hours when the enemy was throwing fiery darts at me. However, thanks to the Sword of the Spirit, the Word of God, also manifested through this website, "All will work together for good for those who love the Lord and are chosen according to his purpose." Praise the Lord, as we believe, praise His holy name!

Amen!

Restored by Doing it Christ's Way!

This is my testimony about how our marriage was saved!! My wife and I are now back together, and this time it is for keeps!!! She now says that she is going to do whatever it takes for our marriage to be saved!!

We now pray together daily and are learning to love each other all over again!!! God has everything under control; that is the good news!!! But, there is difficult news, also (God is not done refining me!).

After we got back together, she began to feel tired and sick. So, she went to the doctor to get a check-up. Hours later, she found out that she was pregnant (not by me). She told me after it was confirmed, which hurt deeply.

I have to admit that I left her for about a week, but praise be to God, I came back under the direction of God. She saw the OM one last time and informed him about the child. Of course, this started another roller coaster of emotions on my part. Then, she reassured me that the OM would have only visitation rights and no personal visits.

We have been going to church. God is in complete control!

Thank you ALL for the much-needed prayers and support!!!

Praise the Lord!! We're RESTORED!

I just want to praise the Lord as my husband moved back home last week, after a year of separation. I hadn't seen any changes, or even seen him in a month. He came by to visit on Sunday evening, came back Monday night and slept on the couch. On Tuesday afternoon, when I got home from work, he was there.

He asked if I would take him back! Praise the Lord! He is so faithful! Even when I kept stumbling and lacked faith, He didn't give up on me. I know we have a long way to go, but the Lord is with us. Praise the Lord!

Restoration in West Virginia!!

Please send me another *How God Can and Will Restore Your Marriage* book. I gave away my last copy and I know yet another lady who needs one. The other lady I gave the book to is RIGHT NOW in church with her husband!!! His adultery is over!! She told me their life is now BETTER than before!! This is AMAZING—only through the LORD could this have happened!! God is WONDERFUL!!

The Power of God moved in my Life!

I have seen the POWER OF GOD move in my life and I have witnessed REAL MIRACLES that cannot be explained by science! I have seen people healed and demons exorcized when God placed my hands on them. I knew the Scriptures, I was a walking concordance and I was a Pharisee!

When my wife left me after three years of marriage, and left our two-year-old son with me, because she couldn't "handle the responsibility," I had no energy to fight for her. I just took care of my son, alone, for almost 12 years. I felt no joy in my life and I never took it to God! Satan had me so blinded that I never even asked God to bring my wife back! WORSE, I told God that "I will not ask!"

My life slowly went downhill! I had girlfriends but could never fall in love, and I was empty! That was when I met a friend I'll call "Betty." I have always obeyed when God told me to do or say something, so when He told me to tell Betty my story, I obeyed Him.

My wife looked at me with amazement! She told me later that she did not understand how I could know the power of God and yet appear so empty! She described me as a "walking dead man"! When we next spoke, I wanted to get to know her better (maybe as girlfriend material), but instead, I told her how messed up my life had been since my wife had left me. Betty actually scolded me for not standing up to the enemy for my marriage!!! I told her that I couldn't pray for that!

My wife asked me what I would like her to pray for and I said, "Pray that I might be made whole again and know the joy of my salvation!" That was two months ago. Since then, God has moved incredibly quickly! I learned how to pray again, and finally asked God to return my wife to me.

Then after 12 years, my wife called me and said she wanted to come home! PRAISE GOD!!!

Restored!! God's Power Will Heal ANY Marriage!!!

I wanted to share with all of you the power of praying for the other woman (or man). My marriage has recently been restored!!

It has not been an easy road. After my husband had been home for almost a month, I found out by accident that he had not totally broken it off with the other woman, nor had he told her that he had moved home. Although he had moved out of her home, she had no idea that he had come back to me.

When I found out, God gave me the peace and wisdom to deal with the situation with a quiet and gentle spirit! My husband seemed almost relieved that the whole truth was finally out. Now all he had to do was tell the other woman that it was truly over. This was something that he had not been able to do for four weeks, but he now had the conviction that he needed to do it.

As we expected, she did not take it well. I immediately got a very hateful and hurtful email from her detailing all the times in the previous few weeks that she had been intimate with my husband. Even though I told myself to be prepared for something like this, it still just took the breath out of me and continues to haunt me at times. [Seek God's protection by deleting such messages as soon as any harmful content is discovered. "For it is a shame to even speak of those things which are done of them in secret" (Ephesians 5:12).]

The part of this story that requires praise is the second email I got from her. (All through this I had been MAKING myself pray for her. It was not easy, and I didn't want to do it, but I knew I had to.) A couple of days after the first email, I got a second email from her. The tone was totally different from the first email. She was repentant!!

She said that she knew what she had done was wrong and she asked for my forgiveness!!! She said that she could not believe that she had turned into the kind of woman that she had always hated and that she had always feared would interfere in her own marriage. Her heart had changed!!!

I believe that God is going to restore her marriage, too!!! I believe that he is going to bring this woman to salvation!! I also believe that had others and I not prayed for her, she would have continued to torment my husband and me as we try to put this marriage back on solid ground.

Please pray for the woman or man who is in an adulterous relationship with your spouse. God is powerful!!! He will do things that you never dreamed He would do and in the process bring great healing to your heart!!

AWESOME Restoration in Cincinnati!

I came to Restore Ministries for help as God lovingly pointed me there, as I begged Him for guidance. He is faithful and true.

I began to read information from the website. I ordered *A Wise Man* and *How God Will Restore Your Marriage*. It was such an incredibly great help!! I began to fast and pray. I filled my time with the Word, prayer and my home church, and with my children. I am amazed how I have grown tremendously. I am closer to God than I ever have been in my LIFE!!

I requested prayer. I posted 500 or more prayer requests worldwide on the web. My wife was gone for ten months, but praise God—she came home last week!!!

God does answer prayer—hallelujah! He turned my wife's heart. We had no discussions of her coming home until that day when she did come home!!

God showed me quite a bit through a few 40-day Daniel fasts. God opened the doors of heaven for me. Thank you, Father, for your greatness.

There is NOTHING TOO HARD FOR HIM! ALL THINGS ARE POSSIBLE!

My wife had told me she would "NEVER COME HOME. I DON'T LOVE YOU. YOU WERE A MISTAKE. WE SHOULD HAVE NEVER GOTTEN MARRIED. I DO NOT CARE IF IT IS GOD'S WILL THAT I SHOULD NOT DIVORCE—I WILL NOT EVER BE BACK."

My wife had found another man and they made plans to marry.

My divorce was two weeks away from final.

I thought that one of the hardest battles was to have God remove the other man (I am still praying every day for him to be saved). The other man has gracefully (by God's Grace) bowed out, and has even taken responsibility for allowing it to happen, and is moving TODAY out of state—praise the Lord!

God gave me Joel 2:25: "And I will restore unto you what the cankerworm has eaten."

Three years ago I nearly lost my wife in labor for our son; he did die three days later. I have experienced bankruptcy, foreclosure on my home, divorce court two weeks away, praying my home off the market, praying the other man out and so much more—praise you Jesus!!! God CAN DO ANYTHING!

Thank you, Restore Ministries!!!

Restored in the Philippines!

I was able to know your ministry through the Internet. I am a pastor who fell into sin against my wife and my God. Since being restored, God has used me, even through the government, to spread His good news about restoration.

My situation was much like yours. It is my personal story as a minister and the way God restored my family and the way my wife responded to it that gave us victory and a ministry for couples today.

Presently, I am able to share the Word of God with local government employees every Monday. We have three satellite churches and more than 300 followers. I'm a full-time minister and I'm committed to go for growth for GOD'S Kingdom. I share some of my ministry background so that I will not be strange to you. May you find interest in sharing more of your ministry here in the Philippines. Are you considering Philippines as one of your mission fields? I desire to facilitate your ministry radio broadcast or television crusade. Our place is peaceful as well as progressive.

I got married when I was 22. Three days into our honeymoon, my wife woke up crying because she had a dream that a lady came to take me. So I told her that it was "just a dream." Years later I had a dream that I would be tested through this kind of temptation, but I just ignored it because I felt I was strong and would stay faithful to my wife.

Then one day I met a lady and the Holy Spirit told me that I needed to be alert; once again, I just ignored it. I was a pastor. To make a long story short, I was tempted and fell terribly into sin for almost a year and half without the knowledge of my wife.

Then the day came when the Lord exposed me because God doesn't want us to go on sinning. When my wife found out about the situation, she became so desperate. Married life with this sin is a terrible situation. At this point, I confessed my faults to my superior in the church because I was an associate pastor. I resigned under a self-disciplinary action. My wife was hurt so much, but she had such a strong commitment to God, and her faith in Him anchored her and gave her hope for our restoration. She even prayed for this woman because the lady confessed her love to me but at the same time asked forgiveness too.

It was a hard time for me too because I didn't know what to do. I felt I was the most miserable person on the face of the earth because of my sin. My wife, instead of having a human reaction, kept on praying and trusting God. Sin hurts not only the sinner (me), but it affects everyone.

It is sad to say but when some of you (like me) share your problems with others "for the sake of unloading and to seek comfort" they will be the source of your miserable fate! There are those who can't help you but they always want to share your personal prayer requests with others!

After all those trials, I've now been restored back to my wife and my ministry. The ministry now is touching the lives of government leaders and even their families. I have so much to tell about "where is God when you are hurt when you sin." Now God is raising me to the level that I will be able to minister to every Filipino family.

The lesson I learned in my experience is don't ignore the early warnings of God. Don't trust your flesh. Keep the family the priority. And overcoming our trials is a way that we can touch and encourage those who are going through the same situation so that they might be overcomers too—in Jesus' name!! God will never give up so you must not give up! Today we are happy and have one beautiful boy who is in kindergarten. My wife and I just forget everything bad we went through and worship the Lord for the great things He has done!!

I have seen a lot of broken families but I believe God has given us a mandate to be part of their restoration. This is my concern. I wish you could have the burden to extend your ministry here in the Philippines. The cases of violence here are very isolated, but I believe the enemy just wants to stop the work of those who have a burden for worldwide ministry like yours, because of the so-called terrorists. The Philippines is good ground for a worldwide ministry because your dollar is 50x in value here. You can have a radio program for only $150 a month, 30 minutes, twice a week. We could hold seminars and conferences. I will pray that you will have a burden for us here. PRAY FOR IT. I hope to hear from you soon.

"Every family we help to (restore) we fix the foundation of our shaking society."

We are sending some tracts for them to distribute and are praying about what more the Lord would have us do. If you have a burden for this country and would like to help them in any way, please contact our ministry.

Restored, Miracles and Healing Wounds!

My marriage has been restored for several months. The Lord did not stop with the restoration; as I apply Scripture and Biblical principles and obey God and His Word, I daily see God changing and molding me! He has done wonderful miracles, both small and big, which appear constantly within our previously wounded family.

I prayed that I would hear my husband tell me that he loved me, with the tenderness he once showed, and now he tells me, and shows me, his love each and every day!! I prayed that God would return my husband to the "wife of his youth" and over and over again my husband tells me that he feels he has his bride back again!!

We have never been happier!!! Last night we went for a bite to eat after doing our grocery shopping (a big task for a family of eight), and my husband told me that his life couldn't be better...he was so content and happy!! Then these dear, dear words were said: "I look forward to coming home to you and our children every day now...I look forward to each day and the time we spend together."

PRAISE GOD!!!!!!!!!!!!

For years and years, I orchestrated our worship and spiritual life. Now, I ask my husband if we will be attending church, and many times he has said "No, not this week." But God needed to separate me from unhealthy relationships in our church community. I worshiped church, not God. I was a Pharisee and had put myself above my husband...I was the Christian "know-it-all and force-it-all" in our family. Now I wait, with joyful anticipation, for the day that God makes my husband the spiritual leader in our family after He has changed me!

He has answered EVERY one of my prayers, and so He will, of course, answer this prayer as well, in the time that is right for us. In the meantime, I continue in my prayer closet, trusting God and thanking God for the miracle of our restored marriage. Thank you Lord!!

Woke Up to Find Husband Home!

I had no idea when I submitted my praise report last week telling people "not to give up" and that "our miracles could be right around the corner" that mine actually was!! Praise the Lord, my husband had moved out on Saturday morning. Then on Saturday night I was reading a book that said "if you are in need of a miracle in your finances, health or marriage, the only reason you don't have it is because you haven't asked for it, believed it and expected it."

Well, that night I prayed and asked God, fully expecting my miracle to happen in HIS appointed time, then I went to bed. That was 11:15 p.m. Then about 1:30 a.m., I was awakened by my husband standing beside the bed. He said, "Do you want me to come home?" I said, "Yes!" and then laughed. He asked what I was laughing about. I said, "YOU WOULD NOT BELIEVE the dream I just had." Then I explained to him that I had dreamt that he was coming home.

Then he said he was tired of going against God and wanted to come home and give it his best effort!!!

We may have a long way to go, but praise the Lord, my husband WANTS to be HERE and is willing to try!!

Please pray for us as we are still in a very vulnerable position and Satan doesn't give up easily. I give Him ALL the praise, as I would NOT have been able to handle this without Him. I know it is His will and He alone can heal this marriage. I only want His will for my marriage and my life. I praise Him and thank Him.

Thank you and your ministry!! Your books and this site have been such a blessing to me during this time! God has done such a work in me and I hope that it will continue.

Restored After Two Years of Separation and a Divorce!

My husband and I were separated two years ago and going through rough times long before then. Financial problems made me bitter and resentful toward my husband. I was not a Christian and he was. That bitterness and anger opened a door for Satan to come in and rob us of our family. We have 13 and 12-year-old sons. My eyes were blinded and my heart was stone cold. I hurt my husband severely, and with a smile on my face! I asked him to leave the house without considering the consequences, listening to advice from non-Christians who would tell me "Just throw him out; things will never change."

After he was forced to find an apartment the devil began to attack his faith (he had prayed for me to be saved during our 15 years of our marriage). He began to go out with friends and stray away.

With my anger and hard heart I pushed for a divorce just to prove that no one could treat me this way. I didn't think about what the true effects would be on our sons. My mother-in-law prayed for us daily and asked that the doors would be closed on the upcoming court date. I still went to court wondering what was going to stop me.

When I got to the courthouse no one was sitting in the section that I was assigned to. I asked a deputy and he informed me that the judge was out of town (no one had told me) and all the petitions had been moved to another court. My name was not on the list. Then my attorney was late but I still insisted on waiting. When he arrived he informed me that there was a problem. The courts had stamped the wrong child support court numbers on my documents. I still insisted that we continue. He searched for a stand-in judge to take my oath at that time. She said she would not touch my case. I still pushed and he found another judge who did swear me in. It says, "Let no man separate" but I had! That was the most horrible mistake I have made in my entire life (I'm 41).

Then as I began to learn about the Word I realized how I allowed the devil to come in and lie to me. I began to fight for my family. I prayed daily and wanted to quit numerous times. Then when what I did to him turned around on me I knew how awful it felt. I repented and asked God for forgiveness and began to seek his Word. This storm caused me to change my direction. It was a long and painful struggle as I was a baby Christian. God held me through all the hurt and I continued to go to church even when things were at their worst.

If anyone had seen how bad things were at that time, and saw us now, they would know this is a MIRACLE! We could not even face each other or speak without lashing out or trying to hurt each other. If it were not for God and other people and family praying for me in prayer groups, I would not have been strong enough to be here today.

One day I asked God to show me when my family would be restored. I had a dream that told me to circle a date on the calendar the following week. I woke up and thought "That's just a couple of days; that can't be my answer." (I still did not know that God can work a miracle instantly!!)

I asked God again the following night and the next morning my husband pulled up in our driveway before I left for work. (For an entire year and a half he would make sure I had left before he came over to get the boys ready for school.) When I heard his truck pull in our driveway I knew instantly that God heard my cries.

We are now happier then we ever were in our first 15 years!!! Our wedding is next week and we will have our sons stand beside us to reclaim what the devil stole from us. Praise the Lord. A co-worker is going through a very similar situation. I asked God to guide me with the words to help her. I forwarded her your website today and will continue to pray for her. Thank you!

Divorce Dismissed Day Before Hearing—Marriage Restored!!

My divorce was to be final on April 19, but my husband had it dismissed on the 18th!!! God works in just the right time, even when I thought it was hopeless and wanted to give up. I kept going back again and again to Erin's book, and praying.

I finally gave up and trusted God to do what I could not do for myself. My husband moved back home and we are sharing what we have learned with others. I have had the opportunity to start a small group in my church and have given books to anyone who has shared with me that they too are going through separation or divorce.

I have something to offer someone else only through the grace of God. I have made friends through this site and hope to one day be able to give as much as I have been given and blessed with.

Through the hard work and determination of Dan and Erin, this experience has truly changed my life!! It has restored and changed my marriage into what God intended for us to have, not another divorce statistic!!!

I have only love and utter gratefulness that this site was there for me when there was no other solution to what I believed to be a hopeless situation. I am reminded every day of the promise He has kept that shows the LOVE my God has for me!!!

ALL THINGS ARE POSSIBLE THROUGH CHRIST. This means your marriage too!!! God bless you and thank you!!!!!

God Did Bring My Husband Home!

God revealed to me this morning, as I sat weeping over the events that are taking place right now in my marriage, that I do, in fact, have a lot to praise Him for. I had been praying for two years that God would bring my husband home (he has lived in other states since we first married 2 years ago).

Glory to God, he is going to church services and functions with me and is heavily involved in remodeling our home. As I sit and think, God has been so faithful but my eyes have been blinded by the events that are still happening (the OW calling our house, etc.). The enemy has blinded my eyes so that I could not see the goodness of God!!!

I had promised my Lord and Savior that I would praise Him from the rooftops for His greatness and His faithfulness in all of this. I want to begin right now giving Him the glory even when things aren't yet completed, for I KNOW that they will be!!

Thank you, Restore Ministries, for your Scriptural guidance and prayers!!! It is funny how God kept telling me a lot of your principles that you speak of in your books long before I ever read them. People told me that I was crazy. I thought I was crazy at times, too. I know that God divinely led my path to meet yours, Erin. He brought me to this ministry right when I needed it most. My God is SO Faithful!!!

Glory to GOD. Thank you, Jesus, for you are faithful!!!!

God Restores in Alabama!

When I first came to your website and read about the lady with the 6 kids who lived in Alabama, I told the Lord that there would be another one soon!!

I just watched the Q&A video (again) last night and it was just what I needed!! My husband is so close to coming home—but I thought 'not yet.' I listened again to when Dan was coming home, but he took a detour and didn't come home—you said on the video that maybe you should not have even said, 'I don't think you should go' (back to the other apartment).

Well tonight—praise God he has decided to come home!!!! Only 8 months ago this marriage was over! He wanted to be let go 'for time served,' but based on God's Word that I found in your books and videos, I am a new creature!!!

He has asked me to decide financially (I'm a retired CPA) if we should keep his house. You see, we often go away for weekends (6 kids) and he thinks his house is cheaper and nicer than hotels. I will "decide" slowly and pray for him to give it up on his own.

I'm so glad I picked that video to watch last night—surely God had his hand on me! When he told me his decision, I didn't scream or get giddy; I just smiled and listened while he told me his 'reasons.' None of these reasons were that he was sorry or loved me—but it didn't matter because they are not important for now. I live by faith and not by sight.

Thank you, Erin, for being a vessel for Jesus. I will keep you posted on moving day—when his things actually come home.

Her second email "Hallelujah!"

Ladies, please quit talking and thinking about praying and DO IT. He will do this!!! My situation is such that I cannot tell the world about my answered prayers, but I can tell you. My husband left me and was gone for over 14 months. Yes, there WAS someone else. Yes, there were attorneys involved. Yes, it was hopeless. Yes, I did everything wrong. When I studied God's word through Erin and Dan's books and tapes—and actually started to apply the principles—I received and received and received.

You must pray and fast and never give up. Your fight is not with your husband but with the devil himself. Prayer will give God the ability to fight on your behalf. He has already defeated the devil, but we need to take the authority in Jesus' name and cut him down at the strongholds. I am so excited about what God has done for me and hope I can encourage you to get busy and quit complaining and start praying!

My husband came home, not because he couldn't live without me, but because he was disabled financially. Still, I praised God. I kept praying. Soon he started to tell me he loved me. He has been to church 4 times, yes!!!!!!! He is not yet ready for Sunday school—so I told the kids to come outside for home Sunday school. My husband said to wait for him. When I picked myself off the floor, I tried not to grin too big. He listened to my prayer and story and Bible reading. Then he said, 'Okay, now we need to pray for Daddy.' He prayed the sinner's prayer and asked Jesus into his life and asked him to guide him in the coming days. I have been praying for this for sooooo long!!!!!!!!!!!!!

I wanted him to come back to the Lord, but I selfishly wanted him to come back to me too. He had been home for over 2 months and he still wasn't ready to be my husband again. Then on my birthday I knew he hadn't had time to get me a gift. After dinner (that I fixed) he fell asleep. So instinctively I went into my prayer closet for a good cry and prayer. When I went to bed my husband woke up, wide awake, and asked if I wanted my present. He got up and put on his wedding ring. God is so GOOD. I had been praying for this since he left.

You can't know how far we have come except that your situation could be much worse—and with God all things are possible!!!!!!!!!!

Whatever the devil steals from us—God can replace sevenfold if not greater!!!!!

I will continue to claim VICTORY for all the troubled marriages that come to this site and pray that those who don't know about this wonderful place will be led here.

This portion is from Erin:

Finally!!!!

Oh, I have been waiting and praying for this, constantly asking the Lord to do it as a favor for me (as if He owes ME anything!).

For those of you who do not know the entire testimony of this Alabama woman, let me share it briefly with you.

Several months ago I received an email. This woman had just had her sixth child when she found out she had breast cancer. After a mastectomy, and losing her hair, at the end of her chemotherapy, she and her husband pulled up in front of a house with a sign that said, "Sold." She thought that her husband was surprising her, that they were getting a "new start." But his words pierced her soul and heart: "This is my new house. I am leaving you. I don't love you. I love someone else."

When I read her email I broke down in tears. I thought that I had heard it all. It was so devastating to my heart that I thought seriously that I could no longer minister in restoration. I could no longer bear to hear and experience the pain.

We received CONSTANT praise reports, which were without a doubt a SACRIFICE of praise. Continual offensive attacks would come and she would praise the Lord with a heart of joy and LAUGHTER. She kept her sense of humor throughout the entire ordeal.

Dan and I both believed her marriage would be restored. Daily she would saturate herself in the books and video tapes, falling asleep as I spoke to her from the tapes.

After this testimony was submitted, we received an SOS Prayer Request. Her husband had "stalled" moving his things back home. He had become surprisingly "cool" in his affections and conversations over the previous few weeks. Then the morning of the SOS she received a surprise visit from a man who told her that his wife and her husband were away together. She politely asked him to leave and said that she could not discuss anything without her husband.

TALK ABOUT A TEST!!!! She did not ask questions, nor did she listen to things that were NOT a "good report," though maybe true.

The next day her husband called and said, "I heard you had an 'interesting' visitor at the house yesterday." As "gentle and quiet" as can be she stated, "Well, no, I don't remember anyone in particular."

THAT'S WHAT DID IT!!!

Her husband was home, for good—GLORY TO GOD!!!

Someday I want to meet this woman, to hug her in triumph. I want to meet her husband, the man whom we prayed for and love because we prayed him home!!!

Update: I did get several hugs when our entire family met this precious woman on a recent trip when we just happened to drive through her city! She now is the president of the women in our Restoration Fellowship. We spent a wonderful week together and God has blessed me with a wonderful friend and encouragement partner!

Restored Times Two!!

My wife moved out 5 months ago in October as a temporary separation, which then turned into her filing for a divorce in February. Over that period of time we were able to see each other a lot because of our 2 boys. She said I was always welcome to come over to see our boys.

Over the last 6 weeks we spent time together eating dinner at the house as well as at her apartment; we watched TV and played rummy, but she never showed any signs of coming home nor would she talk about it.

But I continued to stand on God's Word, although I never acted on the circumstances as everybody was trying to convince me to do (i.e. get an attorney, move your money into a different bank, etc.). I always showed her kindness regardless of how I felt or what I saw.

She came over Friday night and before leaving she gave me a kiss, which totally stunned me. I didn't hear from her again until Easter Sunday, late in the afternoon, when she picked up the boys. She said she'd call later, which she did, and began to tell me that she had some wasps in her apartment. So I went over there with some wasp spray to see if I could help.

We ended up playing rummy and talking about the house and during that conversation she told me that she had been thinking about some things lately, and then she said, 'I want to come home. I want to do family things again and work on the house, but I'm afraid.' We talked and hugged and kissed and she said she needed a few days.

Then, last night (4 days later) she said she is coming home! We are now making arrangements to get her out of her apartment and back home.

Our final divorce hearing was scheduled for April 16th—only 2 weeks away!! She said I would not need to worry about going that day.

All I can say is: 'we serve a mighty God!!!' I know only He could have 'turned her heart'!!

My wife's father told me that she told him only 3 weeks ago that she was 'SURE' that this (divorce) is what she wanted. Only a few weeks before that she had told me regarding the divorce that 'This is something that I feel I need to do, and I want to start new'!! There were many other times when she told me similar things that really hurt, but I continued to trust the Lord, knowing that He always causes me to triumph! God is an awesome God!!

The biggest miracle out of all this is that my Encouragement (Prayer) Partner was scheduled to go to his final divorce hearing on April 5th he and asked me to fast and pray with him. Only two days after my wife told me she wanted to come home, my prayer partner's wife went to the attorney and canceled their divorce!!

Two wives choosing to stop the divorce and restore their marriage in the same week!! I was two weeks away from a divorce and my prayer partner was 3 days!

So those of you who see no change in your circumstances, continue to stand on God's Word and trust Him. My wife told me that she had been thinking about coming home for a few weeks, yet I never saw any difference in her! So don't look at the circumstances! Trust the Lord!! He's always faithful, and always on time!"

ePartner RESTORED too! Glory to God!!

Wow!!! We sure serve an AWESOME GOD!!!!

My wife and I were separated in ugliness in November of 2001. I wanted nothing to do with her and she felt the same about me. I filed for divorce.

Then the Lord changed my heart in February and I rededicated my life to Him (after running from Him for nearly 10 years). I offered Him my life, whether or not He restored my marriage.

There were many trials, but the Lord saw me through and I kept my eyes on Him. I trusted that He would honor my obedience, though the circumstances in the physical realm did not show results.

The court would not dismiss the divorce without my wife's approval, which she did not give.... she wanted it to be over.

I continued to trust in the Lord, accepting that the divorce might go through, but I knew He would restore my marriage (I just didn't know how long the wait would be).

I did not seek men for advice or counsel. I just had people pray and I consulted my Heavenly Father. Yes, I stumbled along the way, but He strengthened me.

My wife's heart turned over Easter weekend and, when we saw each other on Monday, we embraced each other.

She called off the divorce only 3 days before it was to be final! Today we went before the judge to have the divorce officially dismissed. Our kids are so happy and our 8-9 year marriage will now grow longer under His authority!!

Praise God, for He is mighty. I weep for joy at the thought of the Scriptures He gave to me at exactly the right times. I thank Him for giving me the strength to endure, to cry out to Him whenever I had failed or was hurting.

Nothing is impossible with Him. For all of you still waiting, you must believe—keeping your eyes on Him.

The Lord sure placed my Encouragement Partner and me together. His marriage was restored at the same time!!!! Thank you, Father!!

Thank you, Dan and Erin, for being servants of the Lord in your ministry—in an age when most every church only has a 'divorce recovery' group/class and nothing for saving a marriage with the Lord.

Thank you, Jesus, my Wonderful Counselor. All glory to You, my Lord.

Praise God! He Restored Our Marriage!

Here's the praise report and testimony of God's power I have been waiting so long to tell! Today my husband and I went to the court house and got our marriage license! Within the week I will be his wife legally again. What a difference a week can make!

I want to thank all of you who must have prayed for us. I praise God because I know without HIM this would never have happened. I thank HIM that He is using this ministry to give hope to people like me to believe that HE will restore marriages.

After feeling so good about our Christmas together, I still did not hear from him for over a week. I was able to speak to him about our taxes and our conversation turned to what had caused our breakup. Both of us were crying over the phone. I said I knew he still loved me and that I knew we belonged together. After that, we just began making plans to be together again.

So all of you who have any doubt about God's love for you and your families, just hang on! Get into God's Word and His will and pray without ceasing!!!!

Restoration and Salvation in Texas!!

Praise to God for the victory and abundant blessing!

My husband and I were finally restored on February 15, the day after Valentine's Day!

He asked me to pick him up from the other woman's apartment with all his clothes and belongings in tow. My son and I also moved out of my parents' house the same day! Isn't God awesome? Although my parents were very bitter and upset about my decision, I believe God will not put us to shame but reveal His Glory through us.

We had no place to stay, so we stayed at a motel for a week while we searched for a new apartment. I want to emphasize that my credit was destroyed during our separation due to the financial struggle. My husband has very little credit with a couple of outstanding balances. We had to break our last lease due to our separation. The odds were against us, but glory to God, He was our co-signer!

We were able to get a nice 2-bedroom apartment, with washer and dryer in unit, security alarm, and free covered parking in a gated community for a low monthly rent, NO deposit, and NO co-signer (except God's invisible signature) within one week! Another great miracle—He surely is our provider!

As if that wasn't enough, last Sunday was our first Sunday since before our separation to go to church together. My husband asked if we could leave during the altar call. Of course I agreed, but began praying fervently that God would touch his heart and save him.

The pastor asked anyone who had once known God, but had strayed and would like to be forgiven, to raise their hand. I sort of opened my eyes for a moment and saw my husband's hand raised!!! Oh man, I was quivering inside and I prayed harder. Then came the altar call. Lo and behold, my husband squeezed my hand and asked me to go with him to the altar!!

I would like to point out that we have a huge church of several thousand (also televised regularly on TBN). We were seated at the top of the balcony so we had some ways to walk in order to reach the altar, including a long stairway. So it takes a lot of humility and Spirit-led power to stand up and go forward. He then accepted Jesus Christ back into his life! Can you believe it? I was shocked. I had tears running down my face!!

We serve an Awesome God! He is soooo good and He NEVER fails. Now, I can say from experience, He is no respecter of persons. What He did for me, He can do for you. I used to claim it by faith.

Believe it. I did, and it came to pass as it is written in his Word.

I am already excited to see what the Lord will do next. What I have gone through is worth the glory and the experience of the miracles and healing of the Most High God and His Son the Living Jesus Christ!

Hallelujah!!! God Is Awesome!

My marriage has been Restored!!!

I thought to myself that my situation was impossible. But I held on. I went through so much that it is impossible to list everything that happened to me during the time I was believing and trusting God for the restoration of my marriage. Besides, I don't want to slander my husband.

I spoke to him on Friday night and he showed up at our house on Sunday night. He drove across SEVEN states to get home!! He totally surprised me!!! I could not stop thanking GOD!

I often read praise reports from others who said, 'never give up!' Well there were times when I almost did, but I devoted my time to focusing on GOD and not my situation.

Due to my obedience, He gave me all of His promises and restored my marriage.

Tears ran down my face this morning as I drove to work just thinking about how awesome GOD is! He took care of me even when I couldn't take care of myself. He gave me such peace.

I will say to anyone who is thinking about giving up to NEVER GIVE UP!! I know it is hard but He says 'anyone who trusts in Him will never be put to shame' (Romans 10:11). Stand on His Word and His promises – He will never let you down!!"

Marriage "Saved" in Michigan!!!

Thank you so much for your materials!!! They have SAVED our marriage!! My wife and I have decided to use your materials to start a tract ministry! We plan to place your marriage restoration tracts 'At Last There's Hope!' in displays around town and refill them as needed! We are praying for your ministry! THANK YOU FOR EVERYTHING!!"

Restored and New Baby Too!

I have to share this story—it is a perfect miracle from God!!

On November 27th, my husband told me he wanted a divorce. Then on December 26th, almost a month later, I discovered I was pregnant with our first child. I gave my husband the news, but it did not change his feelings. I had to move out of our home January 1. I began reaching to the Lord more than ever. He became my only comfort. I requested prayer for my situation from fellow Christians and began receiving encouraging, spirit-filled emails from a friend in the same situation. These emails were full of God's promises for my marriage, and in one, there was information about how to get a copy of Erin's book on marriage restoration. I was desperate so I sent for it.

I carried her book everywhere and read it whenever I had a spare moment. The promises God has given us in His Word gave me more comfort than I can explain and I began to know in my heart that things would somehow be okay.

I didn't speak with my husband for several weeks and then one day he called and said he had quit his job. I wasn't covered under his insurance anymore and I was 4 months pregnant. It seemed like another struggle, but of course, God planned it perfectly!

Then out of nowhere, on March 26th, my husband asked me to reconcile our marriage!!!

I had prayed it would happen, but didn't realize it would be so soon!

We now have a beautiful 3-month-old son and we are working on our marriage with the help of God every day. It will take time for both of us to completely heal but we've been given a New Beginning by our Heavenly Father and we have so many blessings in our life it brings tears to my eyes when I think of them! God will ALWAYS provide for His children and He loves us more than we could ever imagine!

I am a blessed woman and will forever be humbled by my Lord's power!!"

Restored—Glory be to God!

I thank the Lord for His wonderful promises. God is faithful to those who earnestly seek Him. If you only believe that 'all things are possible'!

My husband moved out in September and went to live with the OW. When I heard it, I am ashamed to say, I tore all his clothes. After a week he told me flat out that he would return only when he wanted to; otherwise, he had decided to live with someone else.

I sought the Lord and cried to Him and that is when I found your website. My friend whom I used to work with had given me your printouts of testimonies of restored marriages. I read them again and again. I then visited your website and finally God helped me.

I began to pray and fast every Tuesday and Thursday while meditating on the Word day and night. I prayed each and every time when the Holy Spirit prompted me.

You know, brethren, God is wonderful because He was working from behind the scenes. When I was almost giving up (saying that there was no change in my situation or in my husband) He WAS working and changing things. My good Lord is able and He allowed it because I learned to wait patiently upon the Lord during these times.

Last month my husband came and said he wanted to come back home, but he wanted to finish first with the other woman. After all that I had learned, I said it was okay with me!

He then started phoning me and coming to my work. I think he was seeing the changes in me. I had been the kind of woman who would shout at him and tell him all sorts of things just to bore him. But now, I am really changed. Now I only listen and agree with whatever he says.

There was no peace with the other woman he was staying with (as his friends would always tell me), so he began wanting to come back home.

Then last night, he finally came home with his bag of clothes!! My marriage is restored!!!

Glory be to the Son of the living God! Thank you Jesus!! Amen."

God is faithful to His promises and He answers prayers. However, so often, too often, the wayward spouse wants to leave their adulterous situation but does not come home. We became involved in a relationship in our church just a couple of weeks ago. The wife, who had left and moved in with another man, accepted the Lord at our altar.

Erin had the privilege of talking to her as an altar worker. Unfortunately, though she doesn't want to be in adultery any more, and though she is now a born-again believer (really running after God) she is afraid of her husband. He has wanted to restore his marriage for the 4 months since she left. He has prayed and gotten on fire for the Lord, but his aggressive behavior toward her is keeping her from coming home. Our prayer is that he would get a hold of the principles that we teach in Restore Ministries so that she would move back home.

Suddenly God Moved and Restored!

I am submitting this praise report to let other women know that God can and will restore your marriage.

My husband and I started having problems after 27 months of marriage. He said he didn't love me anymore and wanted to be single and date. I got connected to this website through a friend and bought the book. Since my husband had moved out I had time to read, meditate and confess the word of God for my marriage. I followed the directions in Erin's book. Two weeks ago I went to the store and I returned home to find my husband's car in the parking lot. He had returned home. He said he was missing God's blessings so he needed to return home.

God has restored my marriage and my husband and I are so happy! God has sent him home in time for Thanksgiving and Christmas. He is so happy that I have forgiven him and I am so happy that God has restored our marriage.

Please, as you read this praise report, understand that there were a lot of things happening during the time that my husband was gone. I suffered a lot and I saw a lot of things that really hurt my heart, but I cried out to God and He heard me and moved heaven and came and made me more than a conqueror.

God is Good, but you must be obedient to His Word as you await the manifestation of your restored marriage. Walk by faith and look not at the things that are seen.

I thank God for Restore Ministries, Erin and her family. May God richly bless you all.

God Restored!

I want to submit a praise report because I need to tell all the readers and members of this ministry how good God is. My husband has not only returned, but our marriage is a lot better than it ever was.

He is happy, and calls me three times a day just to say 'I love you'!!! We go to the movies and the mall holding hands. I know now that ALL the things that Erin said in her book are true. Many times we are not submissive as women. We want to do things our way instead of God's way.

Well, Erin, thanks for teaching me how to be the wife God has called me to be. Women, please don't give up. God is no respecter of persons. He can and will restore your marriage. I am a living example.

Hang in there and watch God put it all back together, and when he does this, no one will be able to open it again unless you do so yourself. I made the mess in my marriage by being contentious and petty.

Let God do his job and 'stand still and know that he is God'!!!

HE IS GOOD ALL THE TIME!!!

Restored Marriage!!

I would like to thank you for your website. It gave me the encouragement to seek God and to believe God for my marriage.

My husband and I got married at very young ages. He was 17 and I was 19 with a 3-year-old daughter, and pregnant with my first son. We thought things would be so great: a family, apartment, children, friends, etc... What we forgot was God. We always ran our marriage and we were surprised when things started going bad. The kids started to grow up, the money started to fade, and we had more bills than we knew what to do with. Both of us thought that the 'grass HAD to be greener on the other side.' We both looked for love in other places.

After my husband's first adultery, we started to work on our marriage. We got into a great church and started taking classes to be in leadership positions in our church. Eventually my husband began to play the bass guitar in the worship group and I began to teach Sunday School to 3rd graders. I thought we had it all under control. We were doing God's work. Our hearts were in the right place, so we thought.

In October 2001, after a very emotional argument, my husband decided to leave his family. He had met someone else at a bar and said he knew he would be happier with her. I was devastated. I think at first I was mostly devastated because he looked so happy and I wasn't. I was jealous because he had someone and I didn't. I tried to date, but every time I would attempt to go out, I would get physically ill and never be able to go. (A blessing from God!)

Two months after my husband left, we started to be able to talk on a civil basis. We had restraining orders against each other, assault charges, and were in a very heated divorce and custody battle. My work performance was horrible; I couldn't eat, sleep, think, or anything. Then one night while looking for divorce 'recovery,' I stumbled over your site. I started crying when I read the first page and decided that night that I was going to turn everything over to God.

My husband would remind me daily that our relationship was over. He would tell me how happy he was with the other woman and how they were going to get married and have more children. This hurt me so much since I had to have a hysterectomy when I was 25 and had always wanted more children. So I cried out to God on a daily basis, not really knowing what to pray for.

On Dec. 20th, I had to have another major surgery. I desperately wanted my husband to be there for the surgery. I asked him to go and he agreed. It was the best feeling to wake up after surgery and feel him giving me a hug.

On Dec. 27th, his birthday, I went over to his house with our two boys and watched them open gifts with their dad. It hurt to be in his home and not be able to tell him how very much I loved him. I remember lying awake at night just watching him sleep and wanting to hold him.

Things began progressing into a friendship and I was thankful for this blessing from God. Then we started talking more. Then one night, I woke to someone standing looking over me—it was my husband standing there. He was drunk and told me he just wanted someone to hold him. The other woman had broken the relationship off the day before his birthday and he was very upset about it. As much as it hurt me to hold him, I couldn't doubt that it was a blessing from God. Slowly things started to progress into a genuine relationship.

Then suddenly my husband came home on January 3!!

At first he said he wasn't moving back in; he was just staying for a little while, but we have been so happy!! I never thought things could be so great! God has truly blessed us with another chance. We realize that our priorities were all messed up. My husband is on his way back into the band and I am going to be teaching a small group.

God is so good!!! He knows just what you need and when. He brought us from a devastating position into an even greater love than either of us ever imagined was possible. I will never forget to put God first in my life. When you put God first, everything else falls into place.

Thank you so much for your encouragement, prayers and help. I think this site was really a gift from God! Without your encouragement, I still believe I would not have found God when I needed Him and would still be on the road to divorce. By the way, that word (the "D" word) does not exist in our home anymore. We have promised to trust in God for all our needs instead of looking elsewhere to satisfy our needs.

Thanks again for all of your help. God bless you both.

Marriage Restored—My Husband's Now Sober!!!

I was a second wife. My husband was married before and had two children from that marriage. I sought God because I was unsure what to do. I kept feeling that God wanted me to stick with this marriage and not give up. I asked God to confirm my feelings and then I read a question from some man (who I don't know—he just emailed a bunch of your questions the day he sent me your website address when I posted my prayer request on a Christian site).

There I saw that you had used Scripture to talk to a woman about a similar situation. I had just prayed on my knees five minutes earlier for a sign of confirmation!!!

God did restore our marriage and He continues to make things better!!

My husband has been drinking heavily for some time. I had been praying that God would take away the drunkard and put a sober man in him. I have been praying this since I heard your suggestion in tape 7.

Get this—he looked at me the other night, for no apparent reason, and said, 'Oh, by the way, I haven't had a drink all day.' I didn't say anything. I have never harped about it even before we had our marriage fall apart. Then two days later, he said he still hadn't had a drink. Last night he told me he still hadn't had a drink. It has been nearly a week without him drinking any alcohol. WOW!

If you only knew the whole story, he used to drink 24 beers a day. Just know that this is from GOD! My husband had a drinking problem, and after I prayed that God would take away the drunkard and replace him with a sober man, HE DID!

God has put us in severe financial ruin to accomplish this and I praise God for answering my prayers!!! Know I am praying for you and your family, Erin."

Restoration and Husband's Salvation in Alabama!!

About 3 months ago I found out my husband was cheating on me, and I kicked him out.

I really didn't know what to do and then his friend bought me the *How God Can and Will Restore Your Marriage* book. I read it and it changed me so much!!!! Then I saw that God had to change the things in me He wanted, before he brought my husband home.

Only one month later, my husband came to spend the weekend with the kids. At the end of the weekend he could see such a difference that he asked to come home!!! He was home for 2 months and then he went with the same friend who gave me your book to a flea market, of all places. There he met a man and my husband got saved right there in the middle of the flea market crowd!!!! Praise be to our God!!!!

Our marriage and our life has been great ever since then! God hears your prayers and has His perfect timing for everything—just obey and let God take over!!!

Couple Saved, Marriage Restored!!!

I just had to write and tell you about our marriage that was miraculously and gloriously restored because of our precious savior. I want you to post it to encourage others who think that their husband (or wife) is so far gone that the Lord can't reach them. I was at the end of my rope when my friend reached out to me and introduced me to her Lord and Savior Jesus Christ. I was alone with two small children. I wept as the group of praying ladies knelt by me and prayed for my marriage. My husband had left and abandoned me. One of the women prayed that my husband would not just come home, but would be saved and have a Saul experience like the apostle Paul had on the road to Damascus!!

Only two weeks after I accepted the Lord, I saw my husband pull up in the driveway and I panicked. But when he walked in, his face was totally changed; his expression was joyful, so different than I had ever seen. He told me he was sorry for leaving us and not telling us where he was going or when he was coming home. That's when I noticed a huge Bible under his arm, the kind that sits on someone's coffee table. He said, 'Sweetheart, while I was gone I accepted Jesus Christ as my Lord and Savior'!!!!! Then he said that his grandmother who had been praying for him for years gave him the Bible!!!! This is such a miracle and an answer to my and everyone else's prayers!!!

My husband has spent hours and hours reading his Bible. No matter where he goes, he carries this huge Bible with him!!!! He also remembers it, everything he reads in the Bible WORD FOR WORD!!!

Three months after my husband came home he told me that God told him to go back to where we used to live, near our families, and that God wanted him to open up a restaurant to feed the poor. I was sooooooo happy he no longer took drugs and drank or was unfaithful to me with all the women, but now he had gone off the deep end!!! But I packed us up and we moved.

We had only been in our apartment a couple of days when my husband went downtown and saw an empty building. He laid his hands on it for God to give it to him. When he came home and told me I was really frightened. I just figured he was high or something. Then I heard someone knocking on the door. It was a man and his wife who handed my husband and me a check and said, 'The Lord told us to give this to you to open the restaurant.' The check was the exact amount of the building my husband had prayed for!! To God be the Glory!!! Hallelujah!!! Thank you Jesus. Nothing is too hard for the Lord. Why did I doubt it????? Why do other Christians doubt that God can do what He says He will????????"

Marriage Restored in Kentucky AFTER a Divorce!!!!

I wanted to email you and tell you that my husband and I were remarried last Friday!! Glory to our God Who ALWAYS leads us to triumph in Christ Jesus! Our God is able to deliver us from the jaws of the lion. I am fully persuaded that our God is able to do that which He has promised! Thank you for your daily encouragement and for the wisdom and counsel of God that you have sown into our lives through your books and website and the preparation that you have shared through the word and your testimony to prepare me for the days ahead. I am excitedly experiencing and expecting that the latter glory of this house shall be greater than the former! Our God is a restorer of more than all we had before. God bless Restore Ministries richly! Our God is truly a Restorer of the ruins, a Repairer of the devastations of our generations and He makes our marriages and families like the Garden of Eden for all to see what the Lord has done!

We Just Got Remarried!! PRAISE GOD!!!!!!!!

My wife and I were remarried July 2 in Gatlinburg, Tennessee! God has completely turned her around! Me too! I am late in telling because I just got back to work after a wonderful vacation with my wife and kids. We had a "Hillbilly Wedding" on the Little Pigeon River in the Smoky Mountains National Park. Just my wife, the children, the Hillbilly preacher, me and God. It was wonderful. I have to get to work now. God does answer prayers. He also had us leave Myrtle Beach early last Friday right before the tornado went right by the campground we would have still been at for one more night. Praise Him!!!

Restoration in Arizona!!

Erin, 2 months ago you kindly responded to an email question I had, even though I had not received your books and was not a member yet. I told you my husband and I followed a Christian/Hindu belief—your gentleness in telling me that the Lord loves all and would restore our marriage even if we are not Christians gave me the encouragement and safety I needed to know Jesus. Thank you for helping me instead of sending me away—*I just wanted you to know that you opened the door to my personal relationship with Jesus in your response—THANK YOU.* And also your being adamant that it was God's will and not my husband's will that was important.

My husband and I separated about 9 months ago. It was a very ugly and painful event. He forced me to leave our home (this was like a knife in my heart). Everything that was good about our life and relationship was suddenly made wrong and ugly in addition to the things that were there that were problems.

I turned to God after the first 2 weeks and noticed that God was already responding to my prayers and beginning the healing in our relationship. Unfortunately, I started going to counseling and my husband and I talked about abuse issues and that sort of thing. You were right about counseling because even though I felt I would have died if it wasn't for my counselor, it seems that all that came from it was hopelessness, more pain and absolutely no love! Instead of helping, the opposite resulted—separation. Thank you for stressing this important point—I cannot deny the truth that God and his love and his Word cures all.

Only 2 months ago I got your book *How God Can and Will Restore...* and the women's workbook *A Wise Woman.* I have to say that I had a LOT of conflict with the contents but noticed that it was truth and as I read on, I felt I was being broken. This was good because I have never experienced such peace as a result. No amount of philosophy, explanations, or anything else could have brought me this peace.

Things began to really turn in our relationship when I confessed to my husband that I had been a contentious woman (only 2 weeks ago). That was the turning point. I almost could feel his tears on the other end of the phone. He exclaimed, 'I never imagined that you would say that. I can't believe I am hearing this.' Then he said something that hurt a bit, but I agreed with him and gratefully to God.

After that conversation, he asked me if I would like to come and visit him and spend some time together. Then that night he admitted that he had been wondering why he didn't just come and get me permanently! He humbly and timidly plucked up the courage to tell me (totally out of character for my husband) that he doesn't understand it all but that he 'KNEW' that we need to keep what we had and build on it. He said he didn't know where I stood because he knows that he hurt me so (the first time he has ever expressed any repentance on his part since the separation) but that he hoped that we can do this. He asked me what I thought (I didn't know what to say but simply agreed!).

Before closing I want to share some direct answers to prayer:

We have spoken for hours on the phone and every interaction has been pure, respectful, innocent. I was in the hospital since our separation and he really didn't care. Then just weeks ago when I told him I developed a complication, he was so sympathetic and wanted to know every detail and asked me to call him with a report after my next appointment. When I did he was so attentive and sympathetic—just like he used to be. Praise you God for your love and kindness!!

Many, many other specific prayers have been answered like: I asked God to make me innocent in my husband's eyes for all things (because he had blamed me for absolutely everything upon our separation) and God did. He told me that he just realized that it wasn't my fault but that we were just doing our best. It just blew my mind—very healing.

I also asked God to place a trust in my husband for me the way a husband trusts his wife in the ways pleasing to the Lord. My husband told me many personal things and said 'I hope you don't mind me telling you all this but you are the only one I can trust to share these things with.' This was after he had totally lost trust in me in EVERYTHING, and I mean everything.

I asked God to turn his heart to loving me—he started flirting with me about 3 weeks ago!!!

I asked God to bring us healing and restoration. My husband said he feels it's time for us to start healing together in our relationship!!!!

I have asked God to change my husband into what he wants him to be and into the husband he wants him to be for me. My husband has shared with me what he could have done differently—things I never ever thought he would see—and I didn't have to say a word!!!! God is amazing and kind and gentle and so generous to us.

Please know everyone that I too was ready to quit (have been on and off throughout) but particularly recently. I was even acting out in my mind filing papers and just being done with the hurt and pain—I had had these thoughts before but was getting ready to act on them and it was not with anger either—yes even then—don't give up!!

I was also resolving myself to the thought that God does want restoration for us (because I had a conflict about whether it was God's will) but that it might take another year or two for me to hear these words. Lo and behold, within 1 week, I received the phone call that he 'doesn't want to lose what we have' and that he doesn't want anyone else (there was not infidelity involved but I could sense from some of the things he had said that there could be—I prayed to God for the hedge of protection just in case!).

I mentioned earlier that there was a huge conflict in me that this may not be God's will and my husband gave me every reason to think that I was being selfish by trying to hold on to our marriage—that it was going against what he needed in his life and career. Then I learned I had to let go and I did!! It was very hard until I realized I could let go without letting go of my commitment to our marriage and still be open to it being restored. My husband 'of his own will' has come back to realizing it is his will to be with me (after God turned his heart). Please note that there was absolutely no manipulation or anything impure involved with this on my part—it all came from God—only God could have shown him what he did—only God could be responsible for this.

I prayed for Jesus to please remove my and my husband's hardened hearts and replace them with his heart, a heart of flesh, and fill it with his word, aspects, patterns and ways. My husband's heart is softened dramatically. Within a month, I saw the changes—thank you Jesus—he even said within the first week of asking the Lord, 'I realize now that I hardened my heart to you because I didn't want anything to stand in my way.' A week later he mentioned his friend who does not believe in God and his comment was, 'I just can't be around people on a daily basis that are "nonbelievers."'. Not only had he never used this term before but he turned away from God about 9 months ago. Is this amazing or what?

I want everyone to know that this all came with a man who told me repeatedly, angrily, blatantly as well as soberly and peacefully that he didn't love me anymore, he couldn't ever live with me again, we held each other back in life—that he had finally understood and accepted this through all our efforts to make our relationship work and that he was moving on to a new life, ALONE, forever, and he absolutely knew it was the right thing. Praise God! Thank you Jesus!!!! He's finally moving back home! Thank you so very much for your prayers. Bless you.

Thank you and everybody for your prayers. I will continue to pray for others—please continue to pray for us.

Again—THANK YOU. THANK YOU. THANK YOU. BLESS YOU. BLESS YOU. BLESS YOU AND YOUR FAMILY.

P.S. I thought I had tried it all—I never thought it would come from God's Word. Your books are an absolute blessing—thank you both for devoting your lives to this cause—what a great service you are doing for God and all of mankind. God bless you. Thank you, God."

Marriage Restored in Missouri!!

Erin, I just wanted to tell you that my marriage has been restored—suddenly!

The last week in May, only nine weeks ago, my husband told me that he was divorcing me, that there was someone that he might start to have a relationship with and that he didn't love me anymore!!

I cried out for God to help me. Then a man sent me a brief email from my prayer post and told me about your website. I received your books and started changing my ways immediately (by the Grace of God). My husband took notice and said I was 'insane' and my family thought I was absolutely crazy. (Even now, my father isn't speaking to me.)

Well, suddenly, shortly after I finished *A Wise Woman* workbook, my husband decided he wasn't going to leave and he never had an affair!!! I don't want to tell you this to shame my husband, but I must because it shows that what is in your book really is true!!! You see, my husband told me one night (only after I opened my mouth to argue about something trivial—the old me!) that he was no longer physically attracted to me and that he would soon become 'intimate' with this other married woman.

When I heard this I prayed to God because I didn't know what to do! My husband said he would sleep on the sofa, but then, after reading in the workbook about how I was to still offer myself to my husband, I said it would still be okay if he slept in our bed even after he had said all this. I still made myself available to my husband and I believe that was the ONLY thing that kept him from having a physical affair! Praise be to the Lord God Almighty!!!!

This threat was so real, Erin. Please let others know how being physically available is so important!! It was the biggest factor in our quick restoration.

Would you believe that my husband is now praising me at work and loves to tell others how he is the leader of our home. He says that if they don't believe it, just to call me and I will agree. AMEN!!

I now seek God for what I need and ask Him to have the Lord speak to my husband about things. Won without a word!!! HE IS EVER FAITHFUL!!!

We have a long journey ahead of us, but I KNOW that the Heavenly Father is working in our lives daily.

This restoration was so sudden. My marriage turned around in a matter of 24 hours after I finally prayed without any DOUBTING that I would give it to God and let Him restore us when He wanted to.

Praise the Lord for giving you these powerful words and for showing you these verses so you could share them with others. I am sharing your website with as many who will listen. I know of 4 or 5 women who are also believing for restoration since I told them of it. If it wasn't for the Lord giving these words to you, they would not be standing. Praise be to God.

I have had 3 or 4 ask for my testimony to put on their websites for encouragement and I said only if they made SURE that it was quite clear that God was the only one who was to be praised for this miracle!!!

Oh, Erin, thank you for your faithfulness to our Father. The Lord has been able to work through you to bring me back to HIM. What an awesome God we share."

We rejoice with you. Oh, what a blessing to see His mercies in action as He draws us to Him and more into His likeness!! What a privilege to learn obedience through the things which we suffer!

We are surrounded on every side by those who turn away from the truth. How good of God to allow us to share in His faithfulness by the grace that He bestows on those who diligently seek Him.

Thank you for sharing your testimony and for your faithfulness in ministering to others. Rev. 12:11 "And they overcame him because of the blood of the Lamb and because of the word of their testimony, and they did not love their life even to death."

She Prayed for the OW!

I read Friday's Q&A Column on praying for the OW so I decided that I should also pray for my husband's OW. I specifically asked God to help her to return to her own husband and that her husband would forgive her. My husband left the next day. On Saturday he moved in with her. ON THE VERY NEXT DAY, on Sunday, he called me and said she was leaving to go back to her husband!! Praise the Lord!!!! (To read the Q&A column and glean the wisdom that this woman read and applied, get the Questions and Answers book available through our ministry office that has transformed and restored many marriages.)

I realized for the very first time that she really does love her husband! My husband came back home and then he asked me if I would talk to her. I did, and she apologized for everything!!! I told her that I would pray for her and her husband. Then I thanked her for talking to me and she thanked me for listening!!!

My God makes even our enemies to be at peace with his people!! Just as the verse says! Glory to God!! Thank you for preaching the Good News that our God is able and willing to heal marriages and our lives!!

Marriage Restored in Kentucky!

In October my husband left me. There was not another woman involved, as far as a lover or adulterous other is concerned. However, my husband had a woman working as his secretary who liked controversy and she enjoyed causing problems with my husband and me. She did a great job and my husband became very dependent upon her, and it seemed to me that she had taken my place as his confidante. I was very hurt and when on her birthday he sent her an expensive bouquet of flowers and did not tell me (I found out from others) I reacted in a way that I know now I should not have. I had already reacted inappropriately many times when she rode with him to meetings out of town, etc. I thought that this should not happen since I disagreed with it! How foolish. Our marriage situation escalated until the end of October when he left me and filed for divorce!

I was devastated. My son was devastated, but my husband appeared to not care. I did all of the wrong things: I talked to others about our situation. I talked to my son about our situation. I called my husband, I argued with my husband, and basically I did everything wrong!!! I also was a Pharisee as I continued to attend our church along with our son and I had no problem crying in public so that everyone would see my pain!!

Somewhere around the first of December, I ordered the *How God Can and Will Restore Your Marriage* book, and I began to apply some of the principles. However, I guess I was not broken enough and I continued to argue with my husband and do the wrong things.

Then, in January I ordered the women's workbook *A Wise Woman* and wouldn't you know that the day that I received it in the mail I fell and hurt my back and was bedfast for about a week (along with my women's workbook)!! After reading *A Wise Woman*, I began to do better: I quit calling my husband; I began to tell the Lord Jesus Christ those things that I wanted my husband to know.

When my back felt better my father had a severe stroke and I spent numerous hours at the hospital with him (along with my women's workbook *A Wise Woman*). My father died soon after.

My husband is the local funeral director. Thus, I had to make the call to him. It so happened that he was en route to the nursing home to see us when my dad died.

During the visitation, funeral, family gatherings etc., my husband was right there as if everything was okay. But immediately after the funeral, he began to withdraw again. It was at this time that I ordered the 'Be Encouraged' audio tapes. (I wanted all of the videos at one time, but I couldn't afford them.) I listened to them nonstop!! With the tapes, along with the reinforcement of all of the principles in the *RYM* book and *A Wise Woman* workbook, I was finally able to let go of the situation and let God do it for me. And He did!!!

My husband began to call me!!! At first sporadically, then practically every day! Then he went out of town. Would you believe, he called me twice on his three-day excursion out of town?!

Upon his return, he called and asked to come out to the house. We were intimate because of the advice I had received from all of your material. Then again we were intimate. Then he called and asked me to go to dinner with him. Then he called and wanted to come out and watch an NCAA game, and we grilled out. The next day he came to church with our son (who picked him up) as I was already there. On that same Sunday, he told me that he was coming home!!! Praise the Lord!! That's when he asked me to go to the regional NCAA games in Philadelphia. Of course, I said 'yes!!!' We had a great time!!

It will soon be 2 weeks since he moved back in!!!! Both of us are so happy to be together again!! The secretary who seemed to cause so many of our problems appears to be looking for another job!! (Please pray she will!!) I had prayed the hedge of thorns prayer around her and also around my husband because I knew that even though he wasn't in adultery with her she was a wrong influence on him.

God is so, so, so GOOD!!!!

It is just a matter of waiting for his timing, our obedience and letting Him do it, instead of us trying to do it ourselves, to restore any marriage!!!!

Your materials helped me to bring my husband home!! Thank you so very, very much!! Please do not use my name, but you certainly can use my testimony!!!"

Marriage Restored after Five-Month Separation!!!

Thank you so much for being obedient and starting this ministry. It has truly helped me. All praises go to God our Father. My marriage was restored, after 5 months of separation!!! My husband called Wednesday at 1 a.m., asking if I would have the garage door open, because he was on his way home!!!! It worked because now I am trusting God and applying the principles that I learned. Thank you so much!!!!"

California Husband Home—Divorce Dropped!

Many things have happened since an online prayer buddy referred me to your website (and also sent me Erin's *RYM* book and *A Wise Woman* workbook for women).

When my husband returned from four months training, this past summer, he informed me he'd had an affair and had fallen in love with another woman. He told me emphatically that he believed our marriage was 'beyond counseling.' So, after much pleading and trying to reason I gave in to his wish (and prayed and cried my heart out to God).

That Monday is when I found your website. I submitted a prayer request that day. That very next Tuesday, my husband came home and had an 'emotional breakdown'! The woman that he had been involved with said she had to 'end' the affair and that he should work on saving our marriage!!!! My husband wasn't ready for that!!! He came to ME and I was here to comfort him in all the confusion he was feeling.

A week and a half later, my husband went in on his own for Christian marriage counseling. I asked how things were going with him. Any changes in his feelings towards her or me? He said, basically, 'no.' This questioning opened the door for him to fill me in on more details than I wanted to know about his adulterous relationship. This, more than ever, made me feel that our case was hopeless. With all that he said I felt I could never live up to being this type of person he thought he wanted. Again it was over!" (We advise to NEVER ask questions. When a spouse is being led by evil, all you will hear is evil and lies, which results in fear and defeat for all concerned!) "However, the VERY NEXT DAY, he said, 'I don't know, but I just can't go through with a divorce!! I can't deal with all the negative changes that would affect us all!'

My husband is home and wants to work on improving our marriage!!! To God be ALL THE GLORY!!

Marriage Restored after She Helped Two Others!!

I was separated from my husband for 16 months from a 23-year marriage. I sought God from the beginning. God led me to three ministries online after I prayed for His guidance. I got your book and read it fervently. I also passed the teachings I learned to many ladies that God brought to me. I watched God restore two marriages of ladies who read your book. One of the ladies has contacted you to translate your book into Spanish.

I would come home and read your website daily for encouragement through this journey. I ordered your cassettes and listened to them and was encouraged tremendously. It is all about obedience and dying to the flesh. I was hardest hit this last six weeks. The principles you showed me, God's Word, was the sword that I used to come against the attacks.

I got a 'suddenly' phone call from my husband last Sunday asking if I would come over and talk to him on Monday. On Monday, he said he wanted to COME HOME!! God had allowed him to lose everything, even his health. He moved out of the OW house and home to his family Tuesday morning!!!!

He came home wounded but God is not through yet. The first day he was home I was applying first aid to his feet where ants had bitten him. As I did that I thought of Jesus washing his disciples' feet. I considered it an honor.

God told me a long time ago that it would be like childbirth and it was true. I don't remember the pain, only the miracle.

My two boys, 10 and 11, ran out in the yard screaming 'Daddy!' when he came home. I knew then and there I was truly blessed!!! It was all worth it!!

I know that now that my husband is home, it is the time to pray harder then ever. The devil is mad, but God is greater. I have reached a new level so new devil!!!

I have not asked my husband any questions, just listened to what he chose to tell me. That is a big growth from the old me.

He recently had major surgery and I was so hurt I couldn't take care of him. Now that he is home I feel so blessed to be able to care for him.

I am still being tested! Last night, he said he wanted to go out and see some of the men at the bar. I didn't say a word. Instead, after he left, I went in and prayed that he would not want to be there any more. He came home ONE hour later and said he felt bad for leaving and wanted to come home!!! PRAISE GOD!!

God is still giving me miracles each day, showing me the changes he is making in my husband. These changes don't happen all at once. As I said, I am still being tested and am still applying what I have learned. What God has started He will finish.

Everyone at work has noticed my glow. I told them my MIRACLE came home!!!!

Praise God for both of you and what you are doing for the Lord. Your reward in heaven will be great.

Marriage Restored in Pennsylvania!!

I'm writing to encourage other women that God IS REAL! My husband and I have been separated for three years. During the course of these three years the Lord has dealt with me and changed my heart. My husband and I have grown so much closer. We are closer now then we've ever been.

My husband was living with his sister, but she decided to get a new apartment. Even though he knew that she was moving, he said he did not have ample time to save and find a place. He eventually found an apartment, but it was not ready before his sister moved and had all of the utilities shut off.

Would you believe, I came home to find my husband asleep in our bed?!! The Lord had directed me to give him his keys back last year!!! He has been there ever since! He said that he would only be here until his furniture arrived. But he now has a furnished apartment and is still finding excuses, like not having sheets for his bed, and not having the money to buy any!!! Every time he talks about the apartment, and all the things he needs, he gets down in his spirit.

God has caused him to become so comfortable at our home that he says he has no desire to leave! I want to praise God because He has humbled me!! And because of the humbling, He allowed my heart to soften. If I was still bitter and holding unforgiveness he would have never considered coming home!

PRAISE GOD BECAUSE HE IS FAITHFUL!!!!!!!

Marriage Restored after a Hard Ten Months!

This woman sent many emails to us for "prayer" only. For many months, I had no idea what her situation was. She REALLY covered her husband's nakedness—even from me! But I KNEW that a humble and praying woman would eventually receive her miracle. Well, here it is! All praise be to God!!

I don't even know where to begin...I guess, first I'd like to say that God continued to help me stand, and believe, and rejoice. He continued to encourage me and gave me manna along the way.

Back in April God removed the OW from my husband's life and brought him to repentance. At that time, he realized he wanted to make things work, but didn't know how to get her off his mind. He had a box of her stuff in his closet for several months. Another 'pray and don't speak moment'! God moved mountains on our behalf once again.

Restoration was slow, but steady. I was so grateful when he was back sharing our bed. Intimacy was lacking for a while, but God continued to restore! Hallelujah!

My husband recently ordered a new wedding band as his was stolen. I am very, very pleased!! Another 'pray and don't speak moment'!

Erin, God has been sooo faithful! He is still working in us both, continuing to heal and restore! Sometimes the enemy will throw doubt, but I am able to recognize it now! It was a long 10-month trial! I am sooo grateful it is over! But I am also grateful we went through it (although I would never have chosen it!).

We truly have a Sovereign God, a merciful God, an Almighty God and a loving God!! There is so much more that I could write. I have really described this miracle in brief!

One more thing. God has been bringing more women into my life with struggling marriages. Please pray for me as I witness and share, and as we seek God's will, not man's. Please, praise God with me, and if we come to mind, please continue to pray for us.

Marriage Restored—Thank You RMI !!

I wanted to thank you for the materials that you have produced. I was on the right track with the Lord even before receiving some of your materials, but the videos and *A Wise Woman* particularly helped to clarify what the Word said, and especially to encourage me during the darkest moments of my life.

Some of the advice Erin gave me was hard to implement, but I walked in faith and did it! I lost a lot of 'friends' along the way, and almost all of the Christians in my life thought I was nuts. They may still! I just know after 9 months of doing things the way the Bible commands, my husband is no longer with the other woman but at home with us.....every night...right after work (this has never been in 12 years).

He asked me to quit my job (that I started out of obedience to him) and he also quit his part-time job. We are continuing to homeschool our children, and the Lord has chosen to bless us with an 8th baby (a real surprise to me!!!). I refuse to believe when people in our fellowship say it is not a 'good' time in our marriage for a baby, since the Lord Himself has chosen it for us. My husband is happier about the baby than I ever remember him being.

Thank you, Restore Ministries, for uplifting me, and for calling me to follow in what the Word says is true. You never asked me to follow your own ideas....only my Savior, and his Word. That is why your ministry is different, and why it WORKS! I know that your entire office prayed for us during our final and most difficult battle, and I am truly grateful for our restoration.

Adultery Over! Wife Says, "Come on Home!"

God is Good! My wife has been involved in adultery for almost two years with a guy she works with. This is the second time she has been involved in adultery in the past three years. She completed divorce papers in April, but had not gone forward in signing them. Yesterday my wife informed me that she is ending her relationship with the other guy today! She also said that she will allow God to restore our marriage!! She asked me to come back to our home!!!

The materials I received from you, *How God Will Restore Your Marriage* and *A Wise Man*, were a Godsend. Also, visiting your web site daily for the past 7 months was a blessing and an inspiration. I was able to draw so much from others and truly see how God was working in their lives.

The key things that God taught me, and it truly was from God as my previous personality would not have done these things, were to humble myself before God and my family and not let pride make my decisions. To fast and pray and take spiritual authority in Christ and do battle.

One point in the book that I took to heart was that my battle was not against my wife but against the enemy attacking her and our family. I learned to pray feverishly and to rely on the Word of the Lord to keep me focused. Also, I was taught the power of prayer; I will never again underestimate the power of prayer and others who pray for you! When two or more agree in prayer it shall be done!!

I learned to be patient, which was the hardest thing of all for me to learn. I always wanted things to happen faster and would then do things in the flesh, which would only make matters worse. God's timing is not my timing, but God's work is eternal.

I also learned to love unconditionally. Love my wife as Christ loves His church. Through this entire process, God has strengthened my love for my wife.

And lastly, TRUST GOD with everything; when I totally submitted to Him, and gave Him my marriage, restoration started.

Dan and Erin, I pray for God's continued blessing on your ministry and your marriage. I will also continue to pray for those seeking God to restore their marriages.

Friend Shares Faith—Marriage Restored!

I gave all of your materials to a friend just after her husband left home. I won't go into detail but the situation looked horrible. Because of the material, I knew the right things to say to encourage her and help her to stay on track regardless of the bleakness of the circumstances. She read the book and watched the videotapes. It was hard for her, but she stayed with it. I was confident because of what I learned in the book and I promised her that God would restore her marriage if she did not listen to her friends and go the way of the world. She called me on New Year's Day to say her husband had returned home. Alleluia!

I thank God I had the material. I was so sure because I believed what I read. I'm grateful to God. Now I just pray that she will continue to reinforce and practice what she learned in the books and tapes. I know, oh too well, how the enemy still looks to destroy the marriage even after the spouse has returned home.

As far as my marriage is concerned, it seems as though God has given me the gift of faith. Also, the Lord has been so gracious by letting me have such a great cloud of witnesses of restored marriages. I know the Lord is working on making me the wife my husband needs me to be and to be the person He has called me to be in Him.

Dan and Erin, I do pray for your family to be kept and shielded by the Lord and that He would continue to prosper you and your relationship in every way.

Thanks!

Awesome Restoration in New Zealand!!!

This man came to our website seeking help. After getting the men's book, he wrote to our Q&A Column with this:

My wife has left. What do I do about seeing our children? I agree with your books on my marriage. The law in NZ is that if I don't contest the custody order then I won't see the children until they are 16. My wife has alleged abuse by me of the children. Should I not fight to see our 7 (age 1-13) children? If I don't go to court and she does then she will have no legal obligation to let me ever see our children again."

This man had not seen his seven children for over SIX MONTHS!!

We advised him to trust the Lord, RELEASE his attorney and not DEFEND himself against the allegations. The magnitude of his decisions and his ultimate trust in the Lord has brought about an AWESOME blessing. Here it is:

After he agreed that trusting the Lord was the ONLY WAY, he experienced a tremendous peace. He was able to work his farm better. Then he called and asked for a large packet of materials to be sent to him to give to all the men he knew who also needed help.

A few weeks later, he wrote about all the Lord was doing in his life. I felt impressed to tell him to agree with Dan and me in prayer that "his wife would need his help and call him." The laws in effect said that she could contact him, but that he would be thrown in jail if he contacted her! We agreed and prayed. Three days later, we received this praise report:

Last night at 7.15 I got a phone call from my wife. First contact with her for just over 6 months!!! I couldn't believe it!! She rang ME! You said you would pray she had a need. She has no money and wasn't going to give the children any Christmas at all. But she (God) decided to ring me only ONE time and ask if I would send her some money for the children. She then talked to me for 7 and a half hours. Yes, till 2.45 this morning!!! I was in a state of shock for much of the call, but thanks to your books etc., must have done some right things for her to talk so long.

I didn't once say 'I love you' even at the end. If she had said it then I would have. I didn't even ask if I could see the children or her or anything like that so there was no pressure for her to do anything for the money. She gave me her address to send some money to (I agreed but she didn't give an amount — left that up to me).

She told me most of what had happened to her and the children during the past 6 months. At about 1 o'clock she said she hadn't meant to talk for so long and then carried on for a lot longer. I tried to listen to her and agree wherever I could. We had a great talk about the Word and God and the good things of God.

There was no mention of another call or anything. I didn't even hint that I was wanting to see her or talk again. When we were talking I wasn't sure if I should be asking her for forgiveness yet or if it was the right time. I couldn't remember if you said I should as soon as possible or not. Because I was unsure I didn't say anything. ???

Her talk about her walk seemed pretty good. She said a lot about rebellion and how bad it was and things like that. How can what she was saying line up with the Word and yet in the area of marriage she can't see it (YET?????)

She also seemed to accept that the marriage was over and it was going to be like her parents (who split when she was 2 and are both on their 3rd marriage). Then she said, 'I don't want it to end like my parents.' ???? This was a miracle!

And yes, I am thanking God. Is there anything I should do now other than pray that God continues to turn her heart back to me?????. This is the scary time because one wrong word could wreck everything. I believe she will ring again. After all she rang once that I didn't expect. (Yes, I know by faith I should have, but after the place I got to last night I no longer did.)

I will try to read through both the books again, today, in case she rings again tonight, but I have a very busy day on the farm (hay time).

I tried not to say anything bad about anything she was doing with the children or the house that she has bought.

I want to praise God and tell everyone who has been praying, but I feel I shouldn't tell anyone (how not to) because she didn't give me any permission to share that she had rung me.

Must go. I got 2 and a half hours sleep and am late leaving for the milking now. I just wanted to share this. Is this awesome or what? I know it's God!! Bless you heaps and heaps.

He did give her a substantial check for the children's Christmas. Then a new test came:

My wife rang again today. Praise God!!!! She wants to work out the money between ourselves and not involve the lawyer. She has already run up $15,000 + legal bills and doesn't want any more. She asked if I would pay off a gift that she got of $30,000 to put a deposit down on the house she bought. She wanted me to give her $100 a week for 6 years. She wants me to keep the farm for the children. She was talking about a divorce and not sure whether to carry on with it. I think she realizes she can't marry again in God's eyes.

I said 'yes' I liked her principle, but could I pray about it before deciding. What I want to do and believe God wants me to do. (If you agree then please pray that my wife will accept it.) I want to give her the $30,000 as a gift so she can not owe these other people. She was not happy because they are already telling her what to do even though it was supposed to be a gift. I can get the money (GOD is great) as a gift to me (real gift) and no one will ever know how she got the money. Is it good for me to do as much as possible for her money wise???

Also I want to offer to pay her mortgage. I can take this from the farm as part of my personal drawings and no one will ever know what it is being used for except my wife and God. Does this sound right???? If I haven't heard from you before she rings again (I believe that she will, GOD is working big time) then this is the offer I will make her.

Also, I want to offer that if she needs money for anything else to ask me first. This seems right to me. Am I right in all this? Should I be doing as much to help as I can ???

She has long-term plans for everything, but I know God has started turning her heart back to me. Why else would she be ringing?

She said today that she has never stopped loving me. I think God is so awesome and awesome.

Here are just three more of his praise reports:

Do you know how awesome it is to pick up the phone and hear 'Hi, it's me here' on the other end! After over 6 months of not hearing her voice and now I've had my 3rd phone call!!! We talked for 4 hours until she was late getting the children from school. Thank you for all your prayers. I can never repay you but God can.

My wife came around tonight for two hours with all 7 children!!! She didn't seem totally comfortable. She talked and came inside and had a coffee. The children got heaps of their things and loaded up the van. It was awesome! Before today, I hadn't seen her or 4 of the children for 6 and a half months. Then in town, and here at our house tonight. This praise report seems impossible—it was just 6 days ago when I talked with her for the first time in 6+ months.

AWESOME AWESOME AWESOME—GOD can surely move fast!!

Then we got this:

When she turned up with all 7 children and their 2 dogs and they all got out of the van it was neat. Then them all staying so long and coming in was awesome. It was hard to not say anything about us!! But I managed. The children all talked to me and shared heaps. As you can guess with 7 of them it was hard to keep track of all the conversations and I always seemed to have one on my lap and another one trying to get on. Praise God!! Do you know how nice all this is?! Bless you for your Godly advice and prayers! Thank you!!

Then we got word that they were either spending time TOGETHER at the farm or her house, but ALWAYS together!! Within about 6 weeks we got news...

Number 8 is on the way!!!

Because of her pregnancy and her being tired with all the children, she was open to more and more help from her husband. Then we got this....

IT'S OFFICIAL—Praise the Lord!!

My WIFE IS HOME!! She has stopped getting the government money and fully moved back. Praise God!!! Now we are relying on God to supply our needs and sort out the rest of our situations. It is official. My marriage has been restored!!!!

Thank you. Thank you. Thank you!

We don't know what the future holds but we are together as a family and that's the most important thing! If anyone has any doubts about your books working, then they haven't tried them, because I can state that they work perfectly! It's only about 4 months from when I started getting to your principles (GOD's) and they have proven true in every way!!!!

I thank you again. You are awesome in God and may He bless you and all you do.

All the questions this man asked and applied related to one of the principles from the Word of God and the course for men hoping for restoration. A man is to protect and therefore can offer support much more than a woman can Biblically.

Update: *Number 8, Meadow Erin, a beautiful baby girl was not their last! Number 10 is now on his/ her way!*

Death Threat Turns into Salvation and Restoration!!!

"My husband and I married too young because I was pregnant. When we were both just 20 years old, we had three little babies to take care of. My husband still hung around with his friends from high school and stayed high on cocaine and later started shooting heroin. As our money got tight, my husband became violent with me. Many times he would hold a gun to my head and tell me he was going to kill me.

I didn't believe in God back then, but I needed someone to help me. One night I heard on the television about a place where 'God had showed up and there were miracles happening. I got on my knees in our living room and asked God to help us get there.

But at the very same time I was praying, my husband was hiding high on cocaine behind our house in some woods. He had his loaded rifle with him and he was waiting for me and the kids to go to bed so that he could come in and kill all of us.

I didn't know he was there so I put the kids to bed and then went to bed myself. That night was the first time in months that I slept in peace. After I was asleep my husband came in the back door and came into our bedroom, but I didn't hear him and then he pointed the rifle at me, but he didn't shoot me. He told me the next day that 'Something or Someone stopped me.' He said that afterwards he went outside and cried.

When I woke up in the morning there he was sleeping on the couch. I told him that we all needed to go to this church I had heard about and he said okay!!!! This was the first miracle that happened.

We loaded up our car that morning and I turned on the Christian radio station (my husband never once said to turn it off!—another miracle) and we headed for the church. It was the longest trip of my life!!! Every few miles, my husband had to stop and throw up. But finally we made it—praise God, praise God, HE IS SO GOOD!!!

We had to wait several hours until the evening service and I kept wondering if he would split before we ever got inside. But he didn't and when the doors opened we were the first people inside. At the end of the service my husband went up and prayed at the altar. I saw him cry for the first time since we were married.

When he stood up, he was not the same man!!!! Glory to God, praise Jesus. He wanted to stay another night so we slept in our car in the church parking lot. In the morning we went to get our boys a haircut. My husband sat there reading the Bible they gave him at the church!!!!

I never would have believed it if I had not seen it with my own eyes. An older woman sat down next to him and they started talking about Jesus. She was not a Christian. When my boys were done my husband said he needed his haircut. This was another miracle!!! His hair was very long (about halfway down his back!!) but he got it all buzzed off with just an inch left.

All I can say is my husband is not the same man I married!! When we got home he went into the bedroom to read his Bible, then he came out with our TV set and threw it in the dumpster!!!

Even though my husband didn't officially leave me, our marriage is a restored marriage thanks to Jesus Christ. Thank you Lord Jesus!!! You are awesome!!!"

Restoration from Atlanta!

"I have a restored marriage that I wanted to write to you about. One night I said, 'I'm leaving. I can't stay in this marriage any longer' to my sister-in-law. But as I got up I heard the Lord speak to me, 'Don't go.' So I sat down. My sister-in-law looked at me and said, 'I thought you said you were leaving?' Then I told her, 'I can't leave him.'

My husband was always high on whatever he could get his hands on—drugs, booze or sniffing glue. He worked in a machinery shop with stuff that he could get caught in. I must repent that sometimes I wished it would happen just to end the nightmare we were living! He was a good guy when we married, but after our son was born severely retarded, he sought comfort by finding something to numb the pain. But I turned to God when he turned to drugs.

But then, two nights after I had heard the Lord tell me not to go, God visited my husband at work. He told me that he was so wasted that he didn't even remember being at work; then all of a sudden he was completely sober. God spoke to him and told him to go to Bible college."

Tragedy Turns to Triumph!!

"When my wife and I met, I was living in rebellion. I was very young, we both were, and when I told my parents our plans to marry, they did all they could to change my mind. But instead, we eloped and my parents cut us off financially. A month after our marriage my wife was pregnant. The new baby, along with our financial stress and our estrangement from family, caused a lot of arguments.

I was not walking with the Lord, though I knew Him, and my wife was an unbeliever. The fights escalated to abuse. We physically fought and there was a lot of emotional and verbal abuse as well. Even though my wife was very attractive, because of our arguing, she was no longer attractive to me. This affected our intimacy and took a major toll on our marriage. When I mentioned divorce I was surprised that my wife was all for it. When we made plans for her to move out, things actually improved a little—maybe because relief was in sight or maybe because we were finally agreeing on something.

Just after she moved out and we divorced, I knew that I had made a mistake. I went to a Promise Keepers meeting and was deeply convicted. I knew I needed to be the spiritual leader of our home and I had failed miserably. When I spoke to my wife about my desire to be a spiritual leader and to get back together, she was totally opposed. I was shocked. I had not expected her to respond that way. The months of rejection that followed were very painful for me. But through this I knew that I had a call on my life and that I had been running from God for years.

During this time I found a song that really ministered to me. It spoke of being a spiritual leader. One day I asked my wife if she would 'just listen to it.' She did, and it began to soften her heart toward me. We decided to move back in together. My parents were very opposed, so once again, they cut us off financially. I knew we should be married, but my wife did not see the need.

During this time my wife became pregnant with our second child. This solidified my commitment to my wife and my family. I just could not imagine another man raising my children! It had to be me! A tragedy happened that really broke me and got me to the point of complete surrender to the Lord. A young man who I had known in high school had recently and radically become a Christian. Because of his talent in sports, he was well known. On the way to speak at an

FCA (Fellowship of Christian Athletes) meeting, his plane crashed and he was killed. Somehow this tragedy brought everything into its proper prospective. Just two weeks later my wife and I were married again. We had a church wedding and invited family and friends this time.

My wife is now a Christian who loves the Lord. She is beautiful on the inside and the outside. I am presently studying to go into the ministry. My opinion about and against divorce is really radical after living through all this. I am adamant against all divorce for any reason and believe people should remain unmarried with the hope of restoration. I believe that I will be able to effectively minister to those facing divorce, separation and rejection since I have been there. I honestly believe that this was all caused by spiritual problems that manifested in marriage problems. Once we get ourselves right spiritually our marriages will also be right.

There are MANY more testimonies that are posted on our website! Five as an introduction, five more to confirm God's ability, and then 33 webpages just to START!

As this book got larger and larger we were unable to keep up with printing all of them in a book!

What you have read is just a *small sample* of the POWER and FAITHFULNESS of God that are told through countless restored marriages!

Don't let ANYONE try to convince you that God cannot restore YOUR marriage! It is a lie. The TRUTH is that He is MORE THAN ABLE!!

Need Help?

We would like to invite you to join our Restoration Fellowship. We have received more praise reports about this area of our ministry and it is growing by word of mouth. When you join our fellowship on the Internet, you receive an ePartner. This is an encouragement, prayer and accountability partner. Men with men and women with women who are going through the same situation and who have a heart to restore their marriages. Go to www.MarrigeHelpOnline.com.

We now have a book that goes into more detail and gives you more help in answering your many questions: *Questions and Answers*. This book has over 300 questions answered through Scripture to the most difficult marital dilemmas you face. This will answer most, if not all, the questions you may now have in terms of the practical walking out of the principles that you have just read or will read.

If you are bombarded with others telling you that your situation is hopeless, I would encourage you to order another testimony book, *By the Word of Their Testimony!* This book (as you have just read) is filled with testimonies of hopeless marriages that God miraculously restored. If your parents, friends, pastor, or coworkers think you are crazy to try to restore your marriage, then give them a "By the Word of Their Testimony!!" book and watch them begin to **encourage** you rather than **discourage** you!

You can order any of the book mentioned by contacting our ministry at 1-800-397-0800 or at **MarrigeHelpOnline.com**.

We look forward to the opportunity to help you through our website and Home Fellowships that are posted on our site.

About the Authors

Dan and Erin Thiele have been blessed to be the parents of four boys, Dallas, Axel, Easton, and Cooper, and three girls, Tyler, Tara and Macy. Erin's faith for her marriage was founded on the rock during her struggle to restore her own marriage. Dan had left her for another woman and eventually divorced her.

Restore Ministries was begun when Erin searched every denomination in her area but was unable to find the help or hope that she needed.

Since Dan's return in 1991, Erin has written many other books with Erin's distinctive style of using the Scriptures to minister to the brokenhearted and the spiritual captives. "He sent **His Word** and healed them, and delivered them from their destructions."

This is another powerful testimony to God's promises and His faithfulness. "For as many as may be the promises of God, in Him they are **Yes**; wherefore also by Him is our **Amen** to the glory of God through us" (2 Cor. 1:20).

Is Your Marriage... Crumbling? Hopeless? Or Ended in Divorce?

At Last There's Hope!

Have you been searching for marriage help? It's not by chance, nor is it by coincidence, that you are here. God has heard your cry for help in your marriage dilemma. He predestined this DIVINE APPOINTMENT to give you the hope that you so desperately need right now!

If you have been told that your marriage is hopeless or that without your spouse's help your marriage cannot be restored, then you need to read the testimonies of those who once had "seemingly" hopeless marriages that are now restored. God is MORE than able to restore ANY marriage, including YOURS!

We know and understand what you are going through since WE, and MANY others who have come to our ministry for help, have a restored marriage and family! No matter what others have told you, your marriage is NOT hopeless!! We KNOW, after fourteen years of ministry, that God is able to restore ANY marriage, even YOURS!

If you have been crying out to God for more help, someone who understands, someone you can talk to, then we invite you to join our RMI Restoration Fellowship. Since beginning this fellowship, we have seen more marriages restored on a regular basis than we ever thought possible!

Who are we and what are we hoping to do?

Restore Ministries helps those who have found themselves in a hopeless situation: men and women whose spouse is in adultery, has left them, has filed for divorce, are already divorced or any other seemingly impossible marital situation. They have often sought help, but everyone (many times even their pastors) has told them it was hopeless. We believe that no marriage is hopeless—regardless of the circumstances. We offer hope, help and encouragement through our website, our Internet and Home Fellowships, our resources.

Erin Thiele founded Restore Ministries in 1990 a year after her husband, Dan, left her for another woman. Even her own pastor (and all the other pastors she spoke to from many denominations) told her that her marriage was hopeless. Yet after seeking the Lord and searching His Word, she knew that it was the Lord's desire to restore her marriage. She promised the Lord that if He would restore her marriage to Dan she would spend the rest of her life proclaiming the truth that "nothing is impossible with God." Just two years after Dan left, and even after Dan divorced her, the Lord kept His word and restored Erin's hopeless marriage "suddenly" in January of 1991. This ministry is the fulfillment of her promise to the Lord.

Erin's ministry to women grew beyond her local area after her first book *How God Can and Will Restore Your Marriage* was published by a Christian publisher and sent all over the world in 1996. Three years later the Lord called her husband, Dan, to join her in ministry when they printed and sent out the men's version of the same book. These books soon became the publisher's most requested books (over their 600 other publications). Restore Ministries began to self-publish their resources when the publisher told the Thieles that they were unable to keep up with the demand for their books.

In 1999 their ministry went up on the Internet and Restore Ministries became an international ministry overnight. Their ministry grew at a phenomenal rate at this point; each month for the first six months on the Internet they doubled or tripled the number of men and women they were ministering to.

In 2001, when they were unable to keep up with the growth, the Thieles established Restoration Fellowship to minister more effectively to the needs of those seriously seeking restoration. Just a year later, in 2002 the fellowship grew to over 400 committed members and increases by an average of five members a day with members from all over the world.

Often accused of being extreme, radical, out-of-balance or legalistic, the message in all of their resources is founded firmly on the Word of God, encouraging those seeking restoration to live the message that Jesus proclaimed, beginning with the familiar Beatitudes.

Their ministry teaches the good news of God's Word to bring healing to the brokenhearted, comfort to those in pain, and freedom to prisoners of despondency and sin through the truth of His Word, giving them the hope that is "against all hope" through the Power of Jesus Christ, the Mighty Counselor and Good Shepherd.

To date Dan and Erin have published 10 books and 22 videos in an effort to minister to the hurting all over the world with the intent of creating a deeper and more intimate walk with the Lord that results in the hurting healed, the bound freed, the lost saved and broken marriages restored.

They minister to men and women from 15 countries including Switzerland, Hong Kong, Singapore, New Zealand, Sweden, Philippines, Brazil and Germany, with large followings in Australia, Canada, and Africa. Both the men and women's books have been translated into Spanish, the women's book into Portuguese and is currently being translated into the Filipino language of Tagalog, Afrikaans, Malayalam the language of So. India, and finally French.

Jesus said that you "will know them by their fruits." Their book *By the Word of Their Testimony* is filled with testimonies of hopeless marriages that were restored, marriages that give glory to God and to the Power of His Word. This book grows at such a phenomenal rate that they are unable to keep up with reprinting due to the number of testimonies that pour into their office.

If you have any doubt about the validly of their ministry, get a copy of this awesome book. It will show you not only hopeless marriages that were restored, but more importantly, it will show you men and women who have been completely transformed into God-lovers and are now committed on-fire Christians, many of whom were saved through this ministry. This ministry was founded and continues to grow on the premise that "if He be lifted up, He will draw all men to Himself" and "the Lord will share His glory with no man."

Restoration Fellowship

Restoration is a "narrow road"—look around, most marriages end in divorce! But if your desire is for a restored marriage, then our Restoration Fellowship is designed especially for you!

Since beginning this fellowship, we have seen marriages restored more consistently than we ever thought possible.

Let us help you stay committed to "working with God" to restore your marriages. Restoration Fellowship can offer you the help, guidance, and support you will need to stay on the path that leads to victory—*your* marriage restored!

Let us assure you that Erin's marriage was restored by GOD (through His Word) as she sought Him to lead her, teach her, guide her and transform her through His Holy Spirit. This, too, is all *you* need for *your* marriage to be restored.

However, God continues to lead people to our ministry and fellowship to gain the faith, support and help that so many say that they needed in their time of crisis.

"I want you to know how MUCH the RMI resources, the fellowship and the website have meant to me. Yes, I will candidly say all you NEED is the Word of God to restore your marriage, but RMI shines a brilliant light on that Word with so much encouragement. I really believe that this would be a much longer more painful journey with a LOT more detours if I had not had the resources of RMI to go back to again and again, leading me to a genuine love for God."
K.H. in North Carolina

Membership Requirement

There is only one requirement to becoming a member: You must **have** and **read** the ***three*** *required resources. We require each of these resources because they are vitally important to your restoration.

To help you get started, we have grouped our *required resources for membership into Membership Packets that will help you get your marriage out of crisis, have given you a 20% Member Discount to use on your Membership Packet, and a FREE membership to our fellowship!

All of our Membership Packets include:

1. The ***Restore Your Marriage*** book. Read this book first. We have heard so many testimonies from men and women who said this book gave them the hope that they so desperately needed, and if you've read the testimonies on our site, you know that it has saved countless marriages. Learn the truth—your marriage is NOT hopeless! $12.99

"All I know now is that ALL the things in this book are true. My spouse has not only returned home, but our marriage is a lot better than it was when we first met. My spouse is happy and calls me three times a day just to say 'I love you'!!! We go to the movies and the mall holding hands. Well, Restore Ministries, thanks for

teaching me how to be the Christian God has called me to be." M.H.

"My spouse said, "I don't love you anymore; I want to be single and date." That's when I bought this book. I followed the directions and two weeks ago I returned home to find my spouse's car who had returned home! God has restored my marriage and my spouse and I are so happy!" G.J.

2. The ***By the Word of Their Testimony!*** The Bible says that we will overcome the wicked by "the word of their testimony." To be able to "endure to the end" and "finish the course," we require that you read and reread these awesome and powerful testimonies every day to build your faith in God's ability to finish the good work He began in you, your spouse and your marriage! $9.99. (Since you have this book, you can replaced it with another one of our resources when purchasing a packet.)

"When I read the testimonies of restored marriages, tears just streamed down my face! Everyone kept telling me it was hopeless, but I just couldn't let myself believe it. Now, after reading so many testimonies I KNOW that God will restore my marriage too!" D.D.

"Others doubted that God wanted to restore my marriage, but once they read enough of the testimonies in this book they got on my side!" K.W.

3. *****A Wise Woman*** or *****A Wise Man***. This book picks up where the *Restore Your Marriage* book leaves off. Neither Dan nor Erin had no clue that their house was on sinking sand. However, through the application of God's principles, which are documented in each of these books, their marriage and family were restored. This book will also help you get your home ready for your spouse to return. $19.99.

"I found this book thoroughly amazing. To be honest with you I found that this workbook was much more helpful than the first book. Obviously that was amazing in it's own way, but I really got to see the mistakes I am making which is a big issue for me and it just has so much more detail. I can honestly say that this book is a must for everyone after the Restore Your Marriage *book."* Hilary **Restored** in South Africa

"A Wise Man is truly a classic piece of Biblical inspiration from two of His anointed—Dan and Erin. The insight and wisdom it

clearly dispenses, coupled with the Restore Your Marriage *book, and second only to the written Word of God, were the most incredibly eye-opening texts that I have ever read in my life. I am still amazed at how penetrating the information is, and how much it helped to begin the transformation process in me. I will never be the same again, and hallelujah for that! Jim in Ohio*

4. Plus on your very first order you can use your **20% Member Discount** (a savings of $8.59).

5. Your final total, using your New Member Discount, will be just **$34.38**.

6. And to help you even further, when you purchase a packet *we* will pay your $35.00 Membership Fee!

7. As an additional bonus, we give you Dan and Erin's Testimony on tape FREE (a $4.99 value).

So, to become a new Member, you pay only **$35.00** (plus shipping) and receive **$82.96** worth of resources and services!

But, you say, you have some of these resources already?

No problem!

We'll let you make other selections of the same value in exchange for any one of these resources.

The easiest way to APPLY for membership and choose any one of the Membership Packets to receive your $35 Membership—FREE is to purchase your packet from our website RestoreMinistries.net. However, if you do NOT have Internet access your host or hostess will be happy to purchase them for you.

When using a credit card, simply order the packet over the Internet at RestoreMinistries.net and fill out the application to join.

*When using a check or money order, include the Membership Packet Fee of $35 (shipping, which is approximately $7 when shipped in the continental U.S. or $43) and then REQUEST an application to be sent in your order.

As a **Home Fellowship** member, you be invited to attend all the Home Fellowship meetings, which will give you special help, support and guidance in restoring your marriage.

You will paired with an **Encouragement Partner** "ePartner," which is another man or woman who is seeking restoration for his/her marriage (men with men, women with women). During the meetings and throughout the week via get-togethers or by phone, you and your ePartner will encourage and pray for each other. We receive so many testimonies from members who say that this has become their most utilized member benefit.

Praise the Lord—I heard from my husband after 18 months of silence! He called and invited me over to his house! This came about after God paired me with my new ePartner. Together, our powerful prayers were heard! Donna

At each **Home Fellowship** meeting we focus on:

- Promises
- Prayer
- Praise
- Fellowship
- And Renewing our minds in Biblical restoration principles via taped lessons.

As a **Home Fellowship** member, you can view the many video/DVD series, which include: the "Be Encouraged!" series; Q&A video series: Alluring & Unconditional Love, Addiction & Submission, Husband Returning or Already Home, Facing Divorce, and Queen Esther; and/or A Wise Woman series.

As a Internet Fellowship Member, you will have access to the "members only" section of our website. You will be given a member number, which will enable you to access special help, support and guidance. For all the MANY benefits, simply visit our website and login with your member number!

Join Restoration Fellowship

"My husband did not talk to me for the first six months after he left but God continued His faithfulness to help me not give up; He used

Restore Ministries to encourage me – I could not have made it without you." Michelle, **Restored** in Wisconsin

"God led me to Restore Ministries, which provided the encouragement I needed at exactly the time I needed it. All of the resources you required for membership helped me. They gave me encouragement, hope and a sense of peace. Stephanie, **Restored** in Kansas

"I cannot thank God enough for His unfailing mercies and for restoring our marriage after five years of marital troubles and separation! I was on the website every day for encouragement. After seeing the changes in me, my husband started to change, he held me and told me he was sorry for all that happened, that that he loved me and always did despite everything!" Lina, **Restored** in Ghana

Join our Restoration Fellowship TODAY and us help YOU **restore YOUR** marriage.

To Join

Visit our website today at

MarriageHelpOnLine.com

Orderline USA: 1-800-397-0800
International Orderline: 417-581-8221

RMI Fellowship: 1-888-721-5253
International Fellowship: 417-485-8111

A

Abraham *175*
adulterous*123, 159, 192, 211, 224, 227*
adultery*5, 8, 11, 13, 116, 134, 155, 157, 158, 164, 169, 190, 211, 213, 226, 231*
affair *222, 223, 227*
agape *105*
alcohol *216*
angry *8, 152, 154, 158, 169, 187*
anniversary *155, 183*
another woman*5, 12, 61, 116, 142, 156, 170, 224, 227, 243*
arguing *138, 160, 240*
argumentative *77, 79*
ask, and you shall receive *187*
Assembly of God *148*
At Last There's Hope *171, 209*
attorney*4, 13, 157, 198, 204, 205, 233*

B

baby*123, 124, 125, 160, 198, 231, 237, 240*
backslidden *63*
Be Encouraged*57, 58, 79, 159, 167, 225*
Bible*2, 12, 62, 63, 79, 94, 104, 105, 127, 137, 152, 202, 217, 231, 239*
bitter.*8, 124, 169, 187, 197, 207, 229*
bitter as wormwood *124*
blood of Jesus *76*
bondage *123*
breakthrough *73, 127*
broken*6, 115, 129, 155, 191, 195, 214, 219, 225*
brokenness *150*
by faith *61*
By the Word of Their Testimony *7*

C

called to peace *11*
cancer *167, 203*
Catholic *148*

children*11, 13, 57, 58, 61, 62, 77, 78, 122, 134, 135, 143, 155, 156, 157, 158, 165, 166, 169, 174, 177, 193, 196, 210, 213, 214, 215, 217, 218, 231, 233, 234, 235, 236, 237, 240*
Christians*7, 11, 187, 198, 209, 218, 219, 231*
church*6, 11, 73, 115, 123, 128, 129, 152, 153, 156, 160, 164, 187, 190, 193, 194, 196, 198, 199, 200, 202, 206, 208, 211, 213, 225, 226, 232, 238, 241*
confessed *125, 189, 194, 219*
contentious*8, 79, 93, 115, 135, 138, 147, 150, 156, 169, 183, 213, 219*
contentiousness *77, 78*
controlling *8, 115, 169*
conviction *192*
counseling*8, 128, 153, 154, 219, 227*
covenant *165, 169*
criticizing *169*
cry out to God *167, 174*

D

Dan*1, 2, 5, 6, 7, 8, 12, 57, 58, 73, 116, 121, 122, 123, 125, 136, 146, 148, 159, 165, 166, 168, 179, 199, 201, 203, 206, 232, 233, 234, 243*
Daniel 3:25 .... *12*
defeat *227*
Delight yourself in the Lord *61*
desires of your heart *61*
despair *8, 152, 155*
didn't love me *128, 212, 221, 222*
disobedience *62*
disobedient *150, 183*
divorce*2, 4, 5, 11, 12, 13, 56, 57, 62, 78, 104, 105, 129, 134, 136, 137, 138, 142, 143, 144, 151, 153, 156, 158, 169, 174, 187, 193, 198, 199, 204, 205, 206, 209, 214, 215, 225, 227, 231, 235, 240, 241*
divorce decree *143*
divorced*5, 7, 12, 104, 146, 165, 240, 243*
don't pursue your spouse *158*
drinking *215, 216*
drugs *217, 239*

E

encouragement partner 78, 152, 159, 204
enemy 57, 58, 80, 150, 151, 157, 163, 165, 167, 189, 191, 195, 200, 230, 232, 233
ePartner............4, 134, 242
e-partner............147
Erin 1, 2, 5, 6, 7, 8, 12, 13, 57, 73, 78, 116, 119, 121, 122, 123, 125, 136, 137, 146, 147, 148, 152, 157, 159, 165, 166, 168, 171, 179, 199, 200, 201, 202, 206, 210, 211, 212, 213, 216, 218, 222, 223, 227, 230, 231, 232, 233, 243

F

Facing Divorce............58, 75
faith 13, 57, 76, 77, 105, 122, 127, 134, 138, 157, 159, 164, 165, 166, 190, 195, 198, 201, 208, 212, 231, 233, 235, 243
fasting............93, 157
Father God............159
fear............58, 119, 154, 158, 227
fellowship............4, 5, 6, 188, 231, 242
fiery darts............189
fiery trial............12
filed for divorce............78, 143
forgiveness 78, 79, 80, 122, 160, 166, 192, 195, 198, 234
funeral............166, 168, 225

G

Galatians 6:9............159
gentle and quiet spirit............150, 157
give up 73, 78, 80, 116, 129, 141, 143, 155, 159, 187, 190, 195, 197, 199, 213, 215, 221
God 4, 5, 6, 7, 8, 10, 11, 12, 13, 14, 57, 58, 61, 62, 64, 71, 72, 73, 75, 76, 77, 78, 79, 80, 93, 94, 96, 101, 104, 105, 107, 115, 116, 118, 119, 121, 122, 123, 124, 125, 127, 128, 129, 130, 134, 135, 136, 137, 138, 141, 142, 143, 144, 146, 147, 148, 150, 151, 152, 153, 154, 155, 156, 157, 158, 159, 160, 161, 162, 163, 164, 165, 166, 167, 168, 169, 170, 171, 174, 175, 177, 179, 180, 183, 187, 188, 189, 190, 191, 192, 193, 194, 195, 196, 197, 198, 199, 200, 201, 202, 204, 205, 207, 208, 209, 210, 211, 212, 213, 214, 215, 216, 217, 218, 219, 220, 221, 222, 223, 224, 225, 226, 227, 228, 229, 230, 231, 232, 233, 234, 235, 236, 237, 238, 239, 240, 242, 243
God's Word 6, 12, 76, 128, 150, 161, 201, 204, 205, 207, 222, 228

H

hard heart............198
harvest............159
hate wall............135, 144
hate walls............78, 79
healing 6, 61, 75, 125, 143, 154, 155, 192, 208, 219, 220
hedge of thorns............226
His Word 5, 6, 7, 10, 58, 77, 128, 137, 142, 143, 151, 159, 163, 164, 169, 196, 209, 210, 212, 243
Holy Spirit............58, 105, 167, 194, 211
hoped against hope............10
hopeless 4, 5, 7, 9, 10, 12, 58, 128, 151, 155, 156, 159, 164, 187, 199, 200, 201, 227, 242
hopeless marriages............4
hopelessness............219
hostile............187
housewife............61, 189
How God Can and Will Restore Your Marriage 5, 13, 62, 79, 153, 159, 164, 190, 193, 216, 225
humble............230, 232
humility............93, 124, 208
hurt 8, 158, 161, 167, 169, 187, 190, 194, 195, 198, 205, 212, 214, 219, 220, 221, 225, 228
husband home 75, 76, 77, 141, 142, 155, 162, 200, 216, 226
husband left home............232

I

I love you 73, 148, 213, 234
idol 57
impossible 5, 10, 11, 12, 13, 72, 75, 80, 144, 148, 159, 164, 188, 206, 208, 236
in the flesh 72, 122, 232
intimate 6, 142, 157, 192, 222, 226

J

Jesus 6, 7, 8, 58, 93, 104, 105, 115, 116, 117, 118, 122, 124, 128, 129, 136, 137, 143, 155, 158, 159, 160, 174, 175, 179, 194, 195, 200, 201, 202, 206, 208, 211, 217, 218, 219, 221, 222, 225, 228, 238, 239
Jesus Christ 6, 104, 158, 159, 208, 217, 225, 239
journey 11, 72, 76, 166, 223, 228

K

know them by their fruits 7

L

lawyer 136, 143, 235
let the unbeliever leave 11
love never fails 11
Luke 1:37 12
lying 174, 214

M

marriage crises 8, 12
married young 156
Men's Manual 171
miracle 10, 13, 72, 76, 80, 118, 134, 141, 148, 152, 158, 159, 160, 167, 168, 175, 197, 199, 205, 208, 209, 217, 223, 228, 230, 234, 238, 239
mistakes 63, 165

N

nagging 135, 169
negative 122, 163, 227
never give up 118, 136, 143, 157, 159, 162, 195, 201, 209
nothing was impossible with God .10

O

obedience 13, 93, 129, 150, 159, 206, 209, 224, 226, 228, 231
obedient 57, 62, 212, 226
OM 156, 166, 190
one flesh 134, 138, 170
other woman 11, 124, 125, 158, 187, 191, 192, 207, 211, 214, 231
overbearing 156
overcome evil with good 10
OW 115, 122, 123, 124, 125, 134, 135, 141, 142, 144, 148, 155, 161, 168, 188, 189, 200, 210, 224, 228, 230

P

pastor 5, 6, 7, 73, 123, 128, 166, 167, 194, 208, 242
peace 12, 76, 77, 80, 118, 122, 142, 144, 151, 152, 154, 157, 163, 169, 171, 192, 209, 211, 219, 224, 233, 238
Pentecostal 187
Pharisee 169, 191, 196, 225
pornography 164
Praise God 8, 115, 116, 134, 136, 141, 148, 156, 158, 175, 206, 207, 222, 229, 235, 237
Praise Reports 14, 78, 127, 135, 141, 164, 189, 203, 209, 236, 242
pray fervently 61
prayer partner 147, 166, 205
prayers 13, 75, 76, 77, 115, 119, 127, 144, 148, 165, 166, 174, 183, 187, 188, 190, 196, 200, 201, 211, 215, 216, 217, 218, 219, 220, 222, 236, 237
praying 93, 105, 117, 123, 127, 128, 141, 142, 143, 147, 156, 157, 159,

160, 162, 163, 164, 167, 168, 187, 191, 193, 195, 196, 198, 199, 200, 201, 202, 208, 209, 215, 216, 217, 224, 230, 235, 238
pregnant *190, 209, 210, 213, 237, 240*
Proverbs *7, 147, 167, 174*
Psalm 119 .... *151*
Psalms *147, 151, 167*

Q

Question and Answer videos *58*
quiet and gentle spirit ... *73, 157, 192*

R

rebelled *62*
reconciliation *123, 161*
rejected *6*
remarriage *134, 147*
remarried *104, 105, 146, 147, 218*
repent *57*
repentance *220, 230*
repented *198*
resentful *197*
respect *105, 155, 177*
respecter of persons.*58*, 61, *208, 213*
restoration *4, 6, 13, 57, 58, 62, 63, 77, 78, 93, 94, 115, 119, 129, 134, 144, 148, 152, 155, 159, 162, 164, 188, 189, 194, 195, 196, 203, 209, 210, 220, 221, 223, 231, 232, 237, 241*
Restoration Fellowship *4*
Restore Ministries *1, 2, 5, 6, 7, 8, 12, 13, 61, 62, 75, 76, 77, 78, 93, 104, 116, 123, 126, 128, 138, 141, 143, 148, 152, 157, 159, 163, 165, 166, 169, 171, 174, 175, 192, 194, 200, 212, 218, 231, 243, 256*
restored *4, 5, 6, 7, 9, 10, 11, 12, 13, 75, 80, 127, 128, 135, 137, 141, 143, 144, 146, 147, 148, 150, 156, 157, 158, 161, 164, 166, 167, 168, 169, 179, 188, 189, 191, 194, 195, 196, 197, 199, 203, 206, 207, 208,*
209, 211, 212, 217, 221, 222, 226, 233, 237, 239, 242
restoredmarriage *4*, 10, 75, 127, 146, 148, 158, 188, 197, 212, 239
rock bottom *177*
Rom. 4:18 .... *13*

S

salvation *80, 129, 148, 191, 192*
Sarah *175*
Satan *77, 150, 157, 158, 159, 160, 165, 168, 179, 191, 197*
Scripture *2, 94, 147, 154, 167, 168, 196, 215, 242*
season *75*
self-righteous *169*
separated *56, 127, 137, 152, 157, 160, 171, 177, 197, 205, 219, 228, 229*
separation *58*, 62, *78, 118, 129, 134, 135, 136, 148, 150, 153, 165, 190, 199, 204, 207, 208, 219, 220, 226, 241*
sin *6, 57, 194, 195*
SOS *159, 203*
spirit-filled *209*
spiritual crises *8*
stop pursuing *79*
submissive *73, 160, 174, 213*
surgery *143, 214, 228*
Sword of the Spirit *189*

T

this marriage was over *153, 201*
tough love *122, 134*
trials *137, 158, 165, 170, 195, 206*
turn my husband's heart *150*

U

unconditional love *76, 179*
unforgiveness *166, 229*

V

virtuous woman 79

W

wedding *134*, *138*, *155*, *158*, *167*, *183*, *199*, *202*, *230*, *241*
wedding band *134*
wedding ring *138*, *167*
what God has joined together, let no man separate *122*
whining *135*
winning without a word *79*
wisdom *8*, *72*, *152*, *192*, *218*, *224*
witchcraft *169*
with God, all things are possible
.... *161*, *164*
Word of God *142*, *159*, *189*
Workers at Home *58*

MarriageHelpOnLine.com

Orderline USA: 1-800-397-0800
International Orderline: 417-581-8221

RMI Fellowship: 1-888-721-5253
International Fellowship: 417-485-8111

Restore Ministries International
POB 830
Ozark, MO 65667